Doxology
and Theology

D1607930

american
university
studies

Series VII
Theology and Religion

Vol. 285

PETER LANG
New York • Washington, D.C./Baltimore • Bern
Frankfurt am Main • Berlin • Brussels • Vienna • Oxford

Paul Galbreath

Doxology and Theology

An Investigation of the Apostles' Creed in Light of Ludwig Wittgenstein

PETER LANG
New York • Washington, D.C./Baltimore • Bern
Frankfurt am Main • Berlin • Brussels • Vienna • Oxford

Library of Congress Cataloging-in-Publication Data

Galbreath, Paul.
Doxology and theology: an investigation of the Apostles' Creed
in light of Ludwig Wittgenstein / Paul Galbreath.
p. cm. — (American university studies. VII, Theology and religion; v. 285)
Includes bibliographical references.
1. Apostles' Creed. 2. Wittgenstein, Ludwig, 1889–1951. I. Title.
BT993.3.G35   238'.11—dc22   2008006444
ISBN 978-1-4331-0148-9 (hardcover)
ISBN 978-1-4331-0441-1 (paperback)
ISSN 0740-0446

Bibliographic information published by **Die Deutsche Bibliothek**.
Die Deutsche Bibliothek lists this publication in the "Deutsche
Nationalbibliografie"; detailed bibliographic data is available
on the Internet at http://dnb.ddb.de/.

The paper in this book meets the guidelines for permanence and durability
of the Committee on Production Guidelines for Book Longevity
of the Council of Library Resources.

© 2008 Peter Lang Publishing, Inc., New York
29 Broadway, 18th floor, New York, NY 10006
www.peterlang.com

Printed in the United States of America

To Jan and Andy,
whose love, support, encouragement, and forbearance
continue to support and sustain
my life and work

Table of Contents

Preface

The bulk of this work was presented as my dissertation at Karl-Ruprechts-Universität in Heidelberg, Germany. I have decided to revise and publish it several years later for two major reasons: (1) My recent work in sacramental ethics grows out of the theological and philosophical work that is presented in this monograph. This hermeneutical study of liturgical language was prompted out of my own existential desire to discover ways in which the language of the church connects with the language of our daily lives. In recent publications, I have worked to build on these connections that are explored in depth here.[1] (2) While a steady stream of literature continues to be produced on language philosophy, hermeneutics, and the work of Ludwig Wittgenstein, my own discipline of liturgical theology remains largely unaffected by this literature. Instead, it mostly continues to rely on other philosophical frameworks. As a result, many of the questions that continue to be raised about the relationship of the liturgy and liturgical language to the life of faith remain open and, in my estimation, lack the analytical approach that would support, clarify, and press for a much closer connection. While liturgical scholars often assume the relationship between liturgical language and the life of faith, our hermeneutical frameworks rarely support the primary, integral relationship between the content and context of the liturgy itself and the ethical actions that are rooted in these acts. Instead, the "meaning of the liturgy" itself is presumed to lie behind the texts and ritual actions (in the minds of the participants or in historical and theological explanations) rather than in the midst of the assembly in the lives of the believers. It is my contention that ethical decisions cannot be secondary or an outcome of what happens in the worshipping community. Instead, the shape of our ethical lives must be integrally rooted in the language and actions of the faithful as they gather around Scripture, font, and table.

There are several significant people who deserve thanks from my time in Heidelberg. I am grateful for the support and direction that I received from Prof. Dietrich Ritschl, who guided the research on this project. Dr. Herbert Hanreich was an especially important conversation partner as I worked on the Wittgenstein literature and dealt with the myriad of interpretations of Wittgenstein's work. In addition, Rudolph and Karen Leube, opened their home in Dossenheim to me, welcomed me as part of their family, and allowed me the freedom and opportunity to finish my work.

More recently, my friend Claudio Carvalhaes urged me to return to the manuscript, work on it, and publish it. I am honored by his friendship and his confidence that this will make a contribution to the scholarly community. I am also grateful for the technological help that I received from Eugene LeCouteur and bibliographical assistance from Quincy Worthington, both of whom are students at Union Theological Seminary and Presbyterian School of Christian Education.

Most of all, my family, Jan and Andy, have been steadfast in their encouragement and support of this work. My wife worked tirelessly to give me the time, space, and opportunity to complete this work. During the course of this project, I have watched my son grow up and become a remarkable adult, whose own commitments serve as an inspiration for me. In the times when it seemed that I would never finish this manuscript, they alone kept the faith on my behalf. For their constant encouragement and unflagging optimism that this book would actually come to fruition, I am deeply grateful and truly blessed.

NOTE

[1]   In particular, a recent publication on the relationship between Eucharist and mission (or outreach) in the church presupposes the theological and hermeneutical lens that is presented in this work. See *Leading from the Table*. (Herndon, VA: The Alban Press, 2008).

Introduction

"Dogmatics is a theological discipline. But theology is a function of the Church."[1] Karl Barth begins his dogmatics with these words. They stand as a bold reminder of the interrelationship of theology and the church. Barth is clear that the church provides the content and the context for theological discussion. The task of theology is to critique and correct the language of the church. The distinction between "wissenschaftliche Theologie" and the "Theologie des einfachen Glaubens–und Lebenszeugnisses und in Unterschied zu die 'Theologie' des Gottesdienstes" is noted at the beginning of the dogmatics. It is the task of dogmatics to examine the language of the church and, as needed, to provide insight and correction. The theologian must remain aware that his/her work occurs within the church since "dogmatics is impossible outside the Church."[2]

Similarly, but more implicitly, Paul Tillich begins his *Systematic Theology* with a discussion of the significance of the theologian's commitment in contrast to that of the philosopher (or scientist). A theologian, according to Tillich, is an interpreter of the church and of its claims of truth. Tillich goes further to define the theologian as one who stands already within the circle of faith. The theological circle predicates a prior and determinative commitment from the theologian.[3] Consequently, theological work is drawn from and dependent on an a priori participation of the theologian within the Christian community.

It is significant that these two theologians, whose lives and work differ in so many ways, began their systematic formulations within this framework. The relationship of the discipline of theology to the proclamation of the church is one of submission: theology draws from the praxis of the church. Theology contributes to the life of the church by doing its work of clarification and, in this manner, Barth spoke of theology directing the language of the church. Although the discussion is circular in nature, ultimately theology must remain dependent upon the church as its source and foundation.

The theological task is a linguistic one. It is done with words and is directed to making clear the words and actions of the church. There is a dialectical element involved in the interrelationship of the ongoing communication between the discipline of theology and the church. The existence of theology is grounded in the life and language of the church. Theology may seek to clarify and at times even alter the church's language, but the a priori nature of the language of the worshipping community as the foundation for any further discussion is a given.

The task of theology, then, is to point to the language of the church and to inquire how it functions. Theology seeks to illumine the meaning of statements made by the church. Theology also seeks to point to the context of statements made by the church (e.g., determining if a statement is primarily a christological or pneumatological statement). These questions are appropriate and significant to the theologian who is seeking to dialogue with and in the church regarding its use of language.

This task becomes more complex due to the relationship of theology to other disciplines. Because theology is involved in dialogue and uses the techniques of other scientific disciplines, it becomes a partner in other conversations, including those of the scientific and academic communities. While this relationship has been explained in various ways (cf. Barth and Tillich), the use and application of language and analytical tools (such as historical–critical methodology) has become an integral part of the theological discipline.

The following study grows out of an understanding of the dialectical relationship between theology and the church. By investigating the use of creedal statements in the church, it seeks to provide information about the function and domain of language in the church. As a theological task, it seeks to be analytical in order to determine the implications of that which is said by the church.

Reference to the language of the church is reference to doxological or liturgical language.[4] The words used by the worshipping community form the basis for any language of faith. Liturgical language is a primary, expressive language of faith. The recitation of the Apostles' Creed or the Lord's Prayer is exemplary of the fundamentally linguistic characteristic of faith. It has frequently been noted that non–liturgical churches have their own "liturgical" traditions (e.g., reading of Scripture, singing of hymns, formulation of prayers). Indeed, the choice of liturgical form is a highly significant one because it carries with it the inherent linguistic field of the believer. In other words, what we say we believe becomes that which we do believe by virtue of its impact on us. Such an understanding is exemplified by conversations with Christians from widely differing traditions. The implications of this study are therefore not restricted to creedal interpretation or any particular liturgical tradition.

In order to accomplish its aim this study, turns first to an historical investigation of the crisis in linguistic interpretation in the church and theological community. There is today a wide-spread discussion regarding questions of meaning and the language of the church. It would be impossible to present an entire historical background for this discussion, but it is hoped that a brief look at the nineteenth century debates within the church in Germany over the meaning and use of the Apostles' Creed will give us insight into the current linguistic dilemma. The presentation of the nineteenth century debates is a theological portrait which seeks to prepare the way for a discussion of alternative interpretations of creedal statements. In chapter two, a philosophical framework is presented through an investigation of particularly significant aspects of Ludwig Wittgenstein's later writings. The choice of Wittgenstein is a methodological one; any attempt to investigate the function of language within the church is bound to consider the functional nature of language itself. Thus, Wittgenstein is seen as a tool in this discussion and not as a philosophical end in itself (similarly the presentation of themes in Wittgenstein's later writings is guided by the theological aim of the work). Needless to say, other theologians and other situations may involve the use of different philosophical perspectives within their investigation. The nature of this particular problem, however, requires a method of analysis which can enlighten us as to how the language of the church functions. If Wittgenstein's work can enable us to understand this activity, then the use of his work can be justified.

Chapter three presents a discussion of the alternative readings of Wittgenstein by theologians. By surveying selected examples, we are looking for examples or parallels of ways in which we can apply Wittgenstein to the interpretation of creeds. The study ends by distinguishing optional approaches to the creeds before presenting an understanding of creedal statements in light of Wittgenstein.

NOTES

[1]   Karl Barth, *Church Dogmatics: The Doctrine of the Word of God*, Vol. 1, Part 1. Translated by G. T. Thomson. (Edinburgh: T. & T. Clark, 1960), p. 1.

[2]   Ibid., p. 18.

[3]   Paul Tillich, *Systematic Theology*, Vol. 1 (Chicago: University of Chicago Press, 1967), p. 23.

[4]   For a fuller discussion of definitions of doxological language, see Teresa Berger, *Theologie in Hymnen? Zum Verhältnis von Theologie und Doxologie am Beispiel der "Collection of Hymns for the use of the People called Methodists" (1780)* (Altenberge: Telos, 1989), pp. 15–19.

Chapter One

Confusion and Controversy:
The Developing Dilemma of
Language in the Church

Preface

The development of difficulties in interpreting liturgical language in the church became evident through a series of conflicts which occurred throughout the nineteenth century in the *Evangelische Kirche* in Germany. Similar controversies over hermeneutical questions arose in other places during this time period. Roman Catholic debate centered around the declaration of papal infallibility following Vatican I. In Great Britain, the discussion was based on the use of the historical-critical method, particularly during the trial of the Old Testament scholar William Robertson Smith. Similar debates about the use of the historical-critical method in the U. S. were evident in the heresy trial of Charles Augustus Briggs in the Presbyterian Church. The present study concentrates on the German debate because it centered on the question of creedal language and its interpretation. The conflicts were based largely on the use and function of the Apostles' Creed, primarily as a required part of worship and ordination vows. The debates over creedal interpretation added to a developing division within the church. These factions have been described by different terms (e.g., positive/liberal). Any attempt to categorize groups carries with it certain dangers. The following study uses the descriptive terms conservative/rationalist, in part because the historical breadth of the period requires that any descriptive adjective be broad enough to include a diversity of opinions within it. These designations indicate the desire of conservatives to preserve particular traditions and interpretations and the attempt by rationalists to include the results of recent critical study.[1] Conservatives and rationalists fought bitterly about the appropriateness and meaning of the creed, but to a large extent failed to reach a consensus. Although there were numerous confrontations, three are highlighted in this study as exemplary of the difficulties occurring within the church. These three episodes demonstrate the lack of clarity about liturgical language which existed both within the conservative as well as the rationalist groups. The conservatives, who were intent upon protecting the church from the influence of liberalism, speculation, and rationalism, saw in the creeds a checklist for doctrinal orthodoxy. Any attempt to redirect or refocus the discussion was rejected as being unfaithful. Unfortunately, rationalists failed to provide a viable alternative as well. The constant criticism of the creed by rationalists placed them in a vulnerable position when conservatives characterized them as attempting to destroy the church.

The following survey seeks to highlight the role that the Apostles' Creed played in these conflicts, while at the same time attempts to present a description of the controversies and the personalities involved in the discussions. While the survey is historical in nature, it is motivated by a theological perspective which seeks to point to an increasing tension in the church's interpretation of creedal statements.

The historical nature of the presentation seeks to underscore dramatically the emerging difficulty of the interpretation of liturgical texts.[2] Conservatives and rationalists alike sought to find the locus of meaning through historical frameworks either by an insistence on the factual accuracy of the statements or an historical investigation to determine the credibility of the claims made by believers. In so doing, both sides gave primary attention to the events pointed to outside of the text and virtually ignored the doxological context as a determinative factor in the meaning of the confession. A survey of major skirmishes over creedal statements provides important insights into differing theological options that were explored during the last century. While the study of nineteenth century theology has paid primary attention to an analysis of particularly significant theological figures, it has often overlooked an analysis of the on-going discussions within the church. If theology, though, is primarily an analysis of the language of the church, then there is a pressing need to include a discussion of creedal interpretation in its ecclesiological setting. The purpose of the survey, then, is to both highlight the discussion of creedal interpretation in its contextual situation and underscore the need for an alternative hermeneutic to help resolve the on-going conflict within the church.

The Background to the Conflict

In the nineteenth century, the *Evangelische Kirche* in Germany found itself increasingly polarized. The growth of rationalism and the on-going work of biblical criticism was an increasing part of the training and work of theologians and ministers within the church. Even though more extreme views of liberalism, in particular David Friedrich Strauss' *Das Leben Jesu* (1835) raised storms of controversy, it is fair to say that rationalism was entrenched not only in the theological universities, but in the church and society as well.[3]

Confessional Lutheranism developed in opposition to the growth of rationalist and liberal tendencies. The movement can be traced to 1817 when Claus Harm's "95 Theses" attacked Enlightenment religion and the church union in Prussia.[4] The basis for future controversy was established through the passage of the Agenda in 1822 which made the Apostles' Creed mandatory in the liturgy as well as a part of the ordination vows.[5] Until this time the creed had been recognized as an important symbol, but it was not until the nineteenth century that the creed was placed in the center of importance and viewed by conservatives as the distinguishing mark of Protestantism. The passage of the Agenda recognized the creeds as a "*Glaubensnorm*" and saw them as a firm foundation for faith.[6] Ernst Hengstenberg was the foremost advocate of the attempts by conservatives to maintain control over the church.[7] Hengstenberg's role was particularly significant through his work as editor of the *Evangelische Kirchenzeitung* (begun in 1827) which became the foremost place of conservative propaganda as well as a weapon for the conservatives in their fight for doctrinal purity and restoration within the church.

> Besonders der Berliner Professor Hengstenberg (1802-1869), der im Zusammenhang mit dem Erstarken des Konfessionalismus durch die von ihm redigierte *Evangelische Kirchenzeitung* einen beträchtlichen kirchen-politischen Einfluß besaß, attackierte in seinem Blatt jede freiere Geisteshaltung.[8]

Usage and interpretation of the confessions became the center of the debate between conservatives and rationalists. The conservatives within the church aligned themselves with the political powers (particularly in Prussia) and viewed themselves as the protectors of order against the "revolutionaries" who sought not only religious change, but political upheaval as well. The use of the confessions underlined the belief in both authority and hierarchy which the conservatives believed had been granted by divine power.

> Der Kampf gegen die Auflösung des Dogmas, positiv: die Rückkehr zur konsequenten Symbolorthodoxie, d.h. zur wörtlichen Verbindlichkeit der Bekenntnisschriften der Reformation war der Versuch, den Protestantismus gegen das rationale Denken zu immunisieren....Die Erneuerung der Religion zur Garantie der traditionellen Ordnung: in dieser Absicht trafen sich religiöse und politische Reaktion.[9]

The conservatives demanded a return to the Lutheran symbols and confessions and the development of a "churchly theology" in contrast to the liberal view of theologians. The attack upon alternative views provided a new drive for purity, since until that time even rationalists had been considered church members.

> Now the church was to be understood as strictly constituted by its confession, which was "the essence of the evangelical church." There was no middle ground between fidelity to the confession and the abandonment of Christianity.... The confession was both the rule of faith and life and the unifying center for fellowship; without agreement here there could be no true fellowship. Not only the doctrine but the very life of the church rested on its confessions.[10]

The rigidity of the conservative position meant that rationalism could no longer be tolerated in the church. When Friedrich Wilhelm IV came to power, the conservatives' view of a Christian state became the doctrine of the Prussian king as well. The change of political leadership brought new laws which included stricter church discipline. In addition, conservatives were able to strengthen their power through academic appointments in Berlin and Halle.

The *Evangelische Kirche* and the Restoration: The Struggle of the *Lichtfreunde* for Alternatives

An initial confrontation between conservatives and rationalists occurred in 1840 as a result of a newspaper article by Rev. Wilhelm Sintenis in Magdeburg. Sintenis criticized the sentimental portrait of Christ which was predominant in the church and viewed prayers directed to Christ as superstitious.[11] The conservatives demanded that Sintenis be dismissed from his church. Sintenis' meeting with church authorities resulted in only a warning, but the effect was a signal to the rationalists in the church that a stricter line would be taken.

As a result of the Sintenis affair, Leberecht Uhlich, minister in Pömmelte bei Schönebeck, invited ministers of a rationalistic persuasion to gather in Gnadau on 29 June 1841 for a discussion of the place of rationalism within the church. Uhlich's invitation included the following statements:

> Sollen wir Geistliche denn, geborgen im Lehnstuhle unserer Pfarrstelle, abwarten, daß Philosophen, Belletristen, Juristen, Mediciner und wer sonst noch, die Sache der Wahrheit führen und für geistige Freiheit Siege erkämpfen? Nein! Wir sind die Geistlichen, also die, welche gegen Buchstaben und Satzung, Form und andres Werk des Staubes die Sache des Geistes zu führen haben. Dazu aber ist's gut, daß man nicht allein stehe. Ein Verein Gleichstrebender hilft dem Einzelnen seine Ansichten berichtigen.[12]

Uhlich concluded by inviting the ministers to a discussion of the events occurring in the church.

Uhlich was a sympathetic man and a minister who was loved by his congregation. He was a trustworthy, honest person, who had a talent for speaking in a way which was understandable to everyone. Rationalism was not simply an academic concern for him, but was a matter of deep commitment for himself and for his ministry. Uhlich sought renewal in the life of the church and believed that rationalism was a way to speak to people about their lives. He combined his rationalistic views with a kind of inner piety which recognized God's presence in all the world.[13]

Sixteen ministers gathered in Gnadau. They discussed ways of attaining more freedom [*Freiheit des Geistes*] instead of the literalistic approach of the conservatives [*Buchstabenglauben*]. The primacy of reason became their rallying point. Statements of faith should be tested by reason. The essential articles of faith were belief in God, immortality, and the dignity of human beings. The group was also in agreement that all should have the right to free research without fear of censorship or reprimand from the church. The group agreed to meet again in Halle in three months.

On 20 September 1841, fifty-six ministers and laypersons gathered in Halle. The group agreed on the name of *Protestantischen Freunde* and was unified on the need to work against domination by the conservatives in order to maintain a pluralistic basis in the church. The group agreed to nine principles which included: (1) a statement of faith in the "simple Gospel" (John 17:3); (2) the need to make reason the basis for statements of faith; (3) the desire to work for the kingdom of God on earth, particularly through fulfilling their calling as ministers and leaders in the church; and (4) an appreciation of the diversity of Christianity and the need for showing tolerance toward those who share in the life of the church (which was based upon I Cor. 3:11 and Gal. 5:1).[14]

Because of their frequent metaphorical use of light, the *Protestantischen Freunde* became known as the *Lichtfreunde*. The *Lichtfreunde* agreed to meet biannually for open discussion and to form local chapters which would provide an on-going forum for the discussion of rationalism and Christianity as well as other topics of local interest.

The *Lichtfreunde* met again on the week following Pentecost in 1842 in Leipzig. On this occasion more then two hundred men gathered, of which three-fourths were theologians. The discussion centered on the task of the group. The established goal was to help build the kingdom of God based upon the "simple Gospel" in keeping with a present-day world view and by using all scientific and educational tools that were available. The *Lichtfreunde* were united in rejecting any attempt to write their own confession, because of fear that this would bring about disagreement and dissension that would splinter the group.

In the fall of 1842, the *Protestantischen Freunde* met on 22 September in Köthen. Out of the one hundred fifty who gathered more than half were school teachers. The group denied accusations that they were trying to split the church. Instead of division, they were advocating freedom and plurality. At the time, H. Karsten noted that both sides of the debate actually shared much in common.

> Denn wenn man hinwies, daß naturalistische Prediger, wie supranaturalistische, beide doch bezwecken wollten, durch ihre Wirksamheit die Anbetung Gottes im Geiste und in der Wahrheit, so wie die sittliche Veredlung der Menschheit, beide doch wollten die kirchlichen Institute gewahrt wissen, den Gottesdienst gehoben, das Abendmahl gebraucht, u.;[15]

Uhlich was the guiding figure throughout these sessions and served as a moderator between those of differing philosophical viewpoints within the group. The discussions were open to all and were based upon democratic principles. The basis for acceptance in the group was acknowledgement of the "simple Gospel" (belief in God, immortality, and the worth of humanity) and an interest in expressing Christian faith in contemporary terms. The group understood one of its major tasks to include outreach to those who had become estranged from the church due to the intolerance of the conservatives. At this point in their development, the *Protestantischen Freunde* were committed to life within the church and encompassed no one political view.

The conservatives continued to become more aggressive and in 1843 warned ministers not to alter the liturgical form or make omissions from the Apostolic confessions.

> Unter dem stärker werdenden Druck der neupietistischen Orthodoxie, ausgelöst durch den Erlaß des Konsistoriums der Provinz Sachsen, der die Geistlichen zum Gebrauch der Agende und des apostolischen Glaubensbekenntnisses verpflichtete (1843) hatten die "Protestantischen Freunde" an die Kirchengemeinden appelliert und die Gemeindemitglieder zu ihren Treffen eingeladen. Von den Rationalisten als unvernünftige Glaubensformeln bekämpft, als unbedingter Glaubensbestandteil angesehen von der Orthodoxie, hatte sich die theologische Kontroverse auf diese beiden Punkte fixiert.[16]

The meeting in the fall of 1843 was held in Köthen where over three hundred fifty persons gathered. The opening prayer included mention of the growing division between a theology based upon sentences of an earlier time and a philosophy that sought to make all things new. With these words a tone was set for the discussion which drew a sharp distinction from the conservatives' attempts at doctrinal purity. The *Protestantischen Freunde* appealed to the diversity of faith within the church and declared that the question of a particular form was secondary.[17] Freedom remained at the center of faith, and any attempt to require a literalistic interpretation of particular expressions of faith was illegitimate. In addition, conservatives were criticized in a decree for their attempts to control the church. The proper place of discussion and decision was in the congregation and to that end the *Lichtfreunde* called for the development of presbyteries that would allow for discussion on a more localized level by both ministers and laypersons.

The *Protestantischen Freunde* enjoyed rapid growth and six hundred members attended the May meeting in 1844. The growth of lay participation resulted in a changed environment. The increasing pressure of the conservatives contributed to a charged atmosphere in which protestant freedom (Luther's principle) became the rallying cry. By connecting freedom with the rationalist position on the confessions, the *Protestantischen Freunde* sought to establish a foundation for openness within the church.

Uhlich spoke to the assembly on the question of truth and its identity and localization in particular confessional statements. Truth presided not in a book or a church council, but in the work of the Holy Spirit in the Christian community [*Gemeinde*]. Uhlich went on to distinguish between theology and religion (religion being understood as a positive Christian term). The theological tradition no longer contained truth which was applicable to the scientific standards of the day, and any attempts to maintain a dogmatic position failed to take into account the on-going work of the Holy Spirit. The truth which did remain present in the old dogmatic systems was encompassed by the rationalistic expressions of faith.[18]

The growing popularity of the rationalist movement was exemplified by a petition (1844) on the Magdeburg Synod that was signed by over one hundred Magdeburg citizens. The petition called for: (1) a purely scientific exegesis of Scripture; (2) omission of the apostolic confessions during baptisms and confirmations; (3) elimination of the Agenda (which was criticized for its similarity to the Roman Catholic mass); and (4) organization of the church according to a presbyterian system. The requests of the petition were based on the interests of the *Protestantischen Freunde*.[19]

This meeting of the *Protestantischen Freunde* reached a climax during an address by Gustav Wislicenus, pastor of the Neumarktskirche in Halle. Wislicenus was a man known for his total honesty. He had studied theology in Halle, where he was a member of a secret society which was committed to working towards a revolution that would produce a free and unified Germany. Because of his participation in this group, he was arrested and charged as a traitor. He was sentenced to twelve years in prison, four of which were actually spent in jail. During his incarceration, Wislicenus studied the Bible diligently. He combined his personal piety with an Hegelian approach and felt compelled to bring clarity to the discussion of the *Protestantischen Freunde*.[20]

In his address "*Ob Schrift, Ob Geist?*" Wislicenus sharply criticized the literal, dogmatic position of the conservatives. He believed that the conservatives were attempting to live in the past, whereas the current *Weltanschauung* required a new understanding of the faith.[21] Wislicenus concluded that, "Wir haben eine andere höchste Autorität. Sie ist der in uns selbst lebendige Geist."[22] The Holy Spirit worked for freedom and truth. According to Wislicenus, Christian truth was not bound to a rigid interpretation of Scripture or any other text, but was the result of the work of the Holy Spirit in the community. Wislicenus left no middle way and his presentation presented an either-or demand to the *Protestantischen Freunde* to accept the position of the conservatives or to embrace a modern rationalistic approach to the Bible and faith.

The conservative response was led by E. F. Guericke who attended the meeting and launched a scathing attack on the *Protestantischen Freunde* and on Wislicenus in particular. Guericke's report in the *Evangelische Kirchenzeitung* (8 Juni 1844) noted that the *Protestantischen Freunde* met in a room which had nude portraits painted on the walls. Uhlich's leadership role was noted, but he remained fairly well insulated from harsh criticism.[23] Guericke commented that Wislicenus' address was so bold and daring in its dismissal of biblical authority that "...jedes noch irgend im Keime schriftgläubige Herz erzittern mußte."[24] Wislicenus was declared a heretic, and the conservatives called for the church to revoke his ordination. For Guericke and the conservatives, Wislicenus became the representative of the rationalist position.

Guericke's article unleashed a flood of attacks and counter-attacks between conservatives and rationalists. The *Missionsverein* called for an investigation by officials of the church and declared that, "Im Namen des dreieinigen Gottes erklären wir, daß...wir die Köthener Lichtfreunde nicht als Brüder in Christo anerkennen können."[25] Other groups followed the lead of the *Missionsverein.* Pastoral conferences declared that any group which subjected the Scripture to the Spirit was no longer a part of the church.[26] The claim that the *Lichtfreunde* should no longer be considered a part of the true church became typical of the attacks by the conservatives.

> Die Juden seien doch ein gescheidtes Volk; sie hätten schon vor achtzehnhundert Jahren gewußt, was die Lichtfreunde erst jetzt fänden, daß es mit Christo nichts sei.[27]

The conservatives continued to insist that their interpretation and use of the creed was necessary in order to preserve the purity of the church.

The conservatives seized the initiative and proclaimed that the *Protestantischen Freunde* were guilty not only of heresy, but sought to provoke a political revolution as well.[28] As a result, the Cabinet banned all meetings that called the reformation confessions into question. Because of the ban, the polemical exchange took place through written exchanges.[29] While Wislicenus continued to fight desperately for freedom in the church, a commission was formed to investigate charges which were brought against him.

Uhlich attempted to diffuse the situation at the next meeting in the Fall of 1844. He tried to soften the drastic contrasts between a literalistic and a rationalistic approach. Wislicenus, however, continued to push for a sharp distinction. He addressed the eight hundred present clarifying his position that he valued Scripture, but he no longer viewed it as authoritative. The meeting ended interestingly enough with a recitation of the Apostles' Creed.[30]

The conservatives, though, would not be pacified. The commission investigating Wislicenus disregarded the testimony of his congregation and suspended him from the ministry. The removal of Wislicenus from his congregation was an indication that conservatives would no longer tolerate rationalists who criticized and questioned the authority of the church.

In the spring of 1845, between two and three thousand people attended the meeting of the *Protestantischen Freunde*. Wislicenus returned from a colloquium to join the afternoon session and was greeted with a warm welcome. The *Protestantischen Freunde* declared their support for Wislicenus. In addition, the group signed a petition on his behalf. Uhlich concluded the meeting once again by stressing the need for freedom and tolerance within the church.

> Was verschulden wir es, und was verschuldet es die protestantische Kirche, wenn eben in dieser Kirche eine Partei ihren ganzen Namen und Beruf mißversteht, und

sich geberdet, als wäre sie mit ihrem starren Festhalten an Formen und Bekenntniss-
chriften einer vergangenen Zeit die Kirche, wir aber die Abgefallenen, die Feinde?[31]

Uhlich appealed to the assembly calling for a new awakening in the church to
help people recapture a new understanding of truth and freedom.[32]

In the summer of 1845, there were a series of regional meetings including
one in Schießwerdergarden which was attended by six to eight thousand people. The alliance between conservatives and the government created a situation
in which the demands of the *Protestantischen Freunde* carried political overtones.
The calls for freedom of research and teaching, and particularly the desire for
more active lay participation through a representative body of the church, were
also latent with political ideals that carried strong implications, particularly to
the Prussian leadership. The conservatives were quick to note these tendencies
and used them in their appeal for intervention by the government. Hensten-
berg claimed that any group that no longer accepted the authority of Scripture
would also not accept political authority (which the conservatives viewed as
ordained by God).[33] A police report from 1845 noted that the opposition to
the king had aligned itself with the rationalists. The report concluded that
"...die preußische Regierung hat einen Feind gegen sich in's Leben gerufen, der
ihr sehr gefährlich werden kann."[34]

As the political pressure mounted, it became more difficult for the *Protestantischen Freunde*. After the decree on 5 August 1845 which outlawed public
and private meetings of the *Lichtfreunde*, it became clear that the struggle for
freedom and plurality in the church would require a high price. The Prussians
claimed that the ban was due to the political character of the *Lichtfreunde*. The
members of the *Lichtfreunde* seemed surprised at the dramatic turn of events.

> Hätten wir es uns denken können, daß wir den Regierungen unangenehm sein
> würden? . . . Ob unsere Versammlungen bei weltlichen Machthabern Gunst oder Un-
> gunst finden würden, darnach zu fragen, war nicht unsre Sache.[35]

The massive outcry of the *Protestantischen Freunde* due to the ban on meetings
led them on a path of escalation in their battle with the conservatives. On 26
September 1845, Dr. D. Schulz in Breslau was dismissed from his position as
Konsistorialrat due to his signing of a petition that protested the banning of the
meetings of the *Lichtfreunde*. This act brought an increased response from the
Lichtfreunde and an outpouring of protest from those of rationalist persuasion.[36]

The first separation from the *Evangelische Kirche* occurred through the case of Julius Rupp, minister in Königsberg. Rupp was an exceptionally educated and well-rounded man who possessed a through knowledge of theology, philosophy, history, and the classics. In addition to serving his congregation, he taught at the *Gymnasium* and was *Privatdozent* in philosophy in Königsberg. He exemplified Christian humanism at its best and denied any kind of external authority. Rupp had already been reprimanded for a lecture in which he criticized the role of the "Christian government." Following this skirmish, Rupp preached against the usage of the Athanasian Creed claiming that it contradicted Scripture. He repeated his position in an article entitled "*Die Symbole oder Gottes Wort*."[37] The result was that Rupp was dismissed from his ministerial duties. Subsequently, on 19 January 1846 the first free church [*freie Gemeinde*] was formed in Königsberg. Over one hundred people joined the congregation and Rupp was chosen as the first minister.

Wislicenus reacted positively to the development. In an open letter, he welcomed the idea of independent congregations. Wislicenus embraced a radical position which included a break with all forms (e.g., vestments) and appealed once again to the principle of freedom. The result of his letter was another investigation by church authorities which led to his dismissal due to failure to adhere to the Agenda. On 26 September 1846, Wislicenus and thirty-two others formed a free protestant church in Halle. The congregation understood itself to be a private organization based upon democratic principles. Their constitution included the following words: "Wir wollen keine abgeschlossene kirchliche Confession, sondern eine freie menschliche Gesellschaft."[38] Indeed, the group viewed as its task freeing people from religious tyranny. The congregation experienced rapid growth and by 1848 had over one hundred members.

Attempts to form a compromise to the escalating debates resulted in a decision by the Prussian *Generalsynode* in 1846 to consider a new statement of faith for ordination requirements. The statement, which was prepared by Karl Immanuel Nitzsch, followed the general outline of the Apostles' Creed but omitted references to the virgin birth, the descent into hell and the resurrection of the body.[39] This statement and further attempts to modify the ordination requirements failed to become law because of the refusal of King Friedrich Wilhelm IV to accept them. The King interpreted the decisions of the Synod as attempts to usurp the place of the Apostles' Creed. In addition, the Synod decisions received harsh criticism from both conservatives and rationalists.[40] The attempt to find a middle ground failed and the conflict escalated.

The next target for the conservatives was Eduard Baltzer. Baltzer was an active member of the *Protestantischen Freunde* and had been outspoken in calling for reforms within the church. He led the struggle for greater freedom within the church, particularly through a democratic church constitution. In the summer of 1845, Baltzer received a call to become the minister of the St. Moritz church in Halle. The *Konsistorium* rejected the call however because Baltzer refused to commit himself to the Apostles' Creed. The approval of a call to the St. Nicolai church in Nordhausen was also denied. Subsequently, Baltzer founded a free protestant church in Nordhausen on 5 January 1847. By the summer, the congregation had over one thousand members (nearly ten per cent of the city's population) and had received recognition as a Christian community from the state.[41]

On 30 March 1847, an act of tolerance which granted freedom to all religious communities became law. The Prussian government saw it as a possibility for channeling and controlling the growing division in the church. In order to be recognized as a religious community, a group had to agree in general with the recognized confessions, submit their own confessional statement, and present a copy of their constitution. Any group that could not meet these demands was classified simply as a political group and was outlawed.

> Die Funktion des Religionspatents erscheint unter diesen Aspekten klar: der religiöse Unruheherd sollte von der Kirche amputiert werden, indem man den Anhängern der religiösen Protestbewegung die Alternative aufzwang, entweder aus der Kirche auszutreten und die negativen Folgen in Kauf zu nehmen oder sich der gegebenen Kirchenordnung konform anzupassen. Das war die Fortsetzung der von Friedrich Wilhelm IV. eingeleiteten Kirchenpolitik unter anderem Namen mit eben dem gleichen Ziel: die herrschende politisch-soziale Ordnung zu stabilisieren.[42]

Throughout these developments, Uhlich remained the prominent figure for the *Protestantischen Freunde* and the most difficult target for the conservatives. Uhlich's stature in Magdeburg was so high and he was so well respected as both a minister and a person that he remained insulated from the initial attacks of the conservatives. As the conservatives moved to crush the rationalists, it was inevitable that Uhlich would not remain unscathed.[43] The occasion for the charges against him was the result of his services on Easter Sunday in 1847. In spite of his attempts at reconciliation, Uhlich was charged with having committed serious damage to the church order, mainly due to liturgical variations and his failure to teach the Apostles' Creed to his confirmation class.[44] On 29 November 1847, Uhlich formed a new congregation (known as the *christliche Gemeinde*). Within weeks its membership was over two thousand. The congregation sought to continue its tradition and stated that, "Wir wollen evangelische Christen bleiben, was wir waren, und uns wieder der Kirche anschließen, wenn sie zur evangelischen Freiheit zurückgekehrt ist."[45]

The *Protestantischen Freunde* sought refuge from the ever-increasing pressure by aligning with the *Deutschkatholizismus* and forming the *Bund freireligiöser Gemeinden*. Before the official unification of these groups, cooperation had occurred at many levels. The *Protestantischen Freunde* had supported and encouraged the development of the *Deutschkatholizismus* from its very beginning. In fact, Rupp's congregation in Königsberg decided not to use the name protestant because they no longer saw the need for differentiation. Cooperation between the two groups occurred at all levels and both groups shared similar goals. Both sought freedom and unity through democratic principles. Many of the leaders of the *Protesantischen Freunde* and the *Deutschkatholiken* played active roles in the *Vormärzrevolution* (e.g., Robert Blum was active in the assembly in Frankfurt until his assassination).

The political role of the religious leaders of the *Lichtfreunde* and the *Deutschkatholizismus* combined with the censorship and propaganda of the conservatives and the government created a situation in which the religious groups evolved into political activists. One noteworthy example of this development can be found in the work of Rudolph Dulon. Dulon was the minister of a Reformed congregation in Magdeburg where he was associated with the *Lichtfreunde*. He spoke out against the required use of the creeds and was subsequently warned by church authorities. In 1848, he was called as the minister of the Unserer lieben Frauen church in Bremen where he became a leader in the democratic movement. His developing political interests led to his dismissal from the church and he eventually immigrated to the United States.[46]

It was a curious phenomenon that developed through the Prussian regulations which to a large extent labeled the groups as outlaws. By changing their status, the *Protestantischen Freunde* were forced into a mold whereby they were transformed from a church to a group that was forced to struggle for its existence. The result was that the *Protestantischen Freunde* came to be seen less as a religious group and more as a political organization that posed a threat to government authorities.[47]

Police observation and judicial persecution became commonplace. The leaders were repeatedly arrested and given warnings, fines, and sentences (usually probated). Offerings were often confiscated which made survival particularly difficult. Publications were banned and the post office refused to deliver any kind of materials printed by the *Lichtfreunde*. Marriages performed by free protestant ministers were not recognized by the state and any children resulting from these unions were declared illegitimate.[48] Gustav Tschirn, a leader of the *Deutschkatholizismus*, claimed that the persecution of the *Freireligiösen* was more drastic than anything that had occurred during the first two centuries of the church.[49]

The process of eliminating the *Lichtfreunde* was to a large degree successful. Following the unsuccessful *Vormärzrevolution*, the *Lichtfreunde* were made the scapegoats. When the Prussians seized power after the inability of the democratic movement to produce a viable plan in 1849, the free religious congregations were mostly exterminated.[50] The struggle simply to survive consumed all of their time. In addition, they were unable to further develop a positive message that could captivate the populace.

In spite of their weaknesses, the *Lichtfreunde* did give testimony to the presence of alternatives within the church and pointed out the need for reform. The greatest loss occurred in the *Evangelische Kirche* which became an authoritarian power obsessed with protecting a particular form which was no longer perceived as adequate or relevant to wide spectrums of Christians. The result was that further segments of the population became estranged from the church.

The demand by conservatives of adherence to a particular use and interpretation of the Apostles' Creed diminished the possibility for dialogue within the church. As a result, the church tended towards stagnation and lost the opportunity to engage and challenge its members.[51]

The Struggle against Literalism:
The Early Years of the *Protestantenverein*

A second major confrontation between conservatives and rationalists occurred through the work of the *Protestantenverein* which sought to provide a place for open discussion within the church. On 30 September 1863, a group of one hundred twenty men met together in Frankfurt, Germany to lay the foundation for the *Protestantenverein*. The group was quite diverse, consisting of theology professors, ministers, doctors, lawyers, businessmen, and a variety of

other professionals. They shared in common a dream of renewal and a revitali-
zation of the church, and pledged to work for a sense of openness and unification in the protestant church in Germany.

In opposition to the conservative movement, Richard Rothe and Daniel
Schenkel, both of whom were members of the theological faculty in Heidelberg, began to discuss the possibility of forming a group of like-minded church
leaders who were interested in reform. Although Rothe and Schenkel were
united in their decision to seek an alternative structure for church reform, they
represented different theological perspectives. Rothe was firmly entrenched
within the camp of nineteenth century liberalism. His main work was the *Theologische Ethik* which remains a classic interpretation of the idealism of liberalism.[52]   In contrast to Rothe, Schenkel was more moderate in his theological
work and less prolific in his academic output. Schenkel had worked as a leader
of the pietists in Baden and had been outspoken in his critique of Strauss and
other theologians who had opted for a more liberal approach.[53] The liberals
became receptive to Schenkel, however, through his battle against the Jesuit
mission in Heidelberg.

Rothe and Schenkel both possessed a wide range of contacts, and in August 1863 at the Durlacher Conference discovered a common theme while
discussing the role of religious education in the school. What united them was
the desire for an organization which would work beyond the local level and
would address the problems and situation of the protestants in Germany.
Whereas the conferences as well as the *Kirchentag* resided under the control of
the conservatives, there was a need for a group which could provide an alternative voice on issues which encompassed the entire church in Germany. Out of
this interest grew the idea to meet in order to discuss the possibility of forming
a national group. The initial motives encompassed not only the need for a national consensus, but also the need for reform in the church to take place
within the context of the congregation [*Gemeindeprinzip*]. A commitment to the
local church was to become one of the main planks in the platform of the *Protestantenverein*.

Schenkel took charge of the arrangements and issued the invitations to the
meeting in Frankfurt. The invitation repeated the interest in the question of
the possibility of a national unification of the protestant church as well as the
need for reform to occur within the context of the life of the congregation (i.e.,
reform was desired to come through the work of church members and not as a
result of decree from ministers and church leaders). It is interesting to note

that added to this agenda was the question of relationships between differing confessions (reformed and Lutheran) as well as the need for tolerance and freedom within the church (inclusion based upon confession of faith in Jesus Christ and the gospel rather than upon reliance in a creedal formulation).[54]

There was, however, a further matter that would appear on the agenda and become a predominant theme of the *Protestantenverein*: the need to overcome the growing division between the church and an increasingly secularized culture. Rothe, who is generally referred to as the "spiritual father" of the movement, had already made it a significant part of his work. Rothe was convinced that Christianity must be complementary and not antagonistic to the contemporary culture and the industrialized world. The oft-repeated critique that Rothe believed that the church would give way to a Christian political and cultural society is (in my opinion) a misinterpretation and simplification of his perspective. It is true that there are passages in Rothe's writings which speak of national interests usurping the role of the church and becoming a kind of apocalyptic symbol,[55] but simply to isolate and highlight those passages presents a one-sided interpretation.[56] Rothe's desire was not for the elimination of the church from society, but for a church that addressed and embraced a contemporary *Weltanschauung* and the changing cultural climate of his time. In this sense, Rothe worked for an opening of the church and a renewal within the church based upon a contemporary appraisal of society. Rothe was first and foremost a churchman, who remained deeply distraught by the disillusionment and estrangement of large sectors of society from the life of the church. The hope to regain those who had left the church was a significant motivating factor in his work and was to become the primary item of importance in the early years of the *Protestantenverein*.

The gathering in Frankfurt quickly united upon the goals of the group with one exception. Should the new group attempt to construct a contemporary confession in opposition to the strict adherence to the ancient creeds advocated by the conservatives? Rothe had already led the critique against dogmatic assertions which were used by conservatives as litmus tests for Christian belief. Could the *Protestantenverein* produce a contemporary statement of beliefs which would avoid controversial assertions? After a lengthy debate, Rothe led the fight against the creation of a theological statement with his insistence that any statement would tend to be used dogmatically in the same manner in which the conservatives were, in his opinion, abusing the existing confessions of the church. The time-bound nature of doctrinal and theological statements convinced Rothe that the church must be freed from all dogmatic proclamations, "Denn an Jesum glauben heißt nicht an das christologische Dogma glauben, sondern an ihn selbst, an seine Person glauben."[57] The *Protestantenverein* concluded that its task was to reject every form of dogmatism which sought to become exclusive in its interpretation. In so doing, they gained a broad basis for membership.[58] The *Verein* advocated the inclusion of diverse theological viewpoints tempered by a reliance upon scientific and historical critical methodology as a basis for theological conviction. The disadvantage was that the failure to produce a positive statement of faith allowed the opposition to seize the offensive. The general public was left with uncertainty about what the *Verein* actually believed, and the conservatives were largely successful in their attempts to portray the group as liberal outsiders. The attempt to find a broad consensus for inclusion within the *Verein* and opposition to the dogmatic assertions of the conservatives were the decisive factors in the decision to avoid a statement of faith. It can be argued that any attempt to define a particular position would have resulted in such a splintering of the theologically diverse group that dissolution would have been inevitable. The on-coming problems of the *Verein* resulted probably as much in historical developments and fate as in the failure to produce a statement of belief. At any rate, the outcome of the first meeting was to agree in principle upon the goals of the organization while avoiding a specific elaboration of a particular theological position.

The group in Frankfurt agreed to form local chapters in which discussion and debate over the goals and ideas of the *Protestantenverein* could be advanced. Many local groups were rapidly founded and the hope of a grassroots organization which could produce results within the life of the church appeared initially conceivable. Shortly over a month after meeting in Frankfurt, Rothe spoke to a group in Heidelberg which had gathered to establish a local chapter. There was a spirit of optimism which ran through Rothe's address. The first local chapter had already been founded in Dresden, and the dream of building a national network through both the local and national organizations appeared to be blossoming. Rothe established the tone and the agenda, once again, in his brief speech to the gathering in Heidelberg. The relationship between culture and the church was the predominant theme. There was a time when the church was the advocate of cultural development and at the forefront of its movement. This was the period during which the church was the predominant political, social, and cultural institution of its day. Since the time of the reformation, however, a transformation had taken place in which the church no longer maintained the sole responsibility for developments within the culture. Rothe's historical perspective was based upon a belief that in the reformation a turning point in the life of the church and its relationship to other institutions (particularly political) had occurred. This transformation resulted in a shifting world-view in which Christianity was forced out of its ecclesiastical boundaries and into the world. The further developments since the reformation (and in particular the changing life-style in the nineteenth century) demanded an opening of the church to the influences of the day. Building upon his under-standing of the reformation as the point of transition, Rothe sought to view contemporary developments as an outgrowth of the change which had oc-curred as a result of the reformation. The political and social developments which were occurring outside of the confines of the church retained for Rothe a basis and a necessity for dialogue with the church because of their growth out of a humanistic and world-embracing spirit which developed during the refor-mation. The contemporary culture should not be seen as antagonistic toward the church, but as a product and offspring of the history of the church. The denial of the culture as a conversation partner by the conservatives within the church had resulted in the growing disinterest and alienation of large numbers of individuals. The attempt by the church to retain control over that which was developing in other areas (political, social, etc.) was viewed by Rothe as a fail-ure to understand the transition which occurred as a result of the reformation and resulted ultimately in a denial of Protestantism.[59]

At times Rothe went so far as to advocate that the protestant ideals had become encompassed within the political and social developments of his time rather than being accepted by the church. "Daß ein moralisches Gemeinwesen, daß der moderne Staat und was er einschließt, Familie, Wissenschaft, bürger-liches Leben, wirklich geworden ist, das ist Christi wahres Werk und nicht die Stiftung einer Kirche."[60] But once again Rothe's words should be tempered by an understanding that this critique of the church is a critique of a particular church: namely, one that resided within the hands of dogmatic literalists who refused to dialogue or interact with the developments of the day. Rothe longed for a church in which Christianity was expressed in terms of contemporary significance. Rothe's address also included a repeated rejection of any attempt at dogmatically encapsulating Jesus in order to provide a basis for acceptance in the church. Instead, a confession of faith in Christ resulted in a change in life-style and a participation in the building of Christ's kingdom. Schenkel re-flected Rothe's position in his own writings when he denounced a theology which was based upon a literal and infallible interpretation of the Bible. Such a theology is an enemy of cultural development and can be viewed as non-Christian when its preoccupation with doctrinal certainty undermines the capacity for Christians to live in a spirit of love and harmony with one another.[61]

The possibility remained for the church to open up to contemporary developments and thereby win back those who had left. While the possibility demanded a denial of dogmatic assertions by the church, it brought with it the opportunity for the growth and renewal of the church. The division between the church and culture could be overcome by a transition from literalistic, dogmatic dependence on confessional and liturgical formulations in favor of a wide consensus that the church was based upon the Gospel. Such a formulation would allow for freedom of belief within a particular (Christian) framework. The result would be not only a return of those who had left the church, but the true meaning of Christianity would be extended to all areas of life and thereby become world-encompassing instead of world-denying. Rothe sought to extend the meaning of Christianity from the confines of a narrow interpretation of the Bible to one that interacted and dealt with the entire world. The renewal of the church was only possible through a return to the principle of protestant freedom in resonance with the entire cultural developments of the day, i.e., Christianity cannot be content with repeating ancient formulations of faith, but it must seek to find new means of expressing its beliefs in ways which address the needs and concerns of contemporary people. A church built upon such a framework could not only expect renewal, but could work toward the unification of the protestant church in Germany. The desire for a national church appeared once again as the goal not only of Rothe's work, but also that of the *Verein*. A German church which bridged over confessional differences (Lutheran and reformed) and provided an opportunity for dialogue was Rothe's vision. Rothe longed for a church which was led by laypersons and not dictated by the clergy. The technical formulations and insistence upon particular dogmatic assertions by the clergy should give way to a praxis oriented church led by the laity. Rothe's vision was one that he shared with the *Protestantenverein*, if not always in his detailed historical interpretation and specific theological perspective, at least in his hope of moving from dogma to praxis in harmony with a modern view of the world.

Thirty local chapters had been formed by the time of the first national meeting of the *Protestantenverein* in Eisenach in 1865. The group had already grown national in character and political dissension was avoided by the inclusion of the Prussians, who had felt excluded by the strong leadership roles of Rothe and Schenkel. Not only the widening national nature of the group was impressive, but even its opponents appeared surprised by the convention. Hengstenberg, who came to the meetings to sharpen his critique of the *Verein*, was impressed by both Rothe and the newly elected president Johann Bluntschli. Hengstenberg commented afterwards that Rothe's manner of speaking was not only intriguing, but moving. Likewise, he viewed Bluntschli as a sympathetic figure who was capable of both charm and compromise.[62]

Once again, Rothe's address on how the church could win back those who had left it provided not only the highlight, but established the agenda of the young organization. The convention was united on its goals and set them forth in a constitutional framework. The primary purpose of the *Verein* was the renewal of the protestant church in Germany in harmony with the cultural developments of the day. This renewal was sought at the parish level and was opposed to any hierarchical attempts within the church which threatened the rights and freedoms of believers. Once again a desire for confessional accord was underscored with the hope of the development of a national protestant church. Over five hundred members attended the convention and ratified the constitution. Church reform was the major item on the agenda. The meetings began with worship, and the foundation of the *Verein* was firmly committed to the life of the church. Rothe had addressed the situation by stating that the church should not become an institution controlled by theologians, but a place for the congregation where Christian principles could be discovered and practiced.[63]

Unfortunately, dark clouds had already appeared on the horizon. Indeed, the first meeting had been delayed by war. Even more seriously damaging was the publication of Schenkel's *Charakterbild Jesu*.[64] Until that time, Schenkel had been able to serve as a mediator between the more liberal participants and the conservative elements both within and to some extent outside of the group. Not only was this possibility destroyed with the appearance of his book, but Schenkel's conclusions were presented by the conservatives as *the* interpretation of the *Protestantenverein*. It was at this point that Hengstenberg led the attack against the new movement. The debate was turned from the question of the principles of the *Verein* (in particular the potentially positive statements regarding congregational life) to an attack on the "godless liberals" who, represented by Schenkel, denied the deity of Christ.[65] Attacks from pulpits on Schenkel and the *Protestantenverein* became commonplace in some areas (particularly Prussia), and literalists were to a great extent successful in their categorization of the *Protestantenverein* as a liberal, philosophical organization which only played with religion. Some ministers went so far as to issue warnings against participation in the *Verein*. The furor resulted in Schenkel receding from the foreground of the movement and withdrawing from his prior leadership role.

Other difficulties were soon to hinder the growth of the *Verein*. Rothe died of blood poisoning in 1867. Following the controversy over Schenkel, Rothe's death could not have been more untimely. In addition, the political climate was once again disrupted by the outbreak of war with France in 1870. In spite of these monumental setbacks, the *Protestantenverein* continued to pursue its agenda while defending itself from attacks from both the left and right. The meetings from 1868-1870 reiterated the desire for freedom of research and the use of contemporary, scientific methods in theology. Freedom from dogma and for the rights of individual believers remained the major themes throughout the early years of the *Verein*. Addresses were given on the authority of Scripture as well as on questions concerning the historical Jesus. Particularly significant popular topics were also discussed, such as questions regarding bi-confessional marriages (Protestant and Roman Catholic). The desire of the *Protestantenverein* to address the needs of the congregation and to serve as a stimulus for renewal at the parish level can be detected throughout its early meetings.

The sharp attacks by the conservatives on both Schenkel and the *Verein* claimed that the goal of the *Verein* was the creation of a new church, if not a new religion. Schenkel complained bitterly in 1868 about the unfair tactics employed by the conservatives, which had involved, to a large extent, personal attacks on individual members of the *Verein* as well as exaggerations and often misinterpretations of the position of the *Verein*.

For the conservatives the standard for protestant Christianity was found in adherence to a particular interpretation of confessional statements. In spite of numerous attempts at defending themselves, the *Protestantenverein* could not escape from the pressure placed upon them by the continual attacks of the conservatives. An example of the tactics of the conservatives can be seen in the statements issued by the Pastor's Conference which met in Berlin in 1868. The resolution accused the *Protestantenverein* of: (1) undermining belief in the Bible by its reliance on critical methodology; (2) denying the authenticity of the biblical miracles in lieu of scientific explanations; (3) rejecting the divinity of Christ because of the decision not to write a statement of faith; (4) dismissing the work of the Holy Spirit in favor of the spirit of the congregation; and (5) undermining belief in the institutional church through an insistence upon congregational rule. The Berlin ministers concluded that there was no contradiction in historical, archaeological, physical, or astronomical matters between science and the Bible. The *Protestantenverein*, in demanding an openness to the contemporary world, had not only erred in its interpretation of Christianity, but was also inaccurate in its scientific world-view. That left the conservative ministers with the duty of proclaiming that the *Protestantenverein* and its members had broken from the teachings of the church and were no longer a part of the Christian faith.[66]

The *Protestantenverein* responded to the attack at their next meeting by reiterating their commitment to the parish and to the work of winning back those who were estranged from the church. Once again, a passion for renewal through non-dogmatic claims was highlighted. In spite of its attempts to redirect the confrontation, the *Protestantenverein* was immersed in a defense of that which it was seeking to escape: namely, dogmatic conclusions. Hengstenberg and the conservatives did not destroy the movement, but their continuous attacks caused the group to alter its constellation.

By 1870, the group had become to some extent a liberal, theological movement rather than a union of various theological perspectives which had agreed on the issues of religious liberty and church reform. The interests of the church and its members gave way to questions of theological and political inquiry.[67] The changing political climate added to their transformation. The political ascendance of the Prussians in 1870 carried with it consequences for the church. The largely conservative Prussian church adopted a more powerful position within Germany. In addition, the Roman Catholic church developed a more conservative tone, as evidenced by the papal decree on infallibility. The result was that the Protestantenverein was pushed to the left by both internal and external forces.[68]

Forty years after its founding, one of its members remarked that the "Protestantenverein nicht zu den Glücklichen gehöre, über deren Leben ein günstiger Stern leuchte."[69] As previously noted, historical developments through wars, politics, and the untimely death of Rothe caused serious repercussions in the life of the young organization. In spite of these circumstances, what did the group accomplish in its early years? In summarizing the results of the history of the *Verein*, Hönig underscored its role in maintaining the interests of certain groups in the church. The *Protestantenverein* clearly did not succeed in its goal of winning back those who were estranged from the church, but its ability to provide a place for dialogue within the context of the life of the church helped prevent, at least temporarily, a further exodus from the church. The group provided an arena for the discussion of not only theological, but social, political, and practical problems within the life of the church. A significant aspect of its work was in its presentation of an alternative to literalism which occurred through its on-going struggle with Hengstenberg and other conservative opponents. At best, the *Protestantenverein* succeeded in preventing the conservatives from gaining complete control of the church and was able to maintain a place for scientific research within the domain of the church. In spite of its successes in combating the *Protestantenverein*, the conservatives were unable to attain their goal of eliminating the voice of liberalism and attaining doctrinal purity.[70]

The most impressive and lasting result of the *Verein* was through its insistence upon the importance of the parish. The conservative faction which had been eager to criticize the *Verein* for its subjectivity and its dismissal of the proper authority structure, ended up adopting the principal of congregational rule for its own use. The cry for a *Volkskirche* became one which conservatives used in their continuing attacks on liberalism.[71] Indeed, the *Protestantenverein* can be partially credited with church reforms which led to a restructuring and a new emphasis on the local parish.

The broader goals of the *Verein* could not be accomplished and the idealism of the group made criticism easy. In the issue of the relationship of church and culture the founders identified a key area which needed to be addressed. Unfortunately, the *Verein* failed to elaborate a viable option which would convince the average layperson. Even in the early days of the *Verein*, the issues were often intellectualized to the neglect of other factors. The result was a group which sought to embrace the changing culture, but was unable to claim a historical perspective that enabled it to accept both tradition and change.

The decision to avoid a statement of belief left the group open to attacks of subjectivity and individualism. Particularly painful was the fact that Schenkel's book became identified as the position of the *Verein* not only for conservatives, but for others within the church. In spite of repeated denials, the failure to adopt a positive statement left a vacuum which opponents of the group readily seized. The desire for a broad theological spectrum disintegrated and led to the withdrawal of more conservative members like Michael Baumgarten.[72]

It is difficult to read the history of the *Protestantenverein* without a degree of sympathy. The clearest lesson the group provided was the need for plurality to be maintained in the church. Schenkel drew attention to this issue when he remarked upon the explicit desire of the *Protestantenverein* to work within the context of the church. Unlike earlier movements (in particular, the *Licht-freunde*) which withdrew from the church to form separate communities, the *Protestantenverein* maintained its commitment to the church. Schenkel noted that, "die Erfahrung hat seitdem zur Genüge beweisen, daß man nicht das Vaterhaus verlassen soll, wo man zum Verbleiben darin ein gutes Recht, ja eine gewichtige Pflicht hat."[73]

Confessing One's Faith:
The *Apostolikumstreit* and the Struggle towards Openness

Throughout the next two decades, sporadic controversies over the meaning and use of the creeds continued. In 1872 disciplinary cases were raised against Adolph Sydow and E. G. Lisco (both of whom were active in the founding of the *Protestantenverein*). Sydow was removed from his congregation in Berlin, but later reinstated and given a warning when he took exception in a lecture to the creedal statement "conceived by the power of the Holy Spirit and born of the Virgin Mary."[74] Lisco also received a warning due to his lecture on the "Leg-endenhafte Bestandteile im Apostolikum.[75]

In 1891, the actions of a young Württemberger minister, Christoph Schrempf, became the new cause for controversy over the use of the Apostles' Creed. Schrempf was reared as a pietist, but his study of philosophy and theology sharpened an interest in a critical study of the Scriptures. Schrempf spoke with *Oberkonsistorialrat* D. von Wittlich before his ordination regarding his commitment to critical theological research and his deviations from the confessions and certain details of Scripture. In spite of these differences, church officials supported his ordination and Schrempf continued his studies and became the minister of a congregation in Leuzendorf.[76]

On 15 July 1891, Schrempf was to preach on the text, "Seek ye first the kingdom of God and His righteousness." He determined that he could no longer make statements of which he was not fully convinced. As a consequence of this decision, Schrempf omitted the Apostles' Creed as a part of the prescribed liturgy at a baptism following the sermon. On the basis of his critical theological judgments, Schrempf denied the validity of certain parts of the creed and was also concerned that central elements of the Christian faith were not included in it.

Although neither the parents of the child nor any members of the congregation complained about the omission, Schrempf reported his act to church authorities and noted his intention to omit the creed in future baptismal services. Twenty years later, Schrempf wrote that he had sought out an occasion to demonstrate the difficult situation of ministers who were required to use the liturgy.[77] It should be noted that Schrempf had already come into conflict with some members of his congregation for his refusal to participate in a veterans' organization [*Kriegerverein*]. Schrempf was a devout, but highly individualistic person who sought to rediscover the foundation of Christian belief through a careful and critical study of the Gospels. His pursuit of truth demanded an outspokenness that required complete honesty regardless of the consequences. Schrempf believed in the necessity of following one's conscience and forming one's own beliefs. "Kann man mit Gott eine andere Sprache reden als die Sprache des eigenen Herzens?"[78] While Schrempf's negative assessment of the validity of the prescribed use of the Apostles' Creed was certainly not new, his willingness to stand up for his beliefs precipitated a new struggle in the continuing battle over liturgical formulations.

The ensuing controversy developed rapidly. Following his notification of church authorities regarding the omission of the Apostles' Creed during a baptism, church officials decided that the next baptism in the congregation should be conducted by another minister. As confusion and controversy rapidly began to develop, reports circulated in Leuzendorf that Schrempf rejected infant baptism and no longer believed in anything.[79] Following a worship service, Schrempf spoke openly to his congregation about his decision in an attempt to calm things down, but the opposition which had already seized the initiative and branded Schrempf as a heretic declared that Schrempf had damaged the spiritual life of his congregation and was no longer worthy to serve as a minister.[80]

Schrempf argued that his position was based on both a study of the Gospels as well as on the Augsburg Confession in which the standard of faith was defined by the preaching of the Gospel and the administration of the sacraments. The conservatives, according to Schrempf, understood Christianity as the repetition of particular statements. Article 15 of the Augsburg Confession stated that the order of services should not offend one's conscience because it has been established by humans and is not necessary for salvation. Schrempf continued his argument by claiming that:

die Benutzung von Symbolen und Schriftworten darf nicht für an sich Gott wohlge-
fällig gelten, und die zweideutige Benutzung von Schrift und Symbol gefällt Gott ge-
wiß nicht. . . . Auch haben die ersten Jünger nur den allgemeinen Glauben, das Jesus
der Christ sei...nicht ein formulirtes Bekenntnis und bestimmte dogmatische An-
schauungen, wie sie auch ohne apostolisches Glaubensbekenntnis einfach auf den
Namen Christi oder des Vaters, Sohnes und Geistes getauft haben.[81]

Schrempf's pleas, however, were disregarded, and on 18 August 1891 the
Church Council [*Konsistorium*] declared that Schrempf had damaged and confused his congregation by the omission of the Apostles' Creed during the liturgy and that he should no longer serve his congregation. In addition,
Schrempf was fined seventy-two per cent of his salary.[82] Schrempf protested the
decision and attacked the necessity of using a prescribed liturgy which he believed required the sacrifice of his conscience. The response to Schrempf's protest was an immediate dismissal and the removal of his pension.

The controversy was flamed by declarations and articles in conservative
publications like the *Stuttgarter Evangelische Sonntagsblatt* which applauded the
church council for defending the confessions against the attack of liberals like
Schrempf. In a more sympathetic review of the proceedings, Martin Rade questioned why the church council handled Schrempf's case solely in terms of its
judicial requirements and refused to address any religious concerns which were
raised by Schrempf. Additionally, Rade wondered why Schrempf was given
only one early meeting with the General Superintendent in order to defend his
position. In another article that appeared in *Die Christliche Welt*, Karl Köhler
claimed that the charges against Schrempf should have been more specific.
Instead, the council made its decision based solely upon Schrempf's alleged
failure to perform his duties.

So erfährt man aus dem Erlaß nicht einmal...wegen welchen Vergehens das Urteil er-
folgt, noch weniger läßt sich die Behörde auf eine Motivierung mittels Darlegung der
Gründe des Urteils ein.[83]

Rade complained that obedience to the church was being defined as a literalistic interpretation of seventeenth century dogmatics.[84] Köhler lamented that
an inflexible dogmatism was gaining power.[85]

The controversy surrounding Schrempf reached new significance when
Adolf von Harnack became involved in the discussion. Harnack's move to Berlin in 1888 had already created a great deal of controversy since the conservatives had fought to keep him out of Berlin. The *Berliner Tageblatt* reported on
Harnack's first lecture in Berlin and was surprised to find it informative and

fascinating, yet devoid of controversy. In spite of this, conservative opponents of Harnack sought continually to attack him at every opportunity.

Following the outbreak of the Schrempf controversy, a group of Harnack's students asked for his advice about whether or not they should circulate a petition calling for the removal of the Apostles' Creed from the liturgical order and the ordination requirements. Harnack responded to the students' question in a lecture which he gave in his church history course. There were nine points that made up his response to the students. Harnack agreed that there was a need to augment the creed with a confessional statement which was clearer and less problematic. The situation brought about by the Schrempf controversy created an appropriate time for an investigation into the meaning and use of the Apostles' Creed. Although he desired an investigation into its usage, Harnack clearly spoke out against abandoning the creed. A rejection of the creed would do violence to the usefulness and tradition which the creed encompassed. The task of seeking change was to work constructively toward a new statement of faith rather than simply dismissing that which is already present.

While Harnack's opening statements disappointed those students hoping for a more radical response to Schrempf's dismissal, his following statements created turmoil in the discussion on the Apostles' Creed and provided conservatives with an opportunity to express their dissatisfaction with Harnack. In the sixth point of his lecture, Harnack noted that:

> Die Anerkennung des Apostolikums in seiner wörtlichen Fassung ist nicht die Probe christlicher und theologischer Reife; im Gegenteil wird ein gereifter, an dem Verständnis des Evangeliums und an der Kirchengeschichte gebildeter Christ Anstoß an mehreren Sätzen des Apostolikums nehmen müssen.[86]

Harnack noted that the church had made alterations in particular statements of the confession (e.g., the communion of saints) and claimed that the resurrection of the body contradicted Pauline teaching. Furthermore, the statements in the creed should not have been treated as bare facts [*nackte Tatsachen*], but were integrally connected with each other.

The portion of the creed which professed belief in Jesus Christ as "conceived by the Holy Ghost, born of the Virgin Mary" was viewed by Harnack as an exception. These two statements were contrary to the beliefs of many Christians who would otherwise find the creed a useful summary. The church needed to find some solution regarding the necessity of agreement with these statements by both clergy and laity. In this case, Harnack questioned whether belief in the virgin birth should be made a litmus test for inclusion in the church.

> Wenn um eines einzelnen Satzes willen, der mindesten nicht im Zentrum des Chris-
> tentums steht, die Fähigkeit, die Gemeinde, in die man hineingeboren ist, zu erbauen
> und an ihrem innern Leben teilzunehmen, aufgehoben sein sollte, so könnte eine re-
> ligiöse Gemeinde überhaupt nicht bestehen.[87]

Harnack did caution that theologians who objected to the virgin birth as a part of the Apostles' Creed should nevertheless be in agreement with church beliefs, and that the individual should be honest about any disagreement and willing to work for change within the church.

In completing his argument, Harnack pointedly rejected the need for students to become involved in an effort to change the usage of the Apostles' Creed. He rejected this based on three grounds: (1) his belief that the creed should not be abandoned; (2) it was not the place of students to enter into such a decision; and (3) theological students had not yet attained the necessary maturity and knowledge to properly address the discussion (and in particular to avoid confusing the laity). Harnack encouraged his students to devote their time to a careful study of church history and the use of the creed so that they might gain a better understanding of it and in order that their service to the church would be more productive.[88]

Although Harnack's comments were not new and were consistent with his previously published remarks, they touched off a storm of protest. Harnack was stunned that his statements became the center of the confrontation in the church.[89] Harnack was attacked in countless resolutions, conferences, synods, and pamphlets. The attacks were often personal and included labeling Harnack as the Antichrist. In some conferences, pastors were asked to pray for Harnack's death [*ihn tot zu beten*], so that the church would be freed from his influence.[90] Harnack's comments on the virgin birth became the focus of the controversy, and one conference which attacked Harnack declared that the virgin birth was the "foundation of Christianity."[91] Interestingly enough, Harnack was also criticized by liberals who felt that he had not gone far enough. The *Protestantenverein* expressed regret at Harnack's *Vermittlungstheologie* and called for a recognition of the Apostles' Creed simply as an historical document from a previous era.[92]

There was one group that remained loyal supporters of Harnack. The friends of *Die Christliche Welt* met in Eisenach on 5 October 1892 and issued a statement of support for Harnack. This statement reiterated Harnack's claim that there was no interest on their part of eliminating the Apostles' Creed, but only in investigating its meaning both as a symbol of the church and the juridical attempts to make every statement within it binding for ministers and laity. The group went on to demand the right of scientific investigation and a thorough study of the historical development of the creed in order to gain a proper interpretation of it. Furthermore, the declaration of the centrality of the virgin birth caused confusion and was contrary to the testimony of the Gospels.[93]

The growing tumult and the need for some kind of resolution resulted in an investigation into Harnack's statements by request of the Kaiser. The conservatives clamored for action to be taken against Harnack, and Minister Bosse called Harnack to meet with him in preparation for his report to the Kaiser. Bosse was a very conservative man who believed in a literal interpretation of the creeds. Harnack's report of his meeting with Bosse, however, praised him for his openness and knowledge. Bosse raised the possibility of issuing a "first warning" to Harnack with the recommendation that he should be more careful in advising students in areas regarding the church and practical ministry ["*das gehe über eine rein wissenschaftliche Stellungnahme hinaus*"].[94] The final result of the investigation resulted in no disciplinary action against Harnack (although conservatives often claimed the opposite). Harnack's insistence upon freedom of research was not threatened, and the only action taken was the decision to add a professor of conservative persuasion to the theological faculty in Berlin.[95]

Though Harnack was continually attacked, he responded in print to only one of his opponents, Hermann Cremer. In opposition to Harnack's desire for historical investigation, Cremer argued that the facts associated with Jesus Christ were not like other historical facts and thereby not subject to historical investigation. These facts were holy facts [*Heilsthatsachen*] and were bound inextricably to the person of Jesus. They have taken on a special significance through Christ's incarnation and life *for us*. The events of Christ's life were not past facts, but a part of one's present experience. Faith in Christ, then, was not a belief in facts, but a belief in the Christ whose sacrifice for us is tied to the "holy facts" of his life, death, and resurrection.[96] Cremer dismissed the preoccupation of theology with the inner life of Jesus. The Apostles' Creed, for Cremer, presented a summary of the Gospels. The church had simply compiled these "facts" in an "objective, purely historical summary."[97] It was this statement of faith that distinguished the church from other traditions.[98] This confession could not be exchanged for the results of historical research which sought to perform the impossible task of producing a portrait of the inner life of Jesus. Questions about the person of Christ could not be answered by means of historical research. They were considered matters of faith only.

Harnack responded to Cremer's critique partly because of his respect for Cremer. The response opened with a word of thanks to Cremer for the manner and tone of his critique.[99] In response, Harnack underlined the necessity of historical research in theology. Until the eighteenth century, religion was based upon tradition. In the eighteenth century, reason became the predominant basis for religious belief. The first half of the nineteenth century witnessed the rise of speculation as a leading force, but the last half of the nineteenth century was the time for historical study to investigate the foundation of religious belief.

> In dem gegenwärtigen Streit um das apostolische Glaubensbekenntnis handelt es sich um das Recht der geschichtlichen Forschung, in der Kirche zugelassen und gehört zu werden. Wird dieses Recht negiert, so wird das Recht der Reformation negiert.[100]

The role of the church in establishing the creed and its tradition was of central importance to Harnack. His research into the early history of the creed pointed out the variations and differences in the formation and tradition of the creed. The controversy over the Apostles' Creed had erupted, according to Harnack, because conservatives refused to admit the place of historical development. Since religion is bound to history and occurs within history, it cannot be made an exception. The church needed historical research in order to discover the historical Jesus. Harnack affirmed this position because the life of Jesus occurred within history.

Harnack did recognize (in partial agreement with Cremer) that historical research cannot provide a basis for faith in Christ. "...die Überzeugung, daß dieser geschichtliche Jesus der Erlöser und der Herr ist, folgt nicht aus der geschichtlichen Erkenntnis, sondern aus der Sünden- und Gotteserkenntnis, wenn ihr Jesus Christus verkündigt wird."[101] Consequently, a confession of faith should be understood only as the work of the Holy Spirit. Harnack was upset about the tendency of conservatives to misuse the confessions. The misuse of the creed was often a result of the prescribed liturgical order which made its use mandatory. The requirement for Christians to accept one particular historically bound statement as the norm for faith was misleading.[102] Harnack had no interest in abandoning the creed, but hoped for new ways of augmenting it and using it in more appropriate places (he suggested usage as a part of a confirmation class). The attempts to word introductions to the creed to make them more "acceptable" led to dishonest compromises. Harnack believed that the questions regarding the creed were of utmost importance to the church. "Hinter all den schweren kirchlichen Kämpfen und Erregungen der Gegenwart aber liegt dieser liturgische Zwang des Apostolikums."[103]

Harnack was asked repeatedly to write a new confession for the church.[104] He rejected these proposals claiming that he was not a reformer. The task for Harnack remained to work within the church for change. He did not seek a dismissal of part of the church's tradition. The Apostles' Creed remained an integral symbol of the church's tradition and continued to serve a significant role in the life of many Christians. Because many Christians found the creed to be useful for their faith, Harnack was adamantly opposed to doing away with it. Instead, he longed for a building process based upon tradition which would clearly address the issues and needs of the day.

> Wir haben die Überlieferung durch die alte Glaubenslehre zu erziehen, und gewiß - wir wollen die Schätze, die in ihr liegen, fleißig brauchen. Wir wollen auch nicht vergessen, daß alles, was wächst, in Rinden wächst, und daß wir überall an die Vergangenheit anzuknüpfen haben.[105]

The central message of the church was to proclaim the gospel of redemption through the forgiveness of sin.

Harnack remained optimistic about change occurring within the church in spite of the problems and controversies which continued to occur throughout his life. He believed that the church was gradually moving toward a more open environment of tolerance. This movement toward more freedom was underscored by the changes in leadership of the Prussian church from the iron-fisted conservative Hengstenberg to men like Kahl and Kaftan.

The importance of speaking about God brought with it both a challenge and responsibility. Harnack believed that every human statement about God was inadequate. Consequently, the insistence by conservatives on a particular word with a specific meaning was illogical. The significant act was for a community to agree upon speaking, for it was the centrality of the word which had been the foundation of the reformation and provided a basic framework for Protestantism. Throughout his work, Harnack sought to bring new life to the words of the church. Through historical research, Harnack tried to discover the parameters of language as it was molded and changed. It was this liveliness of both tradition and language that set Harnack apart from the conservative insistence upon the creed. At the same time, it was his appreciation of this process that set him apart from more liberal elements who sought to eliminate the creed and ignore the traditions in lieu of "modern faith."

The controversy did not come to any definitive conclusion. Harnack was pleased that even the proclamation of the conservative *Oberkirchenrat* did not make use of the Apostles' Creed as a litmus test for the church. Furthermore, Harnack pointed out that the idea of a test of orthodoxy for candidates was rejected by all sides. Such developments were viewed by Harnack as a part of the slow evolution towards a more tolerant church.

Conclusion

There were no winners in the conflicts between conservatives and rationalists in the church. Although the conservatives retained an upper hand in the conflicts, there was recognition of their weakening influence. The ability of the conservatives to squelch politically the rationalists in the 1840s gave way to their inability to discipline Harnack in the 1890s. To that extent, Harnack was correct when he noted the evolutionary movement towards freedom in the church. The major loser throughout this period was the church which lost capable leaders and countless members through the on-going struggles. The movement toward freedom was so slow and painful that many, particularly laity, became disillusioned and inactive or withdrew from the church

In commenting upon the *Apostolikumstreit*, Agnes von Zahn-Harnack noted that the problems had yet to be resolved. "Alle Fragen, die der Apostolikumstreit vom Jahr 1892 aufgeworfen hatte, stehen noch heute offen."[106] Groups remained divided over the use of the Apostles' Creed: some continued to uphold a literal, infallible view of the factuality of its statements; others recited the creed because the minister did; a third group had reservations about particular statements in the creed; some attempted to condition historically their use of the creed. Unfortunately, a large group had withdrawn from the church because they were unable to make the concessions of any of the other groups.

Conflicts regarding the use of the creed continued into the twentieth century and although new issues would be addressed, questions regarding the meaning of the creed remained. Of particular note were the controversies surrounding Carl Jatho und Gottfried Traub, who were disciplined by church authorities for failing to use the creed during confirmation classes.[107] Even more significant than particular disciplinary cases, though, was a spreading concern about the interpretation of creedal statements (as well as Scripture). Throughout the twentieth century the discussions have broadened to include the need for demythologization, the development of secular theologies in the 1960s and the debate over the appropriateness of speaking about revelation (cf. *The Myth of God Incarnate*).

Instead of a resolution to the language crisis, the result was a broadening that would result in renewed conflict within the church. What remained necessary was an hermeneutical approach that would highlight the contextuality of a statement and provide an alternative to the fixation on historical reference. It seems highly ironic that as the battles over creedal interpretation continued that Harnack (as a church historian) would point to the need to pay closer attention to the creed's use in determining its meaning. In so doing, Harnack stands as a figure enmeshed in the close of an era, while at the same time serving as a precursor to a new one. This approach would seek to reorient the discussion and provide a way of gaining a new perspective on the language of faith and its meaning.

NOTES

[1] While "liberal" has often been used, the limitations of it should also be noted. Its association with a particular stream of academic theological thought makes its use more difficult when discussing developments within the church from 1840-1900.

[2] For a discussion of similar changes undergoing the interpretation of biblical literature, see Hans Frei, *The Eclipse of Biblical Narrative* (New Haven: Yale University Press, 1974).

[3] For an overview of rationalism and its importance in the life of the church see J. Wallmann, *Kirchengeschichte Deutschlands seit der Reformation* (Tübingen: J.C.B. Mohr, 1988), pp. 225ff.

[4] Claus Harms, *Ausgewählte Schriften und Prediten*, Vol. 1, ed. Peter Meinhold (Flensburg: Christian Wolff, 1955), pp. 204-225. Cf. Friedrich Wintzer, *Claus Harms: Predigt und Theologie* (Flensburg: Christian Wolff, 1965), pp. 127ff.

[5] The document which declared the establishment of the Union in Prussia can be found in *Die Geschichte der Evangelischen Kirche der Union: Die Anfänge der Union unter landesherrlichen Kirchenregiment (1817-1850)*, Vol. 1, eds. J. F. Gerhard Goeters and Rudolf Mau (Leipzig: Evangelische Verlagsanstalt, 1992), pp. 88-92.

[6] For a summary of these developments, see Wilhelm Neuser, "Agende, Agendenstreit und Provinzialagenden," in *Die Geschichte der Evangelischen Kirche der Union*, Vol. 1, pp. 55-60.

[7] Claude Welch, *Protestant Thought in the Nineteenth Century*, Vol. 1 (New Haven: Yale University Press, 1972), p. 194.

[8] Gerhard Besier, *Preussische Kirchenpolitik in der Bismarckära: Die Diskussion in Staat und Evangelischer Kirche um eine Neuordnung der kirchlichen Verhältnisse Preußens zwischen 1866 und 1872* (Berlin: Walter de Gruyter, 1980), p. 29. For more on Hengstenberg, see Wolfgang Kramer, *E. W. Hengstenberg, die Evangelische Kirchenzeitung und der theologische Rationalismus* (Erlangen-Nürnberg: Diss. phil., 1972). See also Gottfried Mehnert, *Programme Evangelischer Kirchenzeitung im 19. Jahrhundert* (Wittenberg: Luther Verlag, 1972), pp. 44-45.

[9] Jörn Brederlow, *"Lichtfreunde" und "Freie Gemeinden:" Religiöser Protest und Freiheitsbewegung im Vormärz und in der Revolution von 1848\49* (München: R. Oldenbourg Verlag, 1976), p. 18.

[10] Welch, p. 196.

[11] Christian Tischhauser, *Geschichte der evangelischen Kirche Deutschlands in der ersten Hälfte des 19. Jahrhunderts* (Basel: 1900), p. 632. Cf. Leberecht Uhlich, *Bekenntnisse* (Leipzig: Böhme, 1845), pp. 1–8. See also Brederlow, p. 26. Sintenis sought to emphasize the humanity of Jesus and to underline the role of God the Father.

[12] Uhlich in Ferdinand Kampe, *Geschichte der religiösen Bewegung der neueren Zeit*, Vol. 2 (Leipzig: Otto Wigand, 1852), p. 167. See also Uhlich, *Die protestantischen Freunde* (Deßau: Julius Fritsche, 1845), p. 5.

Please note that I have not made any attempt to alter the German in the citations. The use of nineteenth century texts has resulted in minor variations.

[13] See Uhlich's brief autobiographical remarks in *Bekenntnisse*, p. 10. See also Kampe, p. 166, note 1. For examples, see Uhlich, *Predigten gehalten in der St. Catharinen Kirche zu Magdeburg im Jahre 1846* (Magdeburg: Creutz, 1846).

[14] Uhlich, *Die protestantischen Freunde*, pp. 21–22.

[15] H. Karsten, *Die Kirche und das Symbol in ihrem innern Zusammenhange so wie in ihrem Verhältnisse zu Staat und Wissenschaft* (Hamburg: Johann August Meißner, 1842), p. 2. Karsten concluded that the conservatives and rationalists actually shared a similar approach to the Apostles' Creed because they were both overly concerned with the external foundations and failed to recognize the truth that could not be contained in "external forms."

Orthodoxismus und Naturalismus haben also das mit einander gemein, daß sie in der Sphäre der äußerlichen Abstraktion verharren, und unfähig sind mit der göttlichen Wahrheit als einer lebendigen in eine wirkliche Gemeinschaft zu treten. (p. 86, Footnote 1.)

[16] Brederlow, p. 28.

[17] Eduard Baltzer, *Erinnerungen: Bilder aus meinem Leben* (Frankfurt am Main: Deutschen Vegetarier, 1907), p. 59. "Die Bestrebung der 'protestantischen Freunde' jener Zeit hatten den Zweck, die kirchliche Lehrfreiheit gegen den hereinbrechenden ministeriellen Symbolzwang zu schützen."

[18] Cf. Uhlich in Kampe, p. 172. "Im Festhalten einiger mit der Vernunft im offenbaren Widerspruche stehenden alten Kirchenlehren ist das Heil des Christentums nicht zu suchen. Das Heilsame . . . des alten Systems ist auch in unserer Fassung vorhanden."

[19] Brederlow, p. 29.

[20] C. Thierbach, *Gustav Adolf Wislicenus: Ein Lebensbild aus der Geschichte der freien, religiösen Bewegung* (Leipzig: 1904).

[21] See Wislicenus' extended discussion of this point in reply to his critics in *Ob Schrift, Ob Geist?*, 2nd ed. (Leipzig: Otto Wigand, 1845), p. xff.

[22] Ibid., pp. 17–18. Similar claims were made by Wislicenus' brother in Adolf Timotheus Wislicenus, *Beitrag zur Beantwortung der Frage Ob Schrift? Ob Geist?* (Leipzig: Otto Wigand, 1845), pp. 10–12.

[23] It is interesting to note that because of Uhlich's stature and popularity, the conservatives chose to make their initial assault on Wislicenus. Although Wislicenus' address was more pointed, there were certainly strong parallels between his and Uhlich's previous remarks. Wislicenus was a much easier target because of his background and outspokenness.

[24] Guericke in Wislicenus, pp. 1–2. "Es hat niemals eine verderblichere Demagogie, nie ärgere Feinde der Kirche." The personal nature of the attacks were typical of the attempts to

discredit the *Protestantischen Freunde*. For a more systematic interpretation of Guericke's position on the Apostles' Creed, see Guericke, *Allgemeine Christliche Symbolik*, 2nd ed. (Leipzig:
Winter, 1846), pp. 69-81.

[25] Kampe, p. 182.

[26] Wislicenus noted that one hundred fifty ministers had declared that they no longer recognized his ordination and anathemetized him. See Wislicenus, p. iv.

[27] *Der königliche Ausspruch: "daß die Kirche sich durch sich selbst zu gestalten habe" und die Bekenntnisfrage* (Berlin: C. Grobe, 1846), p. 1. Uhlich's response to such attacks are exemplified
by his remarks in *Bekenntnisse*, pp. 1-8.

[28] Uhlich's response to these charges can be found in *Die Throne im Himmel und auf Erden und
die protestantischen Freunde* (Deßau: Fritsche, 1845).

> "Die protestantischen Freunde, nein, sie sind nicht politisch verdächtig und
> nicht politisch gefährlich. Sollen wir in Beziehung auf die Politik betrachtet wer-
> den, nun dann mache ich den Anspruch auf die Anerkennung, daß wir gute,
> treue Verbündete der Regierung sind." (p. 13.)

[29] Cf. Uhlich, *An ihren Früchten sollt ihr sie erkennen: Anmerkungen zu einer Erklärung des Hrn.
Prof. Dr. Hengstenberg in Berlin gegen die protestantischen Freunde in dem Vorwort zu seiner evangelischen Kirchenzeitung 1845* (Leipzig: Kirchner, 1845), esp. pp. 17-22 for a discussion of
the literary exchanges between conservatives and rationalists.

[30] Kampe, p. 175. This act is exemplary of the attempts by the *Protestantischen Freunde* to avoid
confrontation.

[31] *Wislicenus und seine Gegner* (Leipzig: 1845), pp. 10ff.

[32] Cf. Uhlich, *Die protestantischen Freunde*, p. 4. "Weit entfernt, daß wir das Kirchengehen
abschaffen wollten, sind wir vielmehr der Meinung, daß der Kirchenbesuch durch unsre
Versammlungen neues Leben bekommen werde."

[33] Kampe, p. 182.

[34] Report in Brederlow, p. 34.

[35] Kampe, p. 178.

[36] Cf. *Thronrede bei der Eröffnung der sächsischen Ständesversammlung am 14. September 1845 und
die den kirchlichen Bewegungen unsrer Tage gemachten Vorwürfe* (Leipzig: Gustav Brauns, 1845).
See also *Allerhöchste Antwort Sr. Majestät des Königs Friedrich Wilhelm IV. auf die von dem Berliner Magistrat in der Audienz vom 2. Oktober 1845 in Betreff der kirchlichen Angelegenheiten
überreichten Immediat-Eingabe* (Magdeburg: Albert Falckenburg, 1845), esp. pp. 11-12.

[37] Julius Rupp, *Die Symbole oder Gottes Wort? Ein Sendschreiben an die Evangelische Kirche* (Leipzig: Wigand, 1846). A similar controversy broke out as a result of statements made by
Wilhelm Detroit, minister of a French-Reformed congregation in Königsberg. Detroit was
removed from his congregation because of variations to the Apostles' Creed. See Kampe,
pp. 201 and 223.

[38] Wislecenus in Kampe, p. 229.

[39] The statement can be found in *Die Geschichte der Evangelischen Kirche der Union*, Vol. 1, pp.
353-54. A summary of the Synod and its conclusions can be found in Wilhelm Neuser,
"Landeskirchliche Reform-, Bekenntnis- und Verfassungsfragen: Die Provinzialsynoden
und die Berliner Generalsynode 1846," in *Die Geschichte der Evangelischen Kirche der Union*,
pp. 346-66.

[40]   Cf. Leberecht Uhlich, *17 Sätze in Bezug auf die Verpflichtungsformel protestantischer Geistlicher, ausgegangen von der Synode zu Berlin 1846* (Wolfenbüttel: Holle'schen, 1846), esp. pp. 11-13.

[41]   See Baltzer, *Erinnerungen*, pp. 63-69.

[42]   Brederlow, p. 55. See also Besier, p. 25, Note 31.

[43]   Cf. A. R. Findeis, *Ueber die Gesellschaft der protestantischen Freunde und ihre Grundsätze* (Magdeburg: Albert Falckenburg, 1844), esp. pp. 40-53. For a list of works that appeared during this time, see Kampe, p. 188.

[44]   Cf. Uhlich, *Ueber den Amtseid der Geistlichen* (Leipzig: Otto Klemm, 1846).

[45]   Uhlich, *Sein Leben von ihm selbst beschrieben* (Gera: 1872), p. 43.

[46]   For a summary of the process and a commentary on the decision of the theological faculty in Heidelberg to declare Dulon unfit for further ministry, see Daniel Schenkel, *Gutachten der theologischen Fakultät der Universität Heidelberg über den durch Pastor R. Dulon angeregten Kirchensteit in Bremen* (Heidelberg: Karl Groos, 1852). See esp. p. 128 where Schenkel concluded that certain of Dulon's views are no longer religious, but political and social commentary disguised as religious statements.

[47]   There remains a tendency among many historians to evaluate the *Lichtfreunde* in terms of their political activity (e.g., Brederlow). Besier notes the difficulty of separating religious and political opposition. (Gerhard Besier, *Religion-Nation-Kultur: Die Geschichte der christlichen Kirchen in den gesellschaftlichen Umbrüchen des 19. Jahrhunderts* (Neukirchen-Vluyn: Neukirchener, 1992), p.38) While there were certainly political implications to many of the early decisions of the *Lichtfreunde*, it is my opinion that the group began primarily as a religious movement for renewal in the church which evolved into an increasingly political movement due to both internal and external pressures. One central element in evaluating this group is the decision to focus on particular leaders. Uhlich's leadership role (which has been largely overlooked) is a particularly strong factor for arguing for the religious basis of the *Lichtfreunde*. Cf. Uhlich, *Die Throne im Himmel*, esp. pp. 36-40 where following a rejection of political motives, Uhlich discusses the desire to see renewal in the church.

[48]   Cf. Uhlich's discussion of the difficulties he experienced in Magdeburg in *Dissidentische Denkschrift* (Gotha: Stollbergsche, 1859), p. 14.

[49]   Gustav Tschirn, *Zur 60 jährigen Geschichte der freireligiösen Bewegung* (Bamberg: 1904), p. 51.

[50]   Uhlich discussed the attempts by authorities throughout Germany to suppress the congregations of the *Lichtfreunde*. He also cited a Prussian report from 1851 which states that authorities now have the duty to confront the *Deutschkatholiken* and *Freireligiösen* with all possible means [*mit allen gesetzlichen Mitteln entgegenzutreten*]. Uhlich, *Dissendentische Denkschrift*, p. 7.

It was not until 1858 that the Prussian government eased the restrictions on the freireligiöse Gemeinden. See Helmut Obst, "Lichtfreunde, Deutschkatholiken und Katholisch-apostolische Gemeinden," in *Die Geschichte der Evangelischen Kirche der Union*, p. 324.

[51]   Cf. Walter Nigg, *Die Geschichte des religiösen Liberalismus: Entstehung, Blütezeit, Ausklang* (Zürich: 1934), p. 202. "Wie alle lebendige Entwicklung auf dem Gesetz der Polarität beruht, so muß auch der Pendel der Kirche zwischen Orthodoxie und religiösem Liberalismus hin- und herschwingen." For a contemporary discussion of the importance of diversity within the context of community, see Patrick Hill "Religion and the Quest for Community," in *On Community*, ed. Leroy Roumer (Notre Dame: University of Notre Dame Press, 1991), pp. 151ff.

[52]   For a fuller portrait of Rothe, see Dietrich Rössler, "Richard Rothe, in *Theologen des Protestantismus im 19. und 20. Jahrhundert*, ed. Martin Greschat (Stuttgart: W. Kohlhammer,

1978), pp. 74–83 and *Der Protestantismus im Wandel der neuen Zeit*, ed. Kurt Leese (Stutgart: Alfred Kröner Verlag, 1941), pp. 159ff. Nigg described Rothe with the following words, "Man darf Rothe im guten Sinn des Wortes als einen modernen Heiligen charakterisieren." (Nigg, p. 207.)

53 Of particular significance was Schenkel's opposition to Kuno Fischer, a young philosopher whom Schenkel referred to as an atheist and a danger to the church. See Heinrich Hermelink, *Das Christentum in der Menschengeschichte: von der französischen Revolution bis zur Gegenwart*, Vol. 2 (Stuttgart: J. B. Metzler, 1953), p. 438.

54 Copies of the early documents as well as summaries of addresses are attached in an appendix to Daniel Schenkel, *Der deutsche Protestantenverein und seine Bedeutung in der Gegenwart* (Wiesbaden: C. W. Kreidal's Verlag, 1868). See also W. Hönig, *Der deutsche Protestantenverein* (Berlin: 1904), pp. 28ff.

55 "Jener Strom hat sich in der Stille einer Jahrhunderte langen beharrlichen Geschichtsarbeit unvermerkt ein neues Bett gegraben, und in dieses hat er sich jetzt hinüber ergossen; - aus seinem anfänglichen aber nur provisorischen Bett, dem kirchlichen, hat er sich in dasjenige hinüber begeben, das sein bleibendes sein soll, in das sittliche, in das (denn wir brauchen uns des edlen Wortes wahrlich nicht zu schämen) staatliche." Richard Rothe, "Zur Debatte über den Protestantenverein," in Friedrich Nippold, ed., *Gesammelte Vorträge und Abhandlungen Dr. Richard Rothes und seinen letzten Lebensjahren* (Elberfeld: R. L. Friderichs Verlag, 1886), p. 98.

56 It should be noted that other interpretations of Rothe emphasize the role of the state and conclude otherwise. The following interpretation of Rothe is based on his involvement with the *Protestantenverein*. In light of his activity in this organization and his shared concern for the renewal of the church, it seems problematic to highlight only the statements in Rothe in which the state fulfills an apocalyptical role as the bearer of a new religious community. For other interpretations of Rothe, see Karl-Friedrich Oppermann, *Christus und der Fortschritt: Richard Rothes Versuch einer Vermittlung von geschichtlichen Umgestaltungsprozess und christlichem Glauben* (Göttingen: Theol. Fak. Dissertation, 1983). Paul Kessler, *Glaube und Gesellschaftsgestaltung: Die Bedeutung Richard Rothes für das Verhältnis von Kirche und Welt im 20. Jahrhundert* (Essen: Reimar Hobbing), 1969. Hans-Joachim Birkner, *Spekulation und Heilsgeschichte: Die Geschichtsauffassung Richard Rothes* (München: Chr. Kaiser, 1959).

57 Rothe in Adolf Hausrath, *Richard Rothe und seine Freunde*, Vol. 2 (Berlin: G. Grote'sche Verlagsbuchhandlung, 1906), p. 471.

58 Rothe noted that there was a danger that the *Protestantenverein* would be viewed in the same way as the *Lichtfreunde*. Consequently the attempt was made to provide a broad basis for inclusion in the *Protestantenverein* by rejecting an association with one particular theological perspective. See Rothe, "Zur Debatte," pp. 92 and 127.

59 *Der Protestantismus im Wandel der neueren Zeit*, p. 63.

60 Rothe in Hausrath, Vol. 2, p. 469. See also Rothe "Zur Debatte," pp. 96–97.

61 Schenkel, p. 26.

62 Unfortunately Hengstenberg's published comments on the proceedings were quire different. He used Martha's words in John 11:39, "Lord, already there is a stench because he has been dead four days" as the basis for his attack. The *Protestantenverein*, according to Hengstenberg, was already in the process of decay. Hegstenberg in Hausrath, Vol. 2, p. 486.

63 Richard Rothe, "Durch welche Mittel können die der Kirche entfremdeten Glieder ihr wieder gewonnen werden?," in Friedrich Nippold, ed., *Gesammelte Vorträge und Abhandlun-*

gen Dr. Richard Rothes aus seinen letzten Lebensjahren (Elberfeld: R. L. Friderichs, 1886), pp, 129–147.

[64] Schenkel defended the sharp criticism of his work in Die Protestantische Freiheit in ihrem gegenwärtigen Kampfe mit der kirchlichen Reaktion (Wiesbaden: Kreidel, 1865). Of particular note is Schenkel's rejection of the use of the Apostles' Creed as a standard for orthodoxy (See pp. 268ff.). "Das Christenthum verpflichtet uns nicht zur Annahme eines neuen Lehrbegriffes, sondern zum Wandel in einen neuen Leben aus Gott. Lehrsätze und Bekenntnißformeln sind kein Leben, sondern Meinungen und Theorien" (p. 274).

[65] For an indication of the nature of the attacks on Schenkel, see Zeugnisse gegen das Buch des evang. Predigerseminardirektors zu Heidelberg, welches läugnet daß die Bibel Gottes Wort und daß Jesus Gottes Sohn sei (Karlsruhe: Gutsch, 1864). See also Charakterbild Jesu von Dr. Daniel Schenkel oder Bibel? (Karlsruhe: Gutsch, 1864) and Ph. G. Hauck, Dr. Schenkel, seine Freunde und seine Gegner (Karlsruhe: Gutsch, 1865), p. 22, note 1. Of particular note is Hauck's conclusion that Schenkel's work is heretical because it calls into question the church's confessional basis.

D. F. Strauß also entered in the debate by attacking both sides in Die Halben und die Ganzen: eine Streitschrift gegen die HH. Schenkel und Hengstenberg (Berlin: Duncker, 1865).

[66] The plans of the Protestantenverein to meet in Berlin in 1869 were disrupted by the refusal to allow the group to hold worship services and meetings in churches in Berlin. This decision was indicative of the growing pressures being placed on the group. See Hönig, Der deutsche Protestantenverein, p. 11.

[67] Besier's evaluation of the Protestantenverein is largely in terms of political activities. This interpretation is guided by his interest in church-state relationships during this time period. In defense of his interpretation, Besier notes that the goal of the Protestantenverein to renew the church within the context of the congregation [Gemeindeprinzip] was never concretely defined.

> So liegt der Verdacht nahe, daß es dem liberalen Protestantismus nicht so sehr um die Realisierung der freien Kirche im freien Staat zu tun war, als um die Verbreitung liberalen Gedankengutes, um schließlich über einen politischen Systemwechsel noch die kirchliche Herrschaft in den Landeskirchen zu übernehmen. (Besier, Preussische Kirchenpolitik, p. 181.)

In contrast, my interpretation of the early years of the Protestantenverein (1865–70) has emphasized the religious interests of the group. There were, of course, political implications to many of the group's statements and it may in the end be impossible to separate religious and political interests in this instance. It is important, though, not to underestimate the religious interests of the Protestantenverein.

[68] In the early 1900s, the Protestantenverein received a new wave of interest and grew rapidly until it encompassed thirty thousand members shortly before the outbreak of the first world war. The changing times, however, had already brought about significant alterations to the Verein. It often fell prey to intellectualism, and in particular to the speculative-critical theology of liberalism. In spite of this, the Verein survived in some form, continuing to function and finally cooperating with the Bekennende Kirche during the Third Reich. The Protestantenverein eventually became a member of the International Association for Religion Freedom.

[69] Hönig, p. 9.

70 W. Hönig, *Die Arbeit des deutschen Protestantenvereins während seines fünfundzwanzigjährigen Bestehens* (Berlin: A. Haack Verlag, 1888), pp. 30ff.

71 Hönig, p. 31.

72 Besier discusses the increasing sense of isolation felt by more conservative members like Michael Baumgarten who eventually withdrew his membership in 1876. Besier, p. 191, note 393.

73 Schenkel, p. 68.

74 Aldolph Sydow, *Aktenstücke: betreffend das vom königlichen Consistorium der Provinz Branden- burg über mich verhängte Disciplinarverfahren wegen meines Vortrags "Ueber die wunderbare Geburt Jesu"* (Berlin: Henschel, 1873). Sydow called for a reassessment of the creed in light of his reading of the New Testament as well as the progress of modern research. "Wie nun die Kirche Dogmen bildet, so darf und soll sie nach Dogmen umbilden, wenn fortgeschrittene Gedankenarbeit es erfordert und das Bewußtsein der Zeit in der dogmatischen Tradition nicht mehr mit innerer Wahrheit lebt" (pp. 13-14).

75 Lisco, *Das apostolische Glaubensbekenntnis* (Berlin: Henschel, 1872). For a brief overview, see Hermelink, *Das Christentum in der Menschengeschichte*, Vol. 3 , pp. 553ff.

The Sydow and Lisco cases are sometimes referred to as the "first" Apostolikumstreit. Lisco became involved in another confrontation due to his refusal to use the Apostles' Creed with confirmation classes and in worship services. Because of this, he was dismissed from in his congregation in 1895. See Besier, *Religion-Nation-Kultur*, p. 124.

76 Hermann Schultz, "Gedanken zum Fall Schrempf," *Die Christliche Welt*, 15 September 1892, p. 862.

77 Christoph Schrempf, *Religion ohne Religion*, Vol. 1 (Stuttgart: Frommanns Verlag, 1947), p. 48. Schrempf wanted to emphasize that the individuality of the minister should be appre- ciated and that he should not be treated as a machine. There are conflicting reports that claim that Schrempf had not sought out a confrontation. See Nigg, p. 265.

78 Schrempf, p. 70.

79 Martin Rade, "Die Amtsentsetzung des Pfarrers Schrempf," *Die Christliche Welt*, 18 August 1892, p. 761.

80 Schrempf's discussion with his congregation was later reported as a "Polimisieren gegen das Apostolikum auf der Kanzel." In Rade, p. 762.

81 Schrempf in Rade, p. 761. Schrempf's rhetoric against the required use of the Apostles' Creed became even more outspoken following the decision to remove him from his con- gregation. In defense of his actions he wrote that he could no longer accept the creed as a summary of his faith. He believed that the charges against him were unfair because he had spoken out in honesty. Schrempf argued that had he remained silent about his doubts concerning the creed that nothing would have happened. "Somit schient doch insbeson- dere das Apostolikum der heilige, unantastbare Glaube der Kirche zu sein." Schrempf, *Eine Frage an die evangelische Landeskirche Württembergs* (Göttingen: Vandenhoeck & Ruprecht, 1892), p. 52.

82 The fine was later reduced to fifty per cent.

83 Karl Köhler, "Die Amtsentsetzung des Pfarrers Schrempf vom kirchenrechtlichen Stand- punkt aus betrachtet," *Die Christliche Welt*, 15 September 1892, pp. 869-70.

84 Rade, p. 766.

85 Köhler, p. 872.

86 Adolf von Harnack, *Reden und Aufsätze*, Vol. 1 (Gießen: Ricker, 1904), p. 222-23.

87 Harnack, p. 224.

88 Ibid., pp. 225–26.

89 Harnack noted the consistency of his position towards the Apostles' Creed over a 20 year period. See Harnack, *Das apostolische Glaubensbekenntniß* (Berlin: Haack, 1892), p. 35.

90 Agnes von Zahn-Harnack, *Adolf von Harnack* (Berlin: Hans Bott, 1936), p. 204. See also W. Herrmann, *Warum handelt es sich in dem Streit um das Aposolikums?* (Leipzig: Grunow, 1893).

91 Declaration of the *evangelisch-kirchliche Konferenz* in *Die Christliche Welt*, No. 42, 13 Oktober 1892, pp. 948–49.

92 Harnack, *Das apostolische Glaubensbekenntnis*, p. 6.

93 *Die Christliche Welt*, 13 October 1892, pp. 948–49.

94 Harnack's letter to his Father-in-law, cited in Agnes von Zahn-Harnack, *Harnack*, p. 206.

95 Prof. Schlatter accepted this position and enjoyed a cordial relationship with Harnack.

96 Hermann Cremer, *Warum können wir das apostolische Glaubensbekenntnis nicht aufgeben?* (Berlin: Wiefandt and Grieben, 1893), pp. 42–43. "Wir fordern nicht zuerst einen Glauben an Thatsachen also Voraussetzung und Bedingung des Glaubens an Christus, sondern der Glaube an Christus ist und setzt den Glauben an die Thatsache, die Heilsthatsachen, und wir begreifen beides."

97 Cremer in Harnack, p. 278.

98 Cremer emphasized the role of the Apostles' Creed as a baptismal confession and understood it as that which marked a distinction between those within and outside of the church. Cremer, p. 10.

99 Harnack, p. 267.

100 Harnack, p. 289.

101 Ibid., p. 293.

102 Ferdinand Kattenbusch agreed with Harnack in noting the importance of the historical circumstances surrounding the development of the Apostles' Creed. His solution, however was to allow the laity to have one understanding of the creed and avoid a particular interpretation for the educated clergy and theologians. "Aber die Hauptsache ist, daß es überhaupt nicht gestattet ist, bestimmte geschichtliche Vorstellungen über die Herkunft, den 'Sinn' u.s.w. des Symbols vorzuschreiben. In diesem Sinne muß allerdings der wissenschaftlichen Forschung alle Freiheit gewahrt werden." Kattenbusch, *Zur Würdigung des Apostolikums* (Leipzig: Grunow, 1892), p. 49.

103 Harnack in Agnes von Zahn-Harnack, *Der Apostolikumstreit des Jahres 1892 und seine Bedeutung für die Gegenwart*, (Marburg: Elwert, 1950), p. 11.

104 Martin Rade offered an alternative confession in *Der rechte evangelische Glaube* (Leipzig: Grunow, 1892), p. 35. Rade noted that this statement was not intended as a replacement for the use of the Apostles' Creed during worship.

105 Harnack, Vol. 2, p. 155.

106 Agnes von Zahn-Harnack, *Der Apostolikumstreit*, p. 14.

107 For a summary of this process, see Gottfried Traub, *Meine Verteidigung gegen den Evangelischen Oberkirchenrat* (Bonn: Carl Georgi, 1912). Traub's response to the process is also included and is particularly noteworthy, see pp. 121–158.

Chapter Two
Wittgenstein and the Linguistic Turn

Introduction

In the preceding chapter an attempt was made to highlight the growing problems regarding religious language by looking closely at three examples of differences in linguistic interpretation that developed in discussions in the church in Germany during the nineteenth century. In conclusion it was also noted that these debates were not limited to the examples that were given, but in fact have escalated and continue to concern the church today. Throughout the discussions regarding demythologizing, the death of God, and the on-going hermeneutical debate, the meaning of religious language has been the focal point. In the midst of these discussions, an alternative philosophical approach has been developed. This approach, known as ordinary language philosophy, developed out of the work and writings of Ludwig Wittgenstein.[1]

For many years there has been interest in understanding and applying Wittgenstein's thoughts to the theological discipline.[2] In the following chapter, we will look at several of these attempts. Before turning to them, however, it is important that we begin by taking a careful look at potentially significant themes in Wittgenstein's writings.

The attempt to illustrate the distinctiveness of Wittgenstein's approach should not be understood as an artificial effort to manipulate the material to fit a particular outline. Instead, there is an exploration of significant themes in order to develop a possible alternative understanding that will allow us to discover an approach to religious language (creedal statements in particular) which will avoid the dangers and divisions of the past. This study is certainly not exhaustive. While the present study includes a commentary and dialogue with those who have philosopical expertise about Wittgenstein's works, it is guided by an interest in the possibility of the theological application of themes within the later writings of Wittgenstein. The purpose is to sketch out particular passages of Wittgenstein which have been foundational in the theological discussions that will guide the discussion when it turns to an analysis of the role and function of liturgical language.

Wittgenstein was not a systematic philosopher. His own method was to keep journals and notebooks of thoughts and comments which he continued to refine and redact throughout his life. In the following chapter, no attempt is made to try to systematize these aphorisms. Instead, this chapter looks at particular themes within Wittgenstein's writings which could be useful in providing an alternative to the language crisis troubling the church. While Wittgenstein was not systematic, he did take a holistic approach to language. Consequently, any attempt to delineate this perspective will be arbitrary to some extent. Language games, forms of life, contextuality and rules are all interrelated ideas which combine to form a whole. They are separated in this study only to provide clarity to the contributions which they make in forming this whole.

It would also be impossible to provide a comprehensive commentary on these topics in Wittgenstein. The secondary literature on Wittgenstein continues to grow at a rapid pace. Scholars persist in arguing about variant readings and the implications of isolated statements. The following presentation seeks to avoid the dangers of the over–generalized eisegesis of Wittgensteinian themes (see footnote 2) as well as the quagmire of speculative exegesis from inferred nuances.[3] It is important, for now, to gain insight into salient themes of Wittgenstein's work which can serve as a guide. The over–view which is presented in this chapter is guided by the task of seeking an appropriate model for understanding doxological language.

Language

Wittgenstein begins the *Philosophical Investigations* with a discussion about language. His description of language draws on Augustine's conception of language in which definition and description are essential ingredients.[4] The presentation of Augustine's picture of language serves as a model which Wittgenstein proceeds to call into question. While Patrick Bearsley has criticized Wittgenstein as beginning with an inadequate presentation of Augustine's understanding of language, Wittgenstein is concerned primarily with articulating the implications of a view of language that is dependent on ostensive definition. Hence, he uses Augustine as a representative approach to language.[5] Against this background, Wittgenstein sets forth a description of language games in order to show how language functions. The wide varieties of language and its usage demonstrated to Wittgenstein that an understanding of language that was based solely on naming and ostensive definition was too limited.

The introduction of language games is not an attempt to present "another theory, replacing the previous one, but rather a terminology, incorporating a comparison."[6] Although Joachim Schulte argues that Wittgenstein conceived of language in general as a language game as well as identifying different uses of language as language games, Schulte's example of language as a game in general depends on the possibility of isolating a primitive language game.[7] The danger of such a reading is to attribute to Wittgenstein a transcendent point-of-view of language as a whole which would distinctly contradict his insistence on the limits of human knowledge. Wittgenstein weaves the plurality of language games together not through an over-arching theory of language as a game, but through the similarities that these games share with each other (which he refers to as "family resemblances"). Any notion of an "essence" of language is one that develops only out of inference and must include "the round of collaborative activity that generates the human way of life."[8] While Wittgenstein had considered and developed an understanding of language games in previous writings, it became the focal point for an adequate description of language in the *Philosophical Investigations*.[9] The comparison of language and its function to games is reported to have occurred to Wittgenstein as he passed by a football game in progress. This event led him to observe that "in language we play *games* with *words*."[10] For Wittgenstein, language games included a wide variety of associated activities.

> Language like many an individual game or games as a class: (a) is autonomous, (b) requires no justification, (c) is not a process of ratiocination, (d) nor constantly accompanied by parallel thought processes, (e) but is rather a comprehensive form of life combining the most diverse elements, (f) according to rules, which are (g) flexible, and (h) varied, so reveal no essence.[11]

Learning these language games involves learning explanations and examples.[12] "The term 'language game' is meant to bring into prominence the fact that the speaking of language is part of an activity, or of a form of life."[13] Language games are based on a certain agreement in which words are associated with particular pictures or ways of seeing.[14] The language game is a system of communication which is complete in itself.

> When we forget which colour this is the name of, it loses its meaning for us; that is, we are no longer able to play a particular language game with it. And the situation then is comparable with that in which we have lost a paradigm which was an instrument in our language.[15]

When we observe a language game we must explore how it is to be used. It points to a particular use and takes us in. To understand the language game we must find this usage. Since theoretical explanations fail to justify or grasp language games, the task is to look at the language game as it is being played.[16]

There is no need to try to simplify a language game by trying to replace it with a simpler one. Any attempt results in the use of another language game.[17] The point of language games is not in giving precise definitions (which are impossible), but in how we play the game.[18] "Meaning" involves the mastery of a technique and not some kind of hidden mental activity. Wittgenstein claimed that it was redundant to say that one is able to do certain things when one masters a language game. The language game is about doing not knowing.[19] Language games extend our behavior, "For our language game is behaviour."[20]

Language games have no one thing in common, but are related to each other in different ways. Often different language games are interrelated and require the knowledge of similar things, e.g., Wittgenstein compared the relationship to the knowledge of pieces in one game which would allow one to understand what a "king" is in chess.[21] Wittgenstein refers to the commonalities that are shared among language games as family resemblances.[22] There is often the temptation to look for something in common rather than to recognize that language games are related to each other as a family.[23] Instead of searching for an elusive shared element among language games, one can note the parallels which exist in the way that language is used.

Participation in a language game involves acceptance of the practice (and behavior associated with the language game) as well as a certain level of trust. "I really want to say that a language game is only possible if one trusts something."[24] This acceptance of everyday language games is based on shared participation. Criticism is possible only to the extent that one notes the false accounts and connections within a language game.[25] There is no transcendent perspective outside a language game which would allow for analysis and a comprehensive perspective of a language game. In place of such a vantage point, one accepts and participates in language games which enables one to join in the "hurly-burly" of life.

The end result of a language game is a way of acting. Wittgenstein claimed that an integral relationship exists between a language game and a form of life. They are so wed together that "to imagine a language means to imagine a form of life."[26] Because of this the certainty of a statement is found in its accompanying form of life.[27] It is impossible to make a separation between thinking and action. "For the thinking is not an accompaniment of the work any more than of thoughtful speech."[28] Any attempt to differentiate behavior and state of mind is unwarranted for one comes via the other.[29] Wittgenstein's discussion of "private language" (*Philosophical Investigations* §243ff) in this connection has led to an enormous amount of debate and confusion. Robert Fogelin claims that, "At this stage it is not clear whether the private language argument as currently discussed has very much to do with the text that originally generated the discussion."[30] Similarly, Hallett attributes the confusion to the mistaken notion by some readers that Wittgenstein is offering a theoretical discussion of the possibility of private language.[31]

> The point of exploring the private language fantasy is, then, to retrieve the natural expressiveness of the human body, and to reaffirm the indispensability of belonging to a community: two obvious facts that the metaphysically dictated conception of the self trivializes and occludes.[32]

Ronald Suter concurs by concluding that Wittgenstein sought to refute private mental constructs by showing how words draw from our common language, not words intelligible only to an individual. "Words belong to our shared, public language."[33] The inherent relationship between forms of life and language games requires an acceptance of the forms of life as a given part of the language game (which we can only participate in through a certain level of trust). There is no private language to resort to, only a shared, learned one which is based upon our shared actions and agreement.[34] The participation in a language game involves the ability to recognize the patterns and connections (rules) which make up the language and to be able to continue the pattern in the resultant form of life. This requires more than just a parroting of the words, and Wittgenstein noted that one can play a language game without it making any sense.[35] The ability to continue the pattern or form of life is not due to some hidden mental process or state "behind" the statement. Wittgenstein paradoxically wrote that continuing the pattern is not the same as saying a formula, but that does not mean that it is an activity other than saying the formula. Continuing the pattern in a language game means that one makes the connections between the language game and the form of life.[36] Words effect us as they are connected with our lives.[37]

A sign by itself is dead. It is only in its use that it is alive. The use is life.[38] We should not look internally for understanding, but should look to see how it is manifested. Wittgenstein claimed that answers are expressed in a form of life.[39] Gestures and fine shades of behavior may show that one knows one's way about the language game (i.e., one knows how to manifest the connections in the language game).[40] The change that occurs when the student learns to read is a behavioral change. Similarly, the language game finds its justification in how we live our lives. Agreement is not a matter of holding similar opinions but occurs in a form of life.[41]

There is not an ultimate defense or justification for the way in which we act. We can only show points of reference and connections which exist between the language game and form of life. While an attempt has been made to reinterpret Wittgenstein as one who sought to uncover a correspondence between language and reality, Wolfgang Stegmüller opposes such an attempt and argues that Wittgenstein was concerned with the use of language rather than its connection to reality.[42] One must look at the practice of language in order to see these connections because the end result of a language game is a way of acting. Consequently, the certainty of a statement is its accompanying form of life.[43] The importance of consensus and shared agreement in the playing of the language game convinced Wittgenstein that the form of life grows out of a community.[44]

Rules

According to Wittgenstein, learning a language game involves the learning of rules. There is general agreement that Wittgenstein's understanding of the relationship of rules to language and grammar evolved over a period of time.[45] While a certain continuity exists, there is a noticeable difference between the attempts by the "early Wittgenstein" to develop "rules of logical syntax" (*Tractatus*) and the discussion of rules in the *Philosophical Investigations*. One does not explicitly learn the rules, but the practice.[46] These rules are learned implicitly, however, through the practice of participating in the language game. The game is learned practically without the explanation of explicit rules.[47] Friedrich Waismann rejects attempts to define rules as a concept. In place of a definition, Wittgenstein recognized rules as a "family resemblance concept," i.e., they can be understood in terms of similar features.[48] The rules are not stated but are learned through examples.[49] Practice is the only way in which one can be taught how to follow a rule. Because a word is learned under particular circumstances, it carries with it an implied sense of appropriate usage. Rules are associated with pictures which describe what we do. It is rules that make the situation into a game (e.g., chess). "Moving a piece could be conceived in two ways: as a paradigm for future moves or as a move in an actual game."[50] Consequently the rule carries with it two functions. It acts in a particular way within a language game, but also guides future usage within a language game and other related games.

Wittgenstein claimed that there was a correspondence between "rules" and "meaning."[51] To understand a sentence is to be able to follow the guidelines and connections of the rules within that statement. The rules become manifest in the form(s) of life associated with the language game. This inherent relationship grows out of the guidance of the rules and led Wittgenstein to conclude that a rule that is followed is expressed in our lives.[52]

Rules also play a controlling function within the language game. They provide boundaries which enable language games to be differentiated from one another. One must follow these rules or one is playing another game. It does not mean that one is wrong, but it does mean that one will be involved in a different language game (and that one is speaking of something else).[53] There is not a complete list of rules, but rules permit and forbid certain actions. Rules do not restrict all movement, but do fulfill a limiting function. "Practice in the use of the rule also shows what is a mistake in its employment."[54] Rules also provide guidance to the extent that they provide boundaries as to how far one can go in a particular language game. As a result, contradictions become evident when one has passed out of the boundaries of that particular game. In this understanding, rules are similar to walls which prohibit movement outside of a certain space.[55] Contradictions within a statement exhibit the boundaries which have been crossed over. While the rule may attempt to draw sharp boundaries, the usage will never coincide with it since the use of a word never has an exact correspondence. "We don't use language according to strict rules–it hasn't been taught us by means of strict rules, either."[56] Games are unregulated in the sense that we cannot draw a clear boundary marking where they end. While boundaries may be drawn for special purposes they do not, in reality, exist.[57]

Generally, we cannot give rules because there are no precise definitions. Since words tend to look the same in a dictionary, we are deceived into believing that they can all be defined in one way (ostensively). The definition of a word does not lie in a "mental act" which accompanies them, but in its use according to particular rules within a system.[58]

How does one follow a rule? A rule does not foreshadow all that will happen. It does not anticipate all possible events or associate a particular mental act with accompanying words.[59] Instead the rule offers guidance as to interpretations and connections associated with the language game. Wittgenstein wrote that a rule is like a sign-post in that it shows a direction as to where one should go (i.e., which road to take). There may be, however, several signs that are open for different interpretations which leave room for doubt.[60] The guidance offered by a rule consists of enabling the participant to seek connections between the language game and form of life (but not in an internal way). The rule exerts an influence on the patterning of connections (rather than feelings).[61] Rules guide us to the appropriate way to continue. They do not adhere to a particular mental state but are a "signal."[62] As a sign-post or signal the rule trains us to respond in a particular way. This practice occurs as long as there is a "regular use of sign-posts, a custom."[63] For Wittgenstein, then, to obey a rule is a custom. "To understand a sentence means to understand a language. To understand a language means to be master of a technique."[64]

Wittgenstein also compared rules to samples of color which one uses for comparison in order to determine if one is correct (adhering to the standard). In such a circumstance, rules act as aids in teaching the game. The game can be learned by watching others participate according to rules that can be read from the practice "like a natural law governing the play."[65] Rules offer a sense of guidance in leading us to an appropriate response.

> I wanted to put that picture before him, and acceptance of the picture consists in his now being inclined to regard a given case differently: that is to compare it with this rather than that set of pictures. I have changed his way of looking at things.[66]

The rules that are implicitly a part of a given language serve the function of guiding our response and directing us to act in an appropriate manner (i.e., form of life consistent with the guidance of the rules in the language game). Wittgenstein returns us once again to the corresponding relationship between usage and action. Words have a meaning due to their usage, and out of that usage forms of life are exhibited. Rules are the systems of guidance which allow such a practice to cohere.[67]

Meaning as Use

In discussing "meaning as use," George Pitcher emphasizes that Wittgenstein's discussion is intended as a description of *practice* and not as a theoretical construct. Pitcher claims that, "Wittgenstein was mistaken in identifying the meaning of a word with its use in language."[68] Pitcher's point is to underscore the importance of use rather than to continue an illusive search for meaning. To that end, Pitcher quotes John Wisdom, "Don't ask for the meaning, ask for the use."[69] Pitcher's comments are valuable in pointing out the temptation of returning to theoretical positions and linguistic models which Wittgenstein sought to avoid.

Wittgenstein repeatedly attacked the notion of meaning as a mental process. The *Philosophical Investigations* closes with the comment that, "Nothing is more wrong-headed than calling meaning a mental activity."[70] It is not some kind of mental activity which can be separated and labeled as an "inner move of the game."[71] Instead of looking at understanding as a mental process, one should ask under what circumstances this statement is correct. Meaning "all depends on the system to which the sign belongs."[72] One must examine what surrounds a statement in order to understand a sentence. Meaning grows out of a situation (context) and is dependent on the rules of the language game which is being played. This system provides order so that the game can be played. "How words are understood is not told by words alone (Theology)."[73] Thinking is not a separate, interior activity which can be isolated, but is like the "stream which must be flowing under the surface."[74]

Wittgenstein remarked that, "An 'inner process' stands in need of outward criteria."[75] The temptation to provide an inner, other-worldly, or metaphysical basis for language must be avoided at all costs.[76] Words must be returned to their everyday use.[77] Repeatedly, Wittgenstein stressed that meaning is not tied to some "inner process" or "state". There are not "states" that correspond to a statement of belief.[78] Rather than making assumptions that meaning is associated with a mysterious inner process, we should note the circumstances in which we know how to continue the language game.[79] Thinking is not a mental activity, but is the act of operating with signs.[80] Words are instruments which are designated in terms of usage. They can function in different ways, just as tools can be used for more than one task.[81] The meaning of a word, then, is its use in language.[82] "...It is only in use that the proposition has its sense."[83] Elsewhere, Wittgenstein commented that, "A meaning of a word is a kind of employment of it. For it is what we learn when the word is incorporated into our language."[84]

Wittgenstein's critique of the limits of ostensive definition prepared the way for his description of language in which meaning is related to its use rather than its reference point. While ostensive training teaches us to associate words with objects, we confuse the matter by assuming that all language must have ostensive points of reference. The matter is further complicated by a failure to see that it is the function of these words that is the meaning (not the association).[85] Naming is the connection of a word with an object.[86] We have "baptized" the object with the name and forgotten that a name is the result of the connections and uses of the word.[87]

Philosophy should not try to reduce language to this level nor attempt to explain words solely in terms of ostensive reference.[88] Theology, like philosophy, uses language at times to which no ostensive references correspond. The wide-spread acceptance of Augustine's over-simplified notion of language presents a challenging confrontation. Wittgenstein reminded us, however, that the expression of belief "is just a sentence; and the sentence has sense only as a member of a system of language."[89] Once we escape the magical illusion of ostensive reference, we are returned to the network of language itself. What is important is the particular use we make of words.[90] In making this claim, Wittgenstein underscored an understanding of meaning as use as well as the role of the community. Language is founded on convention or the consensus to use words in a particular way (to play a language game).[91] While words may be associated with particular feelings and gestures, this is caused by our use of the words "in a particular system of language."[92] A group plays a formative role in this system by its agreement on the use of language and through its participation in a language game. "Knowledge is in the end based on acknowledgement."[93]

The question of existence is an inquiry into the use of language. A name may be associated with a wide variety of things. There is no exact fixed case, and should one proposition or aspect disappear there are others on which to rely.[94] "No single ideal of exactness has been laid down."[95] With this statement, Wittgenstein again attacked the simplistic reliance on ostensive reference and scientific methodology which have become predominant. Existence is a secondary question which only arises later in a different context. Children do not learn about the existence of objects, but how to get and use these objects. Only later do questions of existence arise.[96]

The meaning of a statement becomes evident in its accompanying form of life. Certainty in belief is shown, not in terms of feelings, but in terms of how it is manifested in action. Consequently, there will always be a subjective certainty.[97] Wittgenstein viewed the understanding and coherence of a statement as a correlative to its expressive response.

> Religion teaches that the soul can exist when the body has disintegrated. Now do I understand this teaching?–Of course I understand it–I can imagine plenty of things in connexion with it.[98]

A language game includes a particular view–point that results in the form of life or service which accompanies it. Truth comes out of the "frame of reference" given in the language game.[99] Understanding is an act of shared participation in a language game and its form of life. The language game is accepted by a community which consents to participation in and adherence to the implicit rules of the game. A major theme throughout Wittgenstein's work was to debunk the notion of meaning as a mystical, internal activity that is hidden in the private mental confines of individuals. In place of such a notion Wittgenstein returns us to the world of shared exchange where language finds its place based on use and agreement.

Contextuality

"We associate a particular use with a picture."[100] What is the relationship between these pictures that are given and the forms of life? Discovering the connections is a way of uncovering the rules and practices of a language game. While the believer may be using the same words as the non–believer, they will take on a very different meaning because they are associated and controlled by different pictures (and occur in a different environment). This linguistic confusion has led to conflict by those of religious faith. Consequently, it is important that these connections are made clearly. The use of pictures leads us back to Wittgenstein 's understanding of grammar and "theology as grammar," since he concluded that "When I say he's using a picture I'm merely making a *grammatical* remark."[101] Any attempts to verify this remark can only be done by observation of the context and *Sitz–im–Leben* of the statement.

Wittgenstein underscored the contextual dependency of any statement. The meaningfulness of a statement is related to the particular circumstances in which it is uttered. "Our talk gets its meaning from the rest of our proceedings."[102] It is only within an entire language that single expressions have a meaning.[103] Once a statement is removed from its context then it appears in a totally different light.[104] A statement's significance comes from its particular surroundings. Understanding requires a familiarity with a particular language game and its associations. This notion of contextual dependency which emerges in Wittgenstein's work is an ever-expanding one. Words find their meaning in particular sentences which have meaning only in the systems in which they belong. "Only in the stream of thought and life do words have meaning."[105] From this perspective Wittgenstein's contextual dependency becomes an interdependency, i.e., there is a mutual dependency on the inner relationships within the language games. Words are given meaning in a particular context, but the use of these words affects the sentences and contexts in which they are uttered. As a result, we are left with the mutual exchange and dependence of the whole system. While knowledge and meaning come through the use of particular words in specific contexts, there are themes within the language game which point beyond themselves to connections and associations with other language games.[106] These do not belong only to a particular occasion, but are part of a pattern of variety that emerges.

Wittgenstein's insistence on the contextual dependency of a statement does not lead us into an isolationist relativism, but returns us to all of life. S. Stephen Hilmy underscores the contextuality and interrelatedness of language in his discussion of "Wittgensteinian relativism and the dynamic view of language." Hilmy argues that Wittgenstein represents a form of "linguistic relativism" since the "meaning of signs is a question about language (the usage of signs), not a question about psychology."[107]

> What determines our judgment, our concepts and reactions, is not what one man is doing now, an individual action, but the whole hurly-burly of human actions, the background against which we see any action.[108]

Wittgenstein escapes subjectivity and solipsism by focusing on the interrelationships between language and all of life.[109] The reciprocal nature between language games and forms of life provides a foundation for this understanding of the significance of the particular context which emerges in a larger context. As the movement of one piece on a chess board affects all other pieces, so too does any contextual change produce ramifications throughout the language game. Consequently, it is of utmost importance that the speaker adheres to the rules and context of a language game. Custom and upbringing lead one to particular styles which produce particular effects and enable one to see certain connections.[110] An expression "tells you 'what happened' only if you are at home in the special conceptual world that belongs to these situations."[111]

Belief develops out of a collection of propositions which are interdependent. It is not a matter of selecting one proposition or finding verification for a particular statement, but learning a "host of things" (i.e., learning to act according to these beliefs).[112] There is not an independent perspective from which one can judge or analyze certain propositions. One already participates in certain language games and from that basis interacts with others.

> All testing, all confirmation and disconfirmation of a hypothesis takes place already
> within a system.... The system is not so much the point of departure, as the element in
> which arguments have their life.[113]

Wittgenstein's remarks are reinforced by his criticism of an over-reliance on ostensive definition. The commitment to the contextual basis of language games and forms of life, coupled with a broader understanding of language, led Wittgenstein to claim that "Christianity is not based on a historical truth."[114] Faith cannot be buttressed by a reliance on ostensive, historical verification, since the aim is not to establish objective truth. A Christian is given a historical narrative and asked to believe, but not in a way appropriate to other historical narratives.[115] Christians are asked to make connections between these statements and their actions. "But the end is not an ungrounded presupposition: it is an ungrounded way of action."[116]

Wittgenstein's repeated insistence on the contextual dependency of a statement was the glue which held his understanding of language together. By emphasizing the context, Wittgenstein was able to re–assert the interdependency between a language game and a form of life. Perhaps even more significantly, he was able to assert the significance of particular statements and their affects while at the same time showing a broader, dynamic portrait.

Religious Belief

Much has been written about Wittgenstein's own religious beliefs and practices.[117] The discussion here avoids it in favor of a continued exposition of significant themes in Wittgenstein's philosophy.[118] Wittgenstein understood that religious faith was also an example of the importance of the inherent connection between language games and forms of life. "Christianity is not a doctrine" or hypothesis about what happened or what may happen, but is a description of that which occurs in human life.[119] Wittgenstein also wrote that, "A confession has to be part of your new life."[120] Indeed, as Wittgenstein put it, belief comes only as a result of a life.[121] This is true for Wittgenstein because belief in God is displayed in one's life.

> I should like to say...the words you utter or what you think as you utter them are not what matters, so much as the difference they make at various points in your life. ...A theology which insists on the use of certain particular words and phrases, and outlaws others, does not make anything clearer (Karl Barth). It gesticulates with words...because it wants to say something and does not know how to express it. Practice gives the words their sense.[122]

This emphatic underscoring of the centrality of the forms of life which accompany the language games pointed to the significance of acting as part of the language game ("Words are also deeds."[123]) This conviction led Wittgenstein to comment that one could persuade someone that God exists by shaping their life in a particular way. Wittgenstein's point here is not to speculate on the "existence of God," but to show that belief in God is a result of experience (not argument).[124]

Participation in language games involves an implicit trust that translates to a shared form of life. Saying that one believes is not the same as believing. This leads one to the misguided notion that there must be certain feelings and mental acts that accompany the words. One tries out the possibility that specific expressions, gestures or tones provide a determinative basis for belief. Upon closer observation it can be seen that there is not a consensus on the right expressions, emotions, or other attributes to accompany belief.

> Many different criteria distinguish, under different circumstances, cases of believing what you say from those of not believing what you say. ...But sometimes what distinguishes these two is nothing that happens while we speak, but a variety of actions and experiences of different kinds before and after.[125]

Believing is an activity or process occurring as it accompanies a statement of belief and thus becoming associated with and guided by this statement. Wittgenstein warned again that the solution to these puzzles was not to be found in a particular state of mind. For Wittgenstein, belief is not a matter of assent to particular statements or a particular attitude, but a way of acting and living one's life.[126] Knowledge regarding one's state of mind may be helpful in providing information about one's intention, but it cannot be equated with belief.[127] Belief is an observable phenomenon because obeying a rule is a practice.

This does not occur privately, but "there is a way of grasping a rule which is not an interpretation, but which is exhibited in what we call 'obeying the rule' and 'going against it' in actual cases."[128]

In the *Lectures on Religious Belief*, Wittgenstein emphasized that belief is related to a particular way of action ("guidance for this life"). Belief is not based on evidence (ostensive or otherwise) or rational claims.[129] "It will show, not by reasoning or by appeal to ordinary grounds for belief, but rather by regulating for all in his life."[130] In some instances, faith does not reside at the same level as other objects of belief. In these situations, the belief operates as a guidance system which interprets and colors the individual's perspective. It allows one to see things in a particular way and provides a framework whereby other events are interpreted.

In *Remarks on Frazer's Golden Bough*, Wittgenstein noted the impossibility of dealing with the religious practices of a people in terms of explanation. Wittgenstein's use of explanation is concerned with the attempt to hypothesize about reasons underlying religious belief.[131] As Ulrich Browarzik notes, "Es war Wittgensteins Entdeckung, daß dem Glauben keine Hypothesen zugrunde liegen."[132] Instead of the attempt to come up with a satisfactory reason (for ourselves) as to why such practices occurred one can simply depict what human life is like. Thomas Tominaga identifies depth grammar as the use made of a particular picture associated with religious belief. Study of this dimension does not have to do with "testable hypotheses" that can be validated by "empirical or scientific evidence," but with the linguistic acts and their connections in praxis.[133] Richard Olmsted shows the relationship of the depth grammar to all aspects of our lives.

> By repeatedly calling our attention through his investigations to the "depth grammar" of our linguistic activities, he [Wittgenstein] reminded us that our talk about the world is more than a matter of words. All the aspects of a particular "swatch" of a man's life provide the context in which his use of a given expression performs its appropriate role. It is only by being given a use in our lives that our words acquire the significance they have.[134]

The attempt to offer explanations for religious behavior assumes that it can uncover the error(s) of religious practice. But "a religious symbol does not rest on any *opinion*. And error belongs only with opinion."[135] While historical investigation may provide information about the development of a practice, it "is only *one* kind of summary of the data."[136]

Although belief may be associated with historical events (or an historical narrative), it is not this historical basis that is determinative for the believer. "It doesn't rest on an historic basis in the sense that the ordinary belief in historic facts could serve as a foundation."[137] The historic facts encompassed in the belief are handled in a different manner than other historic facts. As a result, any attempt to treat them as matters for scientific inquiry or as points of ostensive reference which can provide verification are misleading. By drawing attention to the context, Wittgenstein reminds us that meaning is related to function. Although faith may cite historical data, it uses it in a different way. "Here we have a belief in historic facts different from a belief in ordinary historic facts."[138]

If this is the case, then, are we left only with a myriad of language games and no possibility of offering a critique of those practices?[139] Are all religious activities beyond the realm of criticism? Wittgenstein does offer the possibility of distinguishing between religious practices.[140] "We should distinguish between magical operations and those operations which rest on a false, over-simplified notions of things and processes."[141] Critique is possible when it comes from an internal logic that points out where incorrect steps and claims have been made (e.g., "Baptism as washing. There is a mistake only if magic is presented as science."[142]). Critique is possible only when one has used a picture or expression inappropriately.

The logic of a religious language game is an internal logic which guides the propositions. It is appropriate to inquire about the consistency within the language game. Inquiry may discover a contradiction. But it is inappropriate to apply external standards in an investigation of a language game. Consequently, attempts to import scientific standards of investigation into matters of religious belief inevitably distort the matter. Rather than try to develop explanations, historical or otherwise, for the practice, Wittgenstein turns our attention to "the *environment* of a way of acting."[143] Religious practices depend on the entire range of associations from which they grow. Any attempts to pull those practices out of their contexts inevitably result in doing violence to them. It is only by being attentive to the surrounding linguistic–cultural framework that one discovers the broader connections that are made.

The contextual understanding of religious belief is also underlined in Wittgenstein's *Lectures on Religious Belief*. When discussing disagreements over belief in the Last Judgment, Wittgenstein wrote,

> It isn't a question of my being anywhere near him, but on an entirely different plane,
> which you could express by saying: "You mean something altogether different, Witt-
> genstein."[144]

While the believer may speak of proof, it is a kind of proof that cannot be
demonstrated through reasoning. Instead it is "an unshakable belief" that acts
as a controlling function in the life of the believer. Faith is not a comparison
of mental states, but is a way of seeing, i.e., it provides a set of pictures or perspectives.

> Those who do not use the picture cannot be compared therefore, with those who do
> not believe in a hypotheses. Believing in the picture means, for example, putting one's
> trust in it, sacrificing for it, letting it regulate one's life, and so on. Not believing in
> the picture means that the picture plays no part in one's thinking.[145]

Similarly, faith is not dependent on evidence. On the contrary, Wittgenstein
claims that evidence would "destroy the whole business."[146] Faith operates
within a system or network and any critique must occur from within that context.

> In certain cases you would say they reason wrongly, meaning they contradict us. In
> other cases you would say they don't reason at all, or "It is an entirely different kind of
> reasoning." The first you would say in the case in which they reason in a similar way
> to us, and make something corresponding to our blunders. Whether a thing is a
> blunder or not – it is a blunder in a particular system.[147]

Belief provides one with a particular picture which will entail certain connections (or forms of life). In order to determine if a blunder is being made
within a particular system, one should look at the connections that are a result
of a particular language game.

> In order to see what the explanation is I should have to see the sum, to see in what
> way it is done, what he makes follow from it, what are the different circumstances un-
> der which he does it, etc.[148]

The importance of a statement of belief then is integrally tied to the forms of
life that accompany it. The connections are a result of the rules and practices
that are a part of the language game. This game is always a shared one, since
"if what he calls his 'idea of death' is to become relevant, it must become part
of our game."[149] By underlining the communal nature of language games,
Wittgenstein avoids the critiques of private language which have sometimes
been raised against him.[150] The particular use of a picture provides its own

verification based on the "consequences" which one "does or does not draw."[151] By making this claim, Wittgenstein once again rejects the possibility of verification or definition via analysis based on historical, ostensive, or scientific methodology. Instead the language game is in a certain sense self-contained and investigation of it must occur within its context.[152]

Theology as Grammar

"Grammar tells what kind of object anything is (Theology as grammar)."[153] This quixotic aside is one of the few overt references to theology in Wittgenstein's work. Yet this reference implies that the theological task in light of Wittgenstein would be comparable to the task of the philosopher which is more fully depicted in Wittgenstein's writings. If this parallel is correct, then the theologian (like the philosopher) should not interfere with the actual use of language, but seek only to describe it.[154] The theological task can be corrective as well when the theologian can show how we have become entangled in our rules. At this point, Wittgenstein's analogy for the philosopher who seeks to untangle the knots in the rope becomes appropriate for the work of the theologian as well. The theological investigation is a grammatical one and seeks to clear away misunderstandings about the use of words and analogies. This task may be extended through substituting one form of expression for another or it may spend its time analyzing a particular form.[155] The theological task is, however, fundamentally guided by its commitment to serving the Christian community and to performing its (grammatical) service on the behalf of the community. "An explanation serves to remove or to avert a misunderstanding."[156] Theology as grammar is not concerned with the creation of new systems, but with the faithful task of clarifying the language of the believer in order that the connections in the language games are clearer.[157]

Conclusion

Wittgenstein's approach to language provides an alternative route to the limited paths that were traveled at the time. The debates during the nineteenth century centered on ostensive definition and factuality. By pointing out additional ways in which language functions, Wittgenstein broadened the basis for the discussion. Language games, rules, meaning as use and contextuality provide a different matrix for approaching language which opens up possibilities that can avoid the problems associated with a fixation on ostensive definition.

Furthermore, Wittgenstein's discussion of religious belief and theology serve as reminders that theology can return to its task of serving the church by attending to the language of the faithful. The following chapter turns to a survey of how theologians have applied this approach.

NOTES

1   For an introduction see V. C. Chappell, ed., *Ordinary Language* (Englewood Cliffs, N.J.: Prentice-Hall, 1964). For a brief historical overview of the place of Wittgenstein and the development of this approach, see A. R. Lacey, "Philosophy and Analysis," in *A Dictionary of Philosophy* (London: Routledge and Kegan Paul, 1976), pp. 177-78 and the article on "Wittgenstein," in *A Dictionary of Philosophy*, Antony Flew, ed. (New York: St. Martin's Press, 1979), pp. 374-77. A more detailed presentation is available in Justus Hartnack, *Wittgenstein and Modern Philosophy*, trans. by Maurice Cranston (Garden City, NY: Anchor Books, 1965).

2   Certain remarks in Wittgenstein's writings led to early speculation about their applicability to theology. As early as 1958, Norman Malcolm made a connection between "form of life" and religion (See Malcolm, *Ludwig Wittgenstein: A Memoir*, 2nd ed. (Oxford: Oxford University Press, 1984), p. 62. "I believe that he [Wittgenstein] looked on religion as a 'form of life'..."

    Kai Nielsen's essay on "Wittgensteinian fideism" was of particular importance in developing the idea of religion as a "form of life." (See Kai Nielsen, "Wittgensteinian Fideism," *Philosophy*, 42 (1967), pp. 191-209). Attempts were also made to apply Wittgenstein's description of "language games" to religious activities by Roger Trigg in *Reason and Commitment* (Cambridge: Cambridge University Press, 1973) and Saul Kripke in *Wittgenstein on Rules and Private Language* (Oxford: Basil Blackwell, 1982).

    Malcolm drew both of these lines of thought together in *Thought and Knowledge* where he concluded that, "Religion is a form of life; it is language embedded in action–what Wittgenstein calls a language game." See Malcolm, *Thought and Knowledge* (Ithaca: Cornell University Press, 1977), p. 212.

    A discussion of this development can be found in chapter 2 of Patrick Sherry, *Religion, Truth and Language-Games* (New York: Harper and Row, 1977), pp. 21ff. Fergus Kerr argues that the attempts to apply these two key Wittgensteinian themes with such generalized notions misled the theological community about the importance of Witttgenstein. See Kerr, *Theology after Wittgenstein* (Oxford: Basil Blackwell, 1986), p. 31. The tendency towards over-generalized application of Wittgenstein continues to exist, e.g., Alexander Altmann argues that "metaphysics is no less of a language game or form of life than religion. " See Altmann, "The God of Religion, the God of Metaphysics and Wittgenstein's 'Language Games'," *Zeitschrift für Religions– und Geistesgeschichte* (No. 4, 1987), pp. 289-306.

    The German discussion has proceeded from the work of Ingolf Dalferth, *Sprachlogik des Glaubens: Texte analytischer Religionsphilosophie und Theologie zur religiösen Sprache* (München: Chr. Kaiser Verlag, 1974) and Joachim Track, *Sprachkritische Untersuchungen zum christlichen Reden von Gott* (Göttingen: Vandenhoeck und Ruprecht, 1977),

3   Kerr, pp. 101-105. Kerr explores example of this in his section entitled "Misinterpreting Wittgenstein." In particular, he takes Bernard Williams to task for his idealistic reading of

Wittgenstein. Cf. Bernard Williams, "Wittgenstein and Idealism," in *Understanding Wittgenstein*, ed. G. Vesey (London: Macmillan, 1974).

4   G. P. Baker and P. M. S. Hacker, *Wittgenstein: Meaning and Understanding* (Oxford: Basil Blackwell, 1980), p. 1.

5   See Patrick Bearsley, "Augustine and Wittgenstein on Language," *Philosophy* 58 (1983), pp. 229-36. "Augustine's picture of language might be represented not as an explicit theory, but rather as a proto-theory that shares the development of many philosophical theories of meaning." (Ibid., p. 14.) An insightful discussion of Wittgenstein's appreciation of Augustine can be found in Timothy Binkley, *Wittgenstein's Language* (The Hague: Martinus Nighoff, 1973), pp. 193-202.

6   Garth Hallett *A Comparion to Wittgenstein's Philosophical Investigations* (Ithaca: Cornell University Press, 1977), p. 68. See also *Philosophical Investigations* §131.

7   Joachim Schulte, *Wittgenstein: Eine Einführung* (Stuttgart: Philipp Reclam, 1989), p. 149. See also Ludwig Wittgenstein, *Philosophical Investigations* (New York: Macmillan Company, 1953), § 7.

8   Kerr, p. 58. Wittgenstein takes us not to a point above or beyond from which we can gain a complete view, but returns us once again to the whole "hurly-burly" of life.

9   For a description of the gradual development of language games in Wittgenstein see Merrill and Jaakka Hintikka, *Investigating Wittgenstein* (Oxford: Basil Blackwell, 1986), pp. 176ff. See also S. Stephen Hilmy, *The Later Wittgenstein* (Oxford: Basil Blackwell, 1987), pp. 98ff. and Baker and Hacker, pp. 48ff. See also Garth Hallett, *Essentialism: A Wittgensteinian Critique* (Albany: State University of New York Press, 1991).

10 The story is reported by Norman Malcolm, *Ludwig Wittgenstein: A Memoir*, Second Edition (Oxford: Oxford University Press, 1984), p. 55.

11 Hallett, *A Companion to Wittgenstein's Philosophical Investigations* , p. 69.

12 Ludwig Wittgenstein, *The Blue and Brown Books* (Oxford: Basil Blackwell, 1975), p. 141.

13 Wittgenstein, *Philosopical Investigations*, §23.

14 Wittgenstein, *Zettel* (Berkeley: University of California Press, 1967), p. 76.

15 *Philosophical Investigations*, §57.

16 Ibid., §654-55.

17 Ibid., §64. This is in distinct contrast to the "early Wittgenstein" and his search for "simples." Wittgenstein was influenced by Bertrand Russell and G. E. Moore who undertood the project of analysing propositions into their basic elements. Russell contended that through this process, experience could be "rendered intelligible." (For a summary of logical atomism, see Morris Weitz, "Analysis, Philosophical" in *The Encyclopedia of Philosophy*, Vol. 1 (New York: Macmillan Co., 1967), pp. 97ff.) Russell claimed to have been indebted to Wittgenstein in this undertaking (See Bertrand Russell, "The Philosophy of Logical Atomism," in *Logic and Knowledge: Essays 1901-1950*, ed. by R. C. Marsh (London: George Allen and Unwin, 1956), p. 177). The search for simples in terms of elementary propositions is apparent in Wittgenstein's *Tractatus Logico-Philosophicus* (London: Routledge and Kegan Paul, 1986). For an assessment of the importance of this in the *Tractatus*, see George Pitcher, *The Philosophy of Wittgenstein* (Englewood Cliffs, N.J.: Prentice-Hall, 1964), esp. ch. two. The place of the *Tractatus* in Wittgenstein's subsequent rejection of logical atomism is also discussed by Pitcher, pp. 171-87.

18 *Philosophical Investigations*, §71.

19 Wittgenstein, *On Certainty*, ed.G.E.M. Anscombe (Oxford: Basil Blackwell, 1969), p. 71.

[20]   *Zettel*, p. 96.

[21]   *Philosophical Investigations*, §31. Knowledge of one game prepares the way for an explantion of moves in another game.

[22]   Ibid., §67.

[23]   *Blue and Brown Books*, p. 17.

[24]   *On Certainty*, p. 66.

[25]   *Philosohpical Investigations*, p. 200.

[26]   Ibid., §19.

[27]   *On Certainty*, p. 46. J. F. M. Hunter explores a variety of interpretations in Hunter, "'Forms of Life' in Wittgenstein's *Philosophical Investigations*," in *Essays on Wittgenstein*, ed. by E. D. Klemke (Urbana: University of Illinois Press, 1971), pp. 273-97. Hunter isolates three possible interpretations of Wittgenstein's use of forms of life before he offers a fourth approach: (1) forms of life are distinct entities that can be understood only in relation to language games and are a "formalized or standardized" part of life; (2) a form of life is an associated group of patterns of behavior connected to language games; and (3) a form of life is a way of life (including values, beliefs, etc.) that is related to the characteristics of a group of people. Hunter attributes these three interpretations to the works of A. M. Quints, P. F. Strawson, Norman Malcolm, Stanley Cavell and George Pitcher. See the related essays in *Wittgenstein: The Philosophical Investigations*, ed. by George Pitcher (Notre Dame: University of Notre Dame Press, 1968 and George Pitcher, *The Philosophy of Wittgenstein* (Englewood Cliffs, N.J.: Prentice-Hall, 1964). Following a careful reading of the occurrence of forms of life in the *Philosophical Investigations*, Hunter proposes an "organic" model in which forms of life are understood as a dynamic complex of associated responses that are part of the use of language (pp. 278-79).

    Another helpful introduction to "forms of life" and a warning of the danger of overgeneralizing the concept (particularly in its application to religion) can be found in Sherry, *Religion, Truth, and Language Games*, pp. 21-21. See also T. E. Burke's caution against reducing religion to a form of life or a language game. Burke, "Wittgenstein's *Lectures on Religious Belief*: A Re-consideration, In *Wittgenstein and His Impact on Contemporary Thought*," Proceedings of the Second International Wittgenstein Symposium (Vienna: Hölder, Pitcher, Tempsky, 1978), p. 510. See also Patrick Sherry, "Is Religion a 'Form of Life'?" *American Philosophical Quarterly* (1972), pp. 159-67. John Hick's review of *The Edges of Language* claims that religious language is presented by van Buren as an "autonomous language game." Hick, review of *The Edges of Language* by Paul van Buren, *Journal of Theological Studies* 24 (October 1973), p. 634.

    Richard Bell points out the variety of language games and forms of life that are associated with religious language. See Bell, "Wittgenstein and Descriptive Theology," *Religious Studies* (October 1969), pp. 1-18. In this regard, see also Hilmy, *The Later Wittgenstein*, p. 298, note 427.

[28]   *Zettel*, p. 20.

[29]   *Blue and Brown Books*, p. 105.

[30]   Robert Fogelin, *Wittgenstein* (Boston: Routledge and Kegan Paul, 1976), p. 153.

[31]   Hallett, *A Companion to Wittgenstein's Philosophical Investigations*, p. 306.

[32]   Kerr, pp. 89-90.

33   See Ronald Suter, *Interpreting Wittgenstein* (Philadelphia: Temple University Press, 1989), pp. 117-122. See also *Philosophical Investigations*, §261.

34   A helpful introduction to the discussion can be found in: John Cook, "Wittgenstein on Privacy," In *Wittgenstein: The Philosophical Investigations*, pp. 286-323. Cook claims that the entire discussion has developed out of a misunderstanding of Wittgenstein.

35   *Philosophical Investigations*, §282.

36   *Blue and Brown Books*, pp. 113-14.

37   *Zettel*, p. 78.

38   *Philosophical Investigations*, §432.

39   Wittgenstein, *Culture and Value*, ed. G. H. von Wright with Heikki Nyman (Oxford: Basil Blackwell, 1980), p. 51. See also p. 61.

40   *Philosophical Investigations*, p. 203.

41   Ibid., §241.

42   *Culture and Value*, p. 16. See Stegmüller, *Hauptströmungen der Gegenwartsphilosophie*, 5th ed., Vol. 1 (Stuttgart: Alfred Kröner, 1975), pp. 584ff. Stegmüller is understood as the "received" (accepted) view of Wittgenstein readers by Merrill and Jaakko Hintikka who also associate Fogelin and Pitcher with this position. For a fuller account of alternative attempts to develop the relationship of language and reality, see Hintikka and Hintikka, p. 212ff. and 235, note 3.

43   *On Certainty*, p. 46.

44   Ibid, p. 38.

45   For an overview of the differences, see Baker and Hacker, *Wittgenstein: Rules, Grammar and Necessity* (Oxford: Basil Blackwell, 1985), pp. 34-41. Hintikka and Hintikka discuss the evolution of rules and its relationship to language games in *Investigating Wittgenstein*, pp. 180-190. See also Ernst Michael Lange, "'Einer Regel folgen'-zu einigen neuen Interpretationen Wittgensteins," *Philosophische Rundschau* (1987), pp. 102-24.

46   *On Certainty*, p. 8.

47   Ibid., p. 15.

48   See Friedrich Waismann, *The Principles of Linguistic Philosophy*, ed. R. Harré (London: Macmillan, 1965), pp. 137-140. See Wittgenstein, *Philosophical Grammar*, ed. Rush Rhees, trans. A. J. P. Kenny (Oxford: Basil Blackwell, 1974), pp. 116-17. This leads Baker and Hacker to conclude that, "The generality of a rule lies in its *use*, not (or not necessarily) in its form. We *guide* our actions by references to rules: we teach and explain rule-governed acitivities by citing the rules that govern it." (Baker and Hacker, *Rules, Grammar and Necessity*, p. 44.) In highlighting the use of a rule, Baker and Hacker describe five significant features of rules: (1) instruction; (2) definition; (3) explanation; (4) justification; and (5) evaluation. (For a complete explication of this dimension of rules and their use, see Baker and Hacker, pp. 45-47).

49   *Zettel*, pp. 54 and 59. A helpful discussion of this matter can be found in Dallas High, *Language, Persons and Beliefs* (New York: Oxford University Press, 1967), pp. 82-86. High notes the danger of following some interpreters of Wittgenstein who have reduced languge games to a matter of rule-following.

50   *Zettel*, p. 54.

51   *On Certainty*, p. 10.

52   *Zettel*, p. 55.

53   Ibid., p. 59.

54 *On Certainty*, p. 6.

55 *Zettel*, p. 119.

56 *Blue and Brown Books*, p. 25.

57 *Philosophical Investigations*, §68.

58 *Blue and Brown Books*, pp. 79-80.

59 Ibid., pp. 142-42.

60 *Philosophical Investigations*, §85.

61 Ibid., §171ff.

62 Ibid., §178-79.

63 Ibid., §198.

64 Ibid., §199.

65 Ibid., §54.

66 Ibid., §144.

67 The presentation on rules has avoided the controversy about the place of the community in the concept of rule-following. Saul Kripke argues for a normative use of rules that is established by the community. See Kripke, *Wittgenstein on Rules and Private Laguage* (Oxford: Basil Blackwell, 1982.) Colin McGuin argues against this interpretation and claims that rule following can be understood in "entirely individualistic terms" (McGuin, *Wittgenstein on Meaning* (Oxford: Basil Blackwell, 1984), p. 200.) It must be noted, though, that while McGuin claims to avoid importing ideas (like community) into an understanding of rules, he does admit to "imposing a classification [of individualism] upon his [Wittgenstein's] position" (McGuin, p. 82). My own position is that while there may not be an explicit notion of the role of the community in the concept of rules, the integral relationship between rules, language games and forms of life provides ample evidence of the necessity of the community in the practice. See also C. Peacocke, "Rule-Following: The Nature of Wittgenstein's Arguments," in *Wittgenstein: To Follow a Rule*, eds. S. H. Holtzman and C. M. Leich (London: Routledge and Kegan Paul, 1981), pp. 93-94.

68 Pitcher, *Philosophy of Wittgenstein*, p. 253. Pitcher notes that much of the discussion of this theme in Wittgenstein revolves around a semantical interpretation that even Pitcher recognizes as having "not much consequence." A presentation of the development of this theme in Wittgenstein as well as a defense against the criticisms of it can be found in Garth Hallett, *Wittgenstein's Definition of Meaning as Use* (New York: Fordham University Press, 1967).

69 Wisdom in Pitcher, p. 253.

70 End of Part 1 of *Philosophical Investigations*, §693. Hallett notes that this statement is in distinct contrast to the early Wittgenstein as well as to the work of William James and Bertrand Russell. Hallett, *A Companion to Wittgenstein's Philosophical Investigations*, p. 600.

71 *Zettel*, p. 113.

72 Ibid., p. 41.

73 Ibid., p. 26.

74 Ibid., p. 21.

75 *Philosophical Investigations*, §580.

76 "It is perverse to think of meaning as a mental acitivity because it only entrenches us in a bewildering picture of the world." Kerr, p. 55.

77 *Philosophical Investigations*, §116.

78 *On Certainty*, pp. 7-8 and p. 30.

79 *Philosophical Investigations*, §154.

80   *Blue and Brown Books*, p. 6.
81   Ibid., p. 68. See also *Philosophical Investigations*, §11.
82   *Philosophical Investigations*, §43.
83   *On Certainty*, p. 3.
84   Ibid., p. 10.
85   *Philosophical Investigations*, §6ff.
86   Fahrang Zabeeh rejects Pitcher's claim that Wittgenstein misused "meaning" and "defini-
     tion' as they relate to proper names. See Zabeeh, "Our Language Games and Forms of
     Life," in *Essays on Wittgenstein*, pp. 368-69.
87   *Philosophical Investigations*, §38-39.
88   *Blue and Brown Books*, p. 18.
89   Ibid., p. 42.
90   Ibid., p. 173.
91   *Philosophical Investigations*, §355.
92   *Blue and Brown Books*, p. 79.
93   *On Certainty*, p. 49.
94   *Philosophical Investigations*, §79.
95   Ibid., §88.
96   *On Certainty*, p. 62. By inference one can claim that in worship one learns how to pray or
     recite the creed rather than to raise questions about the existence of God.
97   *Philosophical Investigations*, p. 225.
98   Ibid., p. 178.
99   *On Certainty*, p. 12.
100 Ibid., p. 71.
101 Ibid., p. 72.
102 Ibid., p. 30.
103 *Culture and Value*, p. 75.
104 *On Certainty*, p. 73.
105 *Zettel*, p. 31. See also *Blue and Brown Books*, p. 5.
106 Ibid., p. 31.
107 Hilmy, p. 143.
108 *Zettel*, p. 99.
109 P.M.S. Hacker presents an account of the development of Wittgenstein's thought on solip-
     sism in Hacker, *Insight and Illusion* (London: Oxford University Press, 1972), pp. 185-214.
     Hacker notes distinctions between the early Wittgenstein, Russell, and the Viennese logical
     positivists. The result was alternative interpretations of solipsism. Russell accepted a "solip-
     sism of the moment," while Carnap advanced a "methodological solipsism." Both seem to
     have drawn their positions (at least partially) from the *Tractatus*. (For a discussion of the
     ambiguity of solipisism in the *Tractatus*, see Fogelin, pp. 84-86. and Schulte, pp. 88-89.)
     Hacker claims that the development of Wittgenstein's ideas led to an outright rejection of
     solipsism because of its metaphysical tendencies (p. 197). Wittgenstein's refutation of solip-
     sism occurs in the discussion on the impossiblity of private language (*Philosophical Investiga-
     tions*, §243ff.). The discussion of solipsism is further muddled by the interpretation by some
     readers of Wittgenstein as a behaviorist. Suter adamantly rejects such a reading in *Interpret-
     ing Wittgenstein*, pp. 61-72.
110 *Philosophical Investigations*, p. 201.

111 *Zettel*, p. 29.

112 *On Certainty*, p. 21.

113 Ibid., p. 16.

114 *Culture and Value*, p. 32.

115 Ibid.

116 *On Certainty*, p. 17.

117 See especially Norman Malcolm, *Wittgenstein: A Religious Point of View?* , ed. by Peter Finch (Ithaca, NY: Cornell University Press, 1994).

118 For those interested in pursuing Wittgenstein's own religious views, see Malcom, *Wittgenstein: A Memoir* and *Recollections of Wittgenstein*, ed. by Rush Rhees (Oxford: Oxford University Press, 1981). Also helpful are two recent biographies: Brian McGuiness, *Wittgenstein: A Life* (London: Duckworth, 1988) and Ray Monk, *Ludwig Wittgenstein: The Duty of Genius* (New York: Penguin Books, 1990).

119 *Culture and Value*, p. 28.

120 Ibid., p. 18.

121 Ibid., p. 32.

122 Ibid., p. 85.

123 *Philosophical Investigations*, §546.

124 *Culture and Value*, p. 85.

125 *Blue and Brown Books*, pp. 144–45.

126 See Dallas High, "Wittgenstein on Doubting and Groundless Believing," *Journal of American Academy of Religion* 49 (1981), pp. 249-266.

127 *Blue and Brown Books*, pp. 146–47.

128 *Philosophical Investigations*, §201.

129 D.Z. Phillips discusses the confusion that exists when our preconceptions about language lead us in the wrong direction. "We may assume that all words operate as names and refer to objects. Thus when we come across the word 'God', we start looking for the object it stands for." Phillips, "Religion in Wittgenstein's Mirror," in *Wittgenstein Centenary Essays*, ed. by A. Phillips Griffiths (Cambridge: Cambridge University Press, 1991), p. 136.

130 Wittgenstein, *Lectures and Conversations on Aesthetics, Psychology and Religious Belief*, ed. Cyril Barrett (Oxford: Basil Blackwell, 1966), p. 55.

131 Cf. "But for someone broken up by love an explanatory hypothesis won't help much." Wittgenstein, *Remarks on Frazer's Golden Bough*, ed. Rush Rhees, trans. A. C. Miles (Cross Hill Cottage: Brynmill Press, 1979), p. 3. W. D. Hudson observes that believers and unbelievers operate on the basis of different pictures (rather than hypotheses). Hudson claims that, "Religious beliefs offer explanations of their own kind." His use of explanation, though, clouds the issue and reinforces the notion that religious beliefs can be reduced to another level. See Hudson, "The Light Wittgenstein Sheds on Religion" in *Ludwig Wittgenstein: Critical Assessments*, Vol. 4, ed. by Stuart Shanker (London: Croom Helm, 1986), p. 180. See also Phillips, "Religion in Wittgenstein's Mirror," pp. 137-38 on the danger of description giving way to explanation.

132 Ulrich Browarzik, "Der Grundlose Glaube," *Neue Zeitschrift für systematische Theologie und Religionsphilosophie* 30 (1989), p. 91.

133 Thomas Tominaga, "A Wittgensteinian Analysis of the Depth Grammar of Religious Belief and Practice," in *Philosophy of Religion* (Vienna: Hölder-Pitcher-Tempsky, 1984), pp. 183ff.

[134] Richard Olmsted, "Wittgenstein and Christian Truth Claims," *Scottish Journal of Theology* 33 (1980), p. 130.

[135] Wittgenstein, *Remarks on Frazer's Golden Bough*, p. 3.

[136] Ibid., p. 8.

[137] *Lectures and Conversations*, p. 57.

[138] Ibid., p. 57.

[139] Such a position has been attributed to Wittgenstein particularly through the notion of "Wittgensteinian fideism" from Kai Nielsen. Nielsen argues that if religious concepts have meaning only within a "form of life" or "language game," they are incomprehensible to those who are non-religious. Within these restrictive limitations the participant (believer) has no further basis which leads Nielsen to conclude that "if conceptual relativism is true, religion should totter." Nielsen, *Contemporary Critiques of Religion* (New York: Herder and Herder, 1971), p. 6 and pp. 98-111. One response to Nielsen's claim is by noting the sweeping generalization made in associating religion with a form of life (see note 2). Furthermore, the interrelatedness of language games and forms of life make such sharp divisions impossible. See D.Z. Phillips, "Religious Belief and Language Games" in *Ludwig Wittgenstein: Critical Assessments*, pp. 149ff.

[140] Phillips rejects "Wittgenstein fideism" precisely on these grounds. See "Religion in Wittgenstein's Mirror," pp. 142-44.

[141] *Remarks on Frazer's Golden Bough*, p. 5.

[142] Ibid., p. 4.

[143] Ibid., p. 13.

[144] *Lectures and Conversations*, p. 53.

[145] Phillips, "Religious Beliefs and Language-Games," p. 156.

[146] *Lectures and Conversations*, pp. 54-56.

[147] Ibid., p. 59.

[148] Ibid., p. 62.

[149] Ibid., p. 69.

[150] On this matter see Dean Martin, "Learning to Become Christian," *Religious Education* 82 (Winter 1987), p. 97. According to Martin, the use of a word is "embedded in the language of believers and determined by longstanding consensus."

[151] *Lectures and Conversations*, p. 72.

[152] Dean Martin notes that a criteria does exist in the church for dealing with matters of dispute. Martin appeals to the accepted authority of scripture, decisions by church gatherings (councils) and religious experience. Martin, "*On Certainty* and Religious Belief," *Religious Studies* 20 (1984), p. 604.

[153] *Philosophical Investigations*, §373. Donald Hudson distinguishes between two tasks: (1) the theologian examines the use of the language (pictures) of the believers to determine if they are consistent; and (2) the theologian explores the "depth grammar by looking at presuppositions and logical consequences." See Hudson, *Ludwig Wittgenstein* (Richmond: John Knox Press, 1968), pp. 59-61.

[154] *Philosophical Investigations*, §124. Phillips rejects the attempts to treat Wittgenstein's remark as an exaggeration. See Phillips, "Religion in Wittgenstein's Mirror," p. 135.

[155] Browarzik underscores this understanding of "theology as grammar" by pointing out the theological task of observing how words function rather than searching for foundational definitions. He also observes the on-going task of articulating faith in a dynamic way (lan-

guage games are not static closed systems). In spite of this recognition, Browarzik concludes his discussion by drawing a distinction between faith and language which makes language a secondary activity.

> Wenn nun fides bei ihrem unvermeidlichen und folgenschweren Übergang in Sprache zur Diskussion steht, lebt sie nicht mehr nur in Gewißheit, sondern auch in "Zeremonien" und "Sprachspielen", die Menschen gefunden haben, um dem Glauben zu vollziehen. Fides steht souverän am Anfang. Browarzik, "Der Grundlose Glaube," p. 95.

Lindbeck refutes Browarzik's position by noting that religious experience is dependent on religious language (Lindbeck, *The Nature of Doctrine*, p. 32). D. Z. Phillips concludes from this that, "Religious experience does not stand to language as a melody stands to a song. We can take away the words of the song, and we are still left with the melody. But we cannot subtract the language and behaviour, in the case of religion, and say that we are left with the experience." Phillips, *Faith after Foundationalism* (London: Routledge, 1988), p. 207.

[156]   *Philosophical Investigations*, §87.

[157]   Phillips rejects the possibility of providing foundations or systems (p. 150), but notes that, "taking a pragmatic attitude towards religious practice...does not mean that Wittgenstein lets anyone, participants included,...get away with confused accounts of practice" (Phillips, "Religion in Wittgenstein's Mirror", p. 147.).

Chapter Three
Theological Readings
of Wittgenstein

Introduction

In the previous chapter, we noted that Wittgenstein does not present a systematic view of philosophy that can be contrasted with other philosophical points of view. Instead, Wittgenstein seeks to point out ways in which language function which run contrary to philosophical expectations. Following the aborted attempt to follow Russell in establishing a linguistic approach based on logical positivism, Wittgenstein turned to an analysis of language which sought to see the meaning in the function, the usage of language.

Because of the importance of Wittgenstein in philosophical discussions, his work has received increasing notice in theological presentations. It has become almost commonplace for Wittgenstein to be mentioned at least in the footnotes. There are few theologians who actually dismiss the importance of Wittgenstein's work for theology. In spite of this, there remains a scarcity of theological literature that seeks as a primary task to grapple with Wittgenstein. In place of this, the theological world has largely contented itself with isolated examples and bibliographical references. The situation has been made more difficult by the quixotic nature of Wittgenstein's own religious beliefs and the lack of direct discussion of theological topics in his works.

The preceding critical introduction to major themes in Wittgenstein sought to provide a basis for an approach to language that would enable one to escape the dilemmas of the hermeneutical confusion over creedal interpretation. The application of this approach can go forward only when one has carefully considered and chosen the route by which one can apply this understanding of language. The following survey analyzes the directions that theologically motivated studies of Wittgenstein have taken. The purpose of the presentation is two-fold: to identify possible options of applying Wittgensteinian themes in theological areas *and* to critically interact with major interpretive presentations of Wittgenstein. The selection of the material has been motivated by an attempt to outline a diversity of formats which have been used to interpret Wittgenstein. These options lay along a continuum that moves from mysticism to sociology as the basis for approaching and interpreting Wittgenstein for the theological community. Consequently, three major paths of theological interpretation will be explored and evaluated: mysticism as a key to understanding Wittgenstein; a sociological reading of Wittgenstein; and options that fall somewhere in the middle of this continuum. Additionally, each of the presentations will include a critical interaction with the material in order to highlight profitable material for our goal of approaching creedal interpretation from a new perspective. The chapter will conclude with a summary of the results of the critical survey for interpreting creedal statements.

There is a bipolarity in Wittgenstein's view of religion that has produced a certain tension in the interpretation of his writings and conversations. This dichotomy is not schizophrenic, but it does have distinct differences that are intertwined throughout his writings. Jens Glebe-Møller has drawn attention to two views of religion that exist in Wittgenstein. Glebe-Møller refers to the first view as a "highly subjective or personalized view of religion."[1] This view is marked by references that occur in the first person. Wittgenstein's closing note in *Zettel* noted that, "'You can't hear God speak to someone else, you can hear him only if you are being addressed.'–That is a grammatical remark."[2] According to Glebe-Møller, this comment serves as an interpretive clue for Wittgenstein's personalized view of religion. Glebe-Møller also points out Wittgenstein's remarks (in the Lecture on Ethics) that ethics should be done in the first person.

In contrast, Glebe-Møller points out a sociological dimension of religion that is present in Wittgenstein. Significant in this regard are concepts such as "following a rule." The task of following a rule involves the acceptance of a social structure that we have inherited. Our inclusion in communities involves a learning and acceptance of rules and structures which provide a framework (Glebe-Møller prefers to use the term mythology) for belief and action. Religion, in this sense, develops out of this social foundation and shapes our beliefs and actions by providing both linguistic and behavioral patterns to us from the community. Glebe-Møller's understanding of the sociological dimension in Wittgenstein is centered on a mythological understanding of society that he views as being threatened by the forces of secularization. Glebe-Møller goes so far as "to question if there is such a thing as a shared religion [Y] any longer."[3]

In defining a sociological view of religion as a shared, cultural phenomenon, Glebe-Møller has over-generalized the social role of religion. The demise of cultural religion does not eliminate the social dimension of religion. Instead the disappearance of cultural religion brings about a new emphasis on the role of the religious community. This new role does not need to be based on an individualistic approach, but discovers its identity as a confessing church.

> Rejecting both the individualism of the conversionists and the secularism of the activists and their common equation of what works with what is faithful, the confessing church finds its main political task to lie, not in the personal transformation of individual hearts or the modification of society, but rather in the congregation's determination to worship Christ in all things.[4]

While Glebe-Møller is helpful in identifying the two views of religion in Wittgenstein, his misunderstanding of the nature of the social dimension of religion results in his questioning its continued existence. While the social dimension of religion in Wittgenstein has been often overlooked in the theological discussion, it continues to offer a contrast to the mystical interpretation of religion that is often attributed to Wittgenstein. In order to prepare for a discussion of these viewpoints, this chapter now turns to a representative presentation of Wittgenstein that analyzes various perspectives along the mystical/sociological continuum.

Mystical Interpretations of Wittgenstein

Mysticism and the Demise of Wittgenstein

In 1987, Russell Nieli defined his own interpretive key to Wittgenstein in a comparison of the *Tractatus* and mystic literature. A careful study of the *Tractatus* and a discovery of the reports of Wittgenstein's experiences before World War I convinced Nieli that Wittgenstein had been completely misunderstood. The misinterpretation of Wittgenstein is due partially to the presuppositions of the readers (in particular those of the Vienna Circle and the logical positivists) and the continued ignorance about the literature on mysticism by those in philosophical circles. Once these blinders have been removed, then the *Tractatus* "begins to fall into its proper place once the work is seen in its function as a ladder in the mystical ascent along the *via negativa*."[5] Nieli claims to have rediscovered the "mystical or theocentric vision" upon which the work was based.

Nieli's analysis begins with an overview of the prevailing philosophical schools at the time of the *Tractatus*. The *Wiener Kreis* (in which Wittgenstein participated) formed the basis for the development of Viennese positivism which sought to do away with metaphysical claims. The unlimited capabilities of science led Neurath and Carnap to practice a new philosophy based upon empiricism and logic that rejected the meaningfulness of metaphysical claims. Carnap, in particular, singled out Heidegger's metaphysics as superstitious and logically flawed. Metaphysics is based on deception because it tries to make truth claims that are not verifiable empirically (and consequently can only produce meaningless statements).

The acceptance of Wittgenstein in the *Wiener Kreis* was due to his association with Bertrand Russell and an anti-metaphysical reading of the *Tractatus*. Carnap, in fact, credited Wittgenstein in the Forward of his work *Scheinprobleme in der Philosophie* for demonstrating the senselessness of metaphysical statements. In his autobiography Carnap acknowledged his dependence on Wittgenstein for the "insight that many philosophical sentences, especially in traditional metaphysics, are pseudo-sentences, devoid of cognitive content."[6] The reading of Wittgenstein's *Tractatus* as congruent with the positivistic empiricism of the *Wiener Kreis*, however, depended on certain assumptions and presuppositions that Wittgenstein evidently did not share. By 1929, Wittgenstein had broken with Carnap and indeed Wittgenstein never actually shared all of the views of the group. Carnap noted that Wittgenstein had at times defended metaphysical statements against the critique of members of the *Kreis*. Wittgenstein was also notorious for his reading of the poems of Rabindranath Tagore (a Bengali poet and spiritual leader) during meetings of the *Wiener Kreis*.[7] The group's conversations created a growing division between Wittgenstein and the other members of the *Wiener Kreis*. Carnap noted that re-reading the *Tractatus* caused him (in light of his conversations and confrontations with Wittgenstein) to note the differences between Wittgenstein and his own position.

> Earlier, when we were reading Wittgenstein's book in the Circle, I had erroneously believed that his attitude toward metaphysics was similar to ours. I had not paid sufficient attention to the statements in his book about the mystical because his feelings and thoughts in this area were too divergent from mine. Only personal contact with him helped me to see more clearly his attitude at this point.[8]

Wittgenstein, himself, was despondent about the book's reception. He regarded Russell's introduction to the book as a misinterpretation of his work.

The Preface itself notes that Wittgenstein believed that only a limited number of readers would understand the work. In the discovery that his work was being classified in the school of thought of Russell and the *Wiener Kreis*, Wittgenstein felt abandoned. According to Wittgenstein, "Other than [Paul] Engelmann, not a single person, in fact, really understood it."[9]

The misinterpretation of the *Tractatus* and Wittgenstein's own feelings of isolation provide a foundation for Nieli's alternative understanding of the *Tractatus*. Nieli's interpretation is based on a systematic presentation of mysticism that begins with his exposition of Heidegger (who is presented as an alternative to the empiricism of the *Wiener Kreis* and Carnap in particular). Through an analysis of Heidegger's lecture "*Was ist Metaphysik?*," Nieli attempts to demonstrate the congruence between Heidegger and classical mysticism. Nieli compares Heidegger's attempts to overcome [*überwinden*] metaphysics and his emphasis on the experiential nature of the "Nothing" with literature on the "derealization–depersonalization experience."[10]

Following the interpretation of psychoanalytical theorists, Nieli provides an analysis of the key ingredients of the derealization–depersonalization experience. The experience revolves around a withdrawal from the world and a shattering of the ego. Nieli identifies key common elements of the experience through a presentation of first hand accounts found in the works of William James and in psychiatric literature. The parallels that he notes leads him to include dread as a central experience.[11] Similarities between the psychiatric literature and Heidegger's description of the experience of the Nothing lead Nieli to conclude that "there seems little cause for doubt" that they are describing the same experience.[12]

Following the discussion of Heidegger, Nieli turns to the work of Jean-Paul Sartre for further elaboration of a philosophical portrayal of what Nieli believes is the experience of derealization–depersonalization. Nieli discovers the same parallels between Sartre and psychiatric literature that he found in Heidegger. These parallels convince him of the centrality and significance of this experience as it appears in both philosophical and psychological literature. What is this foundational experience that Nieli has uncovered? Nieli recognizes mysticism at the basis of these diverse experiences. Drawing from such classic works as St. John of the Cross, Meister Eckhart, and Evelyn Underhill, Nieli seeks to demonstrate that the experience of derealization–depersonalization is in reality the experience that mystics have generally termed the "dark night of the soul." Nieli proposes that "the *Tractatus* is in its

entirety, so conceived from the very first lines, an explication and interpretation of an experience of mystic flight."[13] Mystic flight refers to a religious experience that is composed of a feeling of disembodiment of the self and a feeling of absorption into the beyond.

> The experience is pregnant with both emotion and meaning. It is a "break-through",
> "ascent", or "flight" of the soul attaining in its culmination the mystery, wonder, and
> awe of a theophanic Encounter, of a miraculous union between God and man.[14]

Nieli finds support for this interpretation from vastly divergent sources including Buddhists, Augustine, Rudolf Otto, Xenophanes, and the English Puritans.

Integral to the experience of mystic flight is a rejection of metaphysics
(which Nieli understands as "all intellectual arguments and speculations about
the nature and existence of God, of ultimate Being, the Absolute, etc.").[15] The
mystical encounter with God is not a result of intellectual or speculative arguments about the existence of God, but upon the "inner assurance of personal
religious experience."[16] Another characteristic of the mystics and their experience of mystic flight is silence. Silence is an appropriate response because of
the inability of words to describe the experience of the *"ganz andere"*. The reference to silence in the *Tractatus* as well as its anti–metaphysical character lead
Nieli to conclude that Wittgenstein is writing about his own experience of
mystic flight. Nieli's interpretation is influenced heavily by his interpretation
of comments made by Bertrand Russell and other acquaintances of Wittgenstein as well as Wittgenstein's references to an experience that he had before
World War I. Russell wrote in a letter in 1919 to Lady Morrell that he had
met with Wittgenstein and discussed the *Tractatus*.

> I had felt in his book a flavour of mysticism, but was astonished when I found that he
> has become a complete mystic. He reads people like Kierkegaard and Angelus Silesius,
> and he seriously contemplates becoming a monk. ...He has penetrated deep into mys-
> tical ways of thought and feeling, but what I think (though he wouldn't agree) that
> what he likes best in mysticism is its power to make him stop thinking.[17]

In his lecture on ethics in 1929, Wittgenstein described an experience of being "absolutely safe" that Nieli believes to refer to a mystical experience of
1910 or 1911.[18] Nieli concludes that this "mystic–ecstatic experience" is the
"radiating core of the *Tractatus*" and "the key to its interpretation."[19] Being

"absolutely safe", or variations on the same theme, can be easily recognized as an expression of the mystic-flight experience in its disengagement of the self or "I" from identity with the body. As a means of interpreting and expressing this aspect of the experience, it suggests itself quite naturally.[20]

Nieli's reading of the *Tractatus* relies significantly on his interpretation of Wittgenstein's statements about the world. For Nieli, the "in" and "out" of the world statements are understandable only in light of a transcendental encounter outside of the world.[21] Wittgenstein's statement in 6.432 that "God does not reveal himself in the world" is central to Nieli's argument. Nieli contrasts Wittgenstein's comments with those of Schopenhauer. In place of an experiential bonding of inner and outer world, Wittgenstein offers a "radical in-the-world/out-of-the-world paradigm." While aesthetic contemplation and ascetic practice were considered the keys to overcoming the alienation between the inner world of the individual and the outer world of nature and other human beings, Wittgenstein contends (according to Nieli) that the experience of mystic flight causes a radical separation between the world and the experience of the *ganz andere*.

Nieli believes that the centrality of the silence/show-itself [*sagen/sich zeigen*] statements in the *Tractatus* also undergird his mystic flight thesis. Nieli finds parallels in Pseudo-Dionysius which convince him that "they proclaim the same message."[22] The inability of other commentators on the *Tractatus* is due to their ignorance of the experience of mystic flight. Only Engelmann is credited with giving proper emphasis to the mysticism of the *Tractatus*.[23]

The inability of language to capture the mystical experience is in sharp contrast to the logical structure of the world. In such a world, language can only show or point to the experience which is "broken out of" in mystic flight. This leads Nieli to conclude that

> Language and the world do not exist by themselves in the *Tractatus*, but are bounded by a translogical, transcendental realm that manifests itself and its beyondness of the world in a heightened state of consciousness-state of consciousness that also reveals with great clarity the peculiar inner-worldliness and inner-worldly form of all spatio-temporal objects.[24]

Nieli's interpretation of the solipsism in the *Tractatus* provides further support for his argument that Wittgenstein is speaking of a "private experience" and mystical encounter with the Divine. This leads Nieli to conclude that Wittgenstein's mystic experience is (1) private; (2) "an experience in which all statements, churches, sermons, melt away'" (which Nieli interprets as the nonsensical status of metaphysical statements); and (3) a union with the Sacred which cannot be uttered in language.[25]

Nieli is in agreement with other interpreters of the *Tractatus* in regard to Wittgenstein's objections to metaphysical claims. Unlike Russell and the *Wiener Kreis*, however, Nieli contends that Wittgenstein rejects metaphysics not because of its lack of logical structure, but because of its inability to capture the experiential nature of the Divine encounter. "The main villain in the *Tractatus* would seem to be academic metaphysical systems; but the *Tractatus* critique is equally applicable to theological doctrines."[26] The tendency to systematize theological language was rejected by Wittgenstein on the basis of his "private experience(s)."[27] For Carnap and other members of the *Wiener Kreis*, the rejection of metaphysics was based on its inability to provide proper verification. Consequently, all metaphysical statements must be rejected. In Wittgenstein, however, their rejection was due to their inability to express the experiential nature of the divine encounter and thus such statements were regarded as, at best, "*wichtiger Unsinn.*"

> The main target of Wittgenstein's critique of language in the *Tractatus* is metaphysical and theological propositions which talk about God and the Absolute as if they were describing a fact or event in the mundane world displaying no recognition that there exists a problem in using sentences of the observational–descriptive form to express an experience which does not fit this form.[28]

Nieli's interpretation of the *Tractatus* must deal with the problem of Wittgenstein's later writings. The lack of mysticism in the *Philosophical Investigations* and in the later Wittgenstein causes Nieli to distinguish between an early and late Wittgenstein.[29] While such a distinction has been often advocated, it is generally not based on a recognition of an early "mystical phase" in Wittgenstein. In fact the "early Wittgenstein" has generally been placed in the Russell camp from which he gradually emerged. Nieli's reclassification takes on dramatic importance in his work. The pivotal experience in Wittgenstein's transition is the misunderstanding of the *Tractatus*.

> One can speak of nothing less than a revolution in his thought between 1929–1935, and while continuity certainly exists, Wittgenstein's later philosophy must be seen as a radical break with the *Tractatus* in both substance and method.[30]

The later Wittgenstein embraces the sufficiency of ordinary language. Nieli believes that Wittgenstein's despondency due to the failure of readers to recognize the mystical theme of the *Tractatus* resulted in a pre–occupation with everyday language in the hope that at least metaphysical speculation could be avoided in this area.

> Wittgenstein in his later philosophy has resigned himself to the fact that few, if any, can live at the spiritual heights of the *Tractatus*, with its center of meaning in the ladder metaphor and its invocation of silence, but must rest content with the common sense wisdom and common decency of the ordinary man.[31]

The shift is brought about, in part, by Wittgenstein's own experience of estrangement and by the solitary privacy which was produced by his mystical experiences. Nieli hypothesizes that Wittgenstein sacrifices the "Wittgenstein of the *Tractatus*" in an attempt to maintain his sanity. Wittgenstein's later philosophy is thought to be an attempt to re-integrate Wittgenstein in the social culture and milieu in an attempt to maintain his psychological stability.

> Participation in the linguistic life of society, one might say, has come to replace in Wittgenstein's later thought the private meditative experience of the mystic as Wittgenstein's preferred mode of self-transcendence.[32]

Wittgenstein's fragile psychic state could no longer cope with the intense personal demands of the mystical experience and the move to ordinary language sought to provide calm and a social stability that was otherwise lacking. Beyond that, Nieli believes that Wittgenstein's rejection of the private, inner realm in his later material is a result of his "fear of insanity." The turn away from the private mystical-experiential basis of the early Wittgenstein was out of a "fear of the psyche and its depth."[33]

> The inner is permitted to live on only as it is expressed outwardly, either through linguistic or non-linguistic behavior. The obsessive pre-occupation with the external, one might say, is the price of psychic stability; a neurotic form of existence is set forth as a defense against the greater threat of psychotic disintegration and chaos. And thus all sorts of deprecating pejoratives are used in referring to the mind as an inner realm...[34]

Nieli's psychoanalytical reading of the late Wittgenstein allows him to dismiss it totally and declare ordinary language philosophy a "great failure."[35] The inability to maintain a perspective based upon his mystic experiences results in a shift from the freedom of the spirit to the legalism of ordinary language philosophy. Nieli endorses Russell's remark that Wittgenstein has "abandoned his true genius in his later writings."[36] Wittgenstein's goal of a "moral and spiritual" regeneration of society which was sought in terms of "reverential silence" and the "meditative ascent of the soul" in the *Tractatus* gave way to a resignation of the plight of the ordinary person in light of the "corrupting inroads of a positivist-oriented intelligentsia."[37]

Response to Nieli

Nieli's interpretation of the *Tractatus* and assessment of Wittgenstein is based on a highly selective reading. The evidence that Nieli cites for his mystical interpretation is largely reported conversations and Wittgenstein's reading habits. Bertrand Russell's categorization of Wittgenstein as a mystic is a key piece of evidence for Nieli. Needless to say, Russell's definition of mysticism may differ significantly from Nieli. It is also ironic that while excerpts from Russell's letter to Lady Morrell are important evidence for Wittgenstein's mysticism, Russell's influence is otherwise ignored. There is no mention of Wittgenstein's study with Russell and the impact that Russell and his study in Cambridge had on the development of the *Tractatus*. Nieli portrays the *Tractatus* as a "work of art" which was produced by someone who had been seized by the Truth. In contrast, he dismisses the *Philosophical Investigations* as a "tedious and boring work."[38] Such a categorical judgment probably has more to say about Nieli's literary tastes than about the philosophical integrity of Wittgenstein's work.

It is true that Wittgenstein was familiar with a portion of the works that Nieli includes in his systematization of mysticism. Wittgenstein is known to have particularly read and appreciated the works of Tolstoy, Augustine, and George Fox. One must raise the question of whether Wittgenstein's admiration for these thinkers results *de facto* in classifying him as a mystic as well. Indeed, there is a broader question as to whether or not these three thinkers (let alone Nieli's cast of thousand) can be properly categorized as mystics. Nieli's systematization of mysticism gives the reader a false impression that such a school actually exists. If one can speak of mysticism in such a general fashion, it certainly would be difficult to defend Nieli's inclusion of such divergent thinkers of Xenophanes, Kierkegaard, Maslow, and the English Puritans. Nieli's reductionistic model is based upon a psychological reading which seeks to discover mystical experiences behind the text.

Wittgenstein does refer to experiences which he had that Nieli classifies as mystical. While it is impossible to analyze and evaluate these experiences second-hand, it is obvious that Nieli has overplayed their importance in the Wittgensteinian literature. Nieli, for example, places marked emphasis on

Wittgenstein's feeling of absolute safety which is reported by Malcolm and mentioned in the lecture on ethics. This experience, however, does not receive central attention from Wittgenstein in the lecture. It is mentioned (almost in passing) as one example of ethical inquiry. Nieli's declaration that this experience can be "easily recognized" as a mystic flight is at best a highly subjective decision and blatantly overlooks Malcolm's transmission of the stoic nature of Wittgenstein's experience.[39] While Wittgenstein's eccentricities leave a lot of room for speculation, any results which are built largely on psychological readings of his correspondence must make more modest claims than the grandiose systematization offered by Nieli.

In noting Wittgenstein's despondency over the misinterpretation of the *Tractatus*, Nieli is on solid ground. Nieli also develops the distinctions between Wittgenstein and the *Wiener Kreis* in a helpful manner. There has been a tendency (particularly in the philosophical literature) to interpret the *Tractatus* only in terms of Russell and the logical positivists. Nieli notes, in particular, significant differences between Wittgenstein and Carnap. It is ironic, though, that Nieli frees Wittgenstein from the logical positivist entrapment only to bind him in another category (one that is more preferable to Nieli!). There is even perhaps some merit to Nieli's hypothesis that mystic thought (as opposed to mysticism) and an accompanying anti–metaphysical framework may serve as ingredients in understanding the *Tractatus*. All this makes Nieli's recitation of Heidegger even more curious. What is the connection between Heidegger and Wittgenstein (other than Nieli's attempts to make all seminal thinkers subservient to his model of mysticism)?[40] The entire discussion of Heidegger only confuses the presentation by bringing in Heidegger's understanding of "Being" which is subsequently appropriated to Wittgenstein (a practice which is highly questionable).

Nieli's interpretation of the *Tractatus* is in itself problematic. He seems to be more interested in discovering parallels between Wittgenstein and mystical literature than in dealing with the text itself. Nieli's interpretation of solipsism as the "*private* experience" of the divine encounter runs contrary to the rest of the text. In defense of his privatistic concept, Nieli can only point out similarities to Walt Whitman(!) and conclude that "Wittgenstein's notion of the solipsistic 'I' derive from the same experience and stress the same privacy, intimacy, and ultimacy."[41] Nieli also finds the wrong interpretive clue in linking the solipsist passages of the *Tractatus* with the rejection of metaphysics. Metaphysics and the "I" are rejected not on the basis of personal experience but because of the impossibility of such distinctions. The interweaving of the individual in the society is previewed in the *Tractatus* and is a theme that will be further explored in the later Wittgenstein writings.

The attempts to discover a basis for mysticism in these passages leads Nieli to a dualistic interpretation of Wittgenstein. Given such a scenario, Nieli is more than willing to sacrifice the post-*Tractatus* Wittgenstein to his eisegetical interpretation of the Wittgenstein of the *Tractatus*. Because he has created a mystical reading of the *Tractatus*, Nieli is forced to overlook the points of connection between the *Tractatus* and Wittgenstein's later writing. While there are definitely distinctions that can be made between the "early" and "late" Wittgenstein, the bifurcation of the two is only possible through a forced interpretive scheme.[42]

Even more disturbing is the psychoanalytic approach that Nieli employs to justify his interpretation. Wittgenstein's personal problems with depression and even suicide are no reason to accept Nieli's interpretation. Furthermore, Nieli deliberately and selectively plays off Wittgenstein's later period in order to question the sanity of the later work. If one is going to argue from the personal and biographical material (which is a highly subjective and questionable practice), then one should note that throughout his life Wittgenstein was bothered by periods of depression and feelings of isolation. There is no reason to highlight the later stage and conclude that Wittgenstein's philosophical work in this period is somehow flawed because of his "state of mind" or that he produced a philosophy "derived...from his own personal psychic situation" which reflect an attempt to save himself and his own sanity.[43]

While Nieli does offer certain insights that may lead to a more balanced reading of the *Tractatus*, his attempts to force Wittgenstein into his own unified system result in a fundamentally flawed interpretation of Wittgenstein. The result is a clearer picture of Nieli's mystical schema than of Wittgenstein. While Nieli laments the lack of recognition of Wittgenstein's mysticism by the philosophical community, his attempts to expound upon it in such a grandiose and therapeutic fashion lead to more questions than solutions.

Mysticism Throughout Wittgenstein's Writings

Another attempt to interpret Wittgenstein through the lenses of mysticism is offered by Ignace D'Hert. In *Wittgenstein's Relevance for Theology*, D'hert claimed that mysticism was the purpose of the *Tractatus*. This mysticism has often been ignored or viewed as an aberration by interpreters of the *Tractatus*.

In producing a logical analysis of the world, Wittgenstein pointed to the boundaries of language. Beyond this logically demarcated area, however, exists the world of the mystical. According to D'hert, the closing statements of the *Tractatus* point to this world both explicitly and implicitly.

> One can therefore legitimately talk about a twofold sense of the mysticism of the *Tractatus*. One may say that there is the mysticism *in* the *Tractatus* and the mysticism *of* the *Tractatus*. The former points to the fairly clear area of the mystical as outlined in the last part of the book itself. The latter points back to the world and the language of the *Tractatus* to Wittgenstein's whole philosophical undertaking ...[44]

D'hert refers to Wittgenstein's closing statements as the mysticism "in" the *Tractatus*. After arguing for a structured world through a logical use of language, Wittgenstein refers to the area beyond language. Wittgenstein outlined the propositional form so that language could be logically established. Beginning in 6.44, Wittgenstein refers to what is beyond the limits of language. "Not *how* the world is, is the mystical, but *that* it is."[45] The mystical is inexpressible and shows itself (6.522). Wittgenstein concludes in 7 that, "Whereof one cannot speak, thereof one must be silent."[46] These statements lead D'hert to conclude that "the whole point of the *Tractatus* lies in its pointing beyond itself to the sphere of the mystical."[47]

D'hert refers to the mysticism "of" the *Tractatus* as that which comes from the *Notebooks* or from Wittgenstein's letters. Wittgenstein wrote in a letter to Ludwig von Ficker regarding the *Tractatus* that

> The point of the book is an ethical one.... . My work consists of two parts: the one presented here and all that which I have *not* written. And precisely this second part is the important one.[48]

D'hert extends his claim about the centrality of mysticism in Wittgenstein's works by arguing that Wittgenstein tried to show an instance in which "one particular language game" points to the presence of the mystical. "One could put it this way: This is just one example of how one comes to the ultimate by means of one particular language game."[49]

D'hert understands there to be a strong parallel between mysticism (as presented in Wittgenstein) and theology. By drawing from Thomas Aquinas, D'hert seeks to illustrate the inherent relationship between mysticism and theology. Because God transcends the world and even the boundaries of nature, all "talk about God" can only be based on analogy. The mystery of "God" can only be pointed to in language since God's existence is "beyond" what can be expressed. D'hert proposes augmenting the practice of the "analogical use of metaphysical language" which seeks to go beyond boundaries in order to reach the "reality of God." By using "ordinary human experience" which "somehow appears as universal," D'hert believes that another method of analogical God-talk is possible.[50] With this move, D'hert seeks to use the later Wittgenstein material in his theological quest for pointing to the mystery of God. This second method of talking about God shares with theology the task of pointing beyond the boundaries of language to that area of mystical reality which cannot be encompassed in language.

> Since we have to try to conceive of God, try to talk about Him, try to name Him, etc., in function of Jesus Christ, it looks as though the Christian communities are invited to engage in a praxis of creating a variety of God-languages in and through which they attempt to approach "God", the Father of Jesus. Who God is, how we can talk about Him, has to be discovered in function of the multiple ways in which people express their faith in Jesus as the revelation of absolute meaning. I believe that Wittgenstein's conception of language in his later philosophy may prove helpful here.[51]

D'hert's approach allows him to employ concepts from the later Wittgenstein within the mystical system which he proposes is the key to understanding Wittgenstein.

D'hert contrasts his reading of Wittgenstein with the use of Wittgenstein by those in the philosophy of religion. For D'hert most readers of Wittgenstein are seeking to interpret him "from within," i.e., they attempt to adapt certain themes and ideas (particularly from the *Investigations*) to a discussion in the philosophy of religion.[52] According to D'hert, D. Z. Phillips is an example of this approach. "Phillips has produced a typical example of a closed philosophical system under the mask of logical respectability and consistency."[53] Instead of simply spelling out the "grammar of religious beliefs," Phillips has interpreted them in a system which informed believers what they really should do when they pray. The result is a "system in which Christian believers were told in clear terms what they actually mean when they talk. ..."[54]

In contrast to this approach, D'hert attempts to present a more comprehensive view of Wittgenstein by trying "to *express* what *shows itself* in his *Investigations*."[55] This method is what D'hert refers to as reading Wittgenstein "from without." In attempting to do this, D'hert employs Heidegger to bring out a comprehensive interpretation of Wittgenstein. The reading of the *Investigations* via Heidegger discloses the centrality of meaning in language. D'hert believes that Wittgenstein's over-arching concern was to point out the "presence of meaning in any given language."

> And this is what I would like to call the mysticism of the *Investigations* which lies at the very basis of Wittgenstein's philosophical activity. It is the awareness of this givenness of meaning as a kind of mystery which, although in itself inexpressible, is alluded to throughout his investigations, the experience of meaning in the particular language-games. Wittgenstein's mysticism is shown forth in his constantly alluding to this mystery which was there, on the surface, though only to be encountered in experience.[56]

D'hert sees a strong parallel between Heidegger's use of *Sein* and Wittgenstein's understanding of meaning. According to D'hert there is an "inexpressible unity" in Wittgenstein that comes out of the meaning that is present in all language games. This sense of mystery allows for transcendence that is not beyond this world but is available through the world.[57] While D'hert notes that there are no explicit statements of his thesis in the later Wittgenstein, he claims that the purpose of the *Investigations* is to show that the mystical "is *that* there is language."[58] The *Tractatus* was more explicit because it was dealing with a particular language game, but the *Investigations* are dealing with the totality of language games so that any specific statement would violate the approach since "one cannot *talk about* the totality when one is actually engaged in it."[59]

D'hert presents an overview of key concepts in the later Wittgenstein (e.g., language games, forms of life) and seeks to find ways to employ them in his over-all mystical interpretation of Wittgenstein. While recognizing the way which others have employed these concepts, D'hert insists that a systematic approach is needed in order to avoid relativism. This approach, which occurs "from without," is possible through D'hert's equation of "meaning" in Wittgenstein with the theological use of the word "God."

> We did not want to interpret this as a merely relativistic system but much more as a total view, based on and meant to lead to the recognition of some kind of mystery. The mystery itself was never named by Wittgenstein, but we have interpreted it as the presence, the givenness of meaning, and Wittgenstein's approach as an openness, a reverence for this mystery.[60]

The task of theology, then, is to use language to point to the mystery of God who remains "hidden, yet present." This involves a negative view of theological language, since theological language can only seek to grasp that which is ungraspable.

The equation of "meaning" and "God" allows D'hert to "discover" the underlying and implicit unity in Wittgenstein while at the same time placing "the language game of theology" on a unique footing.[61] The centrality of meaning is then, subsequently, given a Christological status. In the life of Jesus, "meaning has become a historical reality."[62] The significance of Jesus is also due to the transcendence that was present in his life and which shows that a human has "the capacity to transform the world to which he belongs into that which constitutes meaning for him."[63]

Within the framework of meaning as a mystical unifying force (which D'hert understands as "God"), D'hert develops ideas from the late Wittgenstein. These themes are centered around theology as praxis.

> A theological praxis in Wittgenstein's sense will primarily consist in questioning the particular theological language-games (including scripture, systematic theology, historical theologies, etc.), the meanings of which it should display. It should spell out the grammar of the different forms of life involved in Christianity such as prayer, liturgy, preaching, art, etc., and ultimately the form of life of Christianity itself. It can only indicate the very remarkable character of this form of life, the extreme oddness of its doctrinal statements, the almost inextricable logic of its language; it could draw attention to the apparent fulfillment people draw from it to its influential character on other forms of life, etc. And at best this kind of grammatical analysis may want to indicate that this extremely rich and diversified variety of language-games and forms of life appears to build up something like a "field of force" which may become an inspiration even to outsiders. Here again is the mystery of meaning in reality which by Christian believers is called "God".[64]

The belief in God that develops out of this configuration is the result of a certain training that occurs through a shared language and form of life. This form of life is unique because it is based on a mystical experience to which Christian language points.

Response to D'hert

D'hert has written an imaginative work that relies heavily on Thomas Aquinas for a theological orientation while at the same time espousing a position of classical mysticism that seeks to claim Wittgenstein as an advocate. D'hert depends heavily on his interpretation of the closing statements of the *Tractatus* and rejects the attempts to adapt other ideas from Wittgenstein because of the tendency to employ these ideas in the context of another philosophical system. Unlike Nieli's attempt to argue for a mystical interpretation of Wittgenstein based largely on a biographical reading of selected instances in

Wittgenstein's life, D'hert attempts to illustrate mysticism in Wittgenstein by highlighting similarities between Wittgenstein and other writers. As a result, the distillation of Aquinas and Heidegger in terms of mystical categories is brought to bear upon Wittgenstein in order to demonstrate the viability of D'hert's own presuppositions. D'hert's a priori commitment to mysticism, however, causes him to import meaning into the language games that he is attempting to define. While D'hert notes that his interpretation is based on a reading of Wittgenstein from "without," he fails to justify the necessity of approaching Wittgenstein from this perspective.

This problem is further compounded by D'hert's highly selective reading of Wittgenstein. Rather than providing a comprehensive basis for approaching Wittgenstein, D'hert is content to select isolated passages (largely from the earlier writings) to fit with his preconceived ideas. Those passages which might prove problematic to D'hert are virtually ignored.

A second major critique of D'hert grows out of his understanding of the relationship between mysticism and theology. If the task of theology is to examine the language of the church, then how does theology point beyond the boundaries of language while still taking its linguistic limits seriously. While D'hert seeks to maintain the uniqueness of the "theological language game," at some points he tries to maintain that all language games lead to the mystical, while at the same time he strives to hold on to a concept of the uniqueness of Christianity. One can begin by questioning D'hert's understanding of language games in Wittgenstein. Is there really one particular language game in the *Tractatus* (as D'hert claims)? Even more problematic is D'hert's discussion of the "theological language game." D'hert fails to provide an example of this phenomena. Is there such a thing as one language game which encompasses all theological talk? Finally, one must ask, what is the point of insisting on the uniqueness of Christianity when all language games point to the place of mystical meaning?

D'hert's approach does offer the reader of Wittgenstein a significant critique of the tendency of theologians to try to discover the "true meaning" of believer's statements. The task of the theologian, as D'hert notes, is not to tell the believer what he or she is actually doing. Such an approach conceals a kind of modern gnosticism in which only the theologians have the special knowledge of what belief actually entails. While the temptation of reductionism does not justify the need to read Wittgenstein "from without," it is an important reminder that those who seek to include Wittgenstein's work in theological

areas should not presume to use it to uncover the "true meaning" of statements but seek to point out inconsistencies in the variety of games in which
the religious community participates.[65] While D'hert's critique at this point is
insightful, he falls prey to the same fallacy by employing a systematic approach
that is explicitly dependent on mysticism and Aquinas to interpret Wittgenstein. Even more ironic is the importation of Heidegger into the discussion.
D'hert's a priori commitment to mysticism causes him to see everyone's work
through these lenses. This view is particularly unsuccessful in dealing with the
later Wittgenstein and suffers from an attempt to view reality from outside of
the language boundaries which is the very approach rejected by Wittgenstein.

A second major contribution of D'hert's work is his attempt to find a way
to avoid relativistic interpretations of language games. While one can again
seriously question whether D'hert is justified in resorting to an "external"
reading of Wittgenstein, he does point to a major area of concern of theological readers of Wittgenstein: Does the loss of an external view-point imply that
all language games are equally valid? The need to discover internal methods of
critique remains a significant challenge to theologians who employ Wittgenstein.[66]

Between Mysticism and Sociology

Existentialism and Implicit Mysticism

A major attempt to think theologically following Wittgenstein has been
offered by Paul Holmer. The results of his work are available in a collection of
essays entitled *The Grammar of Faith* (and in another collection of essays in his
honor in *The Grammar of the Heart*). Holmer's primary concern is to address
the relationship between academic theology and "the language of faith." Holmer distinguishes between the language "about" faith and the language "of"
faith. Language about faith is the secondary reflection that is undertaken in
much of academic theology and is characterized by a third-person mood.
Holmer compares this theology to grammar. Theology about God seeks to explore and extend the rules of theological language (which Holmer refers to as
the "divine grammar").[67] While Holmer recognizes the importance of aspects
of theology about God, He insists that it is secondary to the language of faith.
"Real theology" is that which occurs in the first person mode in which the
individual appropriates that which he/she has learned.

> At best, the theological research that goes on does not quite issue in real theology—instead it prepares people a bit, at the most, for appreciating the real thing. It is like logic in respect to thinking and grammar in respect to writing prose.[68]

Holmer concludes that the major task of "real theology" is to attend to the language of faith.

Holmer believes that academic theology has been distracted from the language of faith. Instead of attending to what believers say and do, theologians have become caught up in playing their own language games. Holmer is particularly concerned by the plethora of theologies that have developed. The development of theologies based on philosophy (e.g., process) or political issues (e.g., liberation, feminist) results in an ideology that attempts to rectify the outmoded theology of the church by addressing itself to contemporary human issues. "Whatever their momentary appeal, such theologies do very little by way of recommending Christianity; instead they recommend causes that do not usually need such extraneous supports anyway."[69] The problem with a great deal of modern theology is that it believes that its task is to uncover (or recover) the true meaning of religious language. Rather than starting with the language of faith much of theology seeks to discover something that is missing by positing a unifying schema that is implicit (or believed to be necessary) in the language of faith.

> One must never entertain, therefore, a picture of a Christian theology as a net of causes and reasons, an intellectual proposal, which by constant assimilation of novelties, by continual adaptation to new circumstances, will reclaim the masses by its sweet reasonableness.[70]

Theology is not something that we can design ourselves. Instead, theology is grammar in that it seeks to point out the rules that underlie the language of faith. These rules "have become embedded in the speech textures themselves."[71] Consequently, what is needed is not a system that will import meaning into the language of faith. Holmer contends that the language of faith as taught by the Scripture, creeds, etc., is sufficient. "For most, these are more than enough."[72] Christians do not need theologians to tell them what they really mean when they pray, confess their sins, etc.

According to Holmer, the question of meaning has come to play a central role in theological discussion. Many theologians contend that the language of faith has become obsolete. The meaning in these statements is still viable; however, it has become buried (in a pre–scientific worldview). The task of the-

ology, then, is to uncover these meanings in order for the language of faith to be intelligible. Such an understanding is based on a bifurcation of meaning and language. It is believed that meaning can somehow be separated from language.

> Thus words, whether spoken or written, seem to be substitutes for, expressions of, and vehicles respecting the nonphysical stuff that is being transferred or communicated with the words.[73]

Holmer refers to this approach as a "spiritualization of language" in which "meaning is mentalistic."[74] The result is a kind of dogma that insists that meaning occurs inside an individual's head in a privatistic way. At this point, Holmer is quick to apply Wittgenstein's arguments against the mentalist, private notion of meaning.

Instead of searching for a system that will revitalize the meaning that is supposed to be hidden in an antiquated language, Holmer proposes a return to the language itself. "Meaning belongs to words when uses for them are at hand."[75] The theological task is not to develop a theory that will be meaningful, but to "suggest the 'learning how' and all [that] that involves in the religious life."[76] The proper theological task is to discover appropriate uses of the language of faith in ways that will teach people *how* to be religious. A functional language is not without meaning! While many theologians express concern over the emptiness of much of religious language,

> ...there is no short road to restoring meanings. This is why the contemporary pleas for a new theological scheme is so lamentable: it suggests that an artificial linguistic context, abstract at that, is really the best matrix for the very important words of faith to come to life; whereas the fact of the matter is that ordinary life–everyday existence—is that matrix.[77]

The meaning of a word is in its use.[78] Consequently, if religious words have lost their meaning it is not because they have been defined incorrectly, but because they have lost "the practice with which they were associated."[79]

For Holmer, modern theology has become preoccupied with a search for foundations. This quest has been based on a presupposition that beliefs must have a foundation if they are to taken seriously. This search for a foundation for faith seeks to isolate the distinctive beliefs (which are deemed as somehow separable from the praying, saying, singing, etc. that accompanies them).[80] According to Holmer, the search for a foundation for faith often turns to metaphysics. Often overlooked are the presuppositions which accompany metaphysical inquiry. Among them is an implicit belief in an underlying system which causes the theologian to search for a kind of common denominator to provide a basis for the beliefs that are espoused. There is also a desire to determine the universal(s) which are present in reality in its search for the building blocks of the foundation for faith. "The concept of 'being' is the most general way of referring to the *fundamentum in re*."[81]

The use of ontological categories centers on "being" as the universal element. If all things have being, then it follows that everything is connected. The significance of this step must not be overlooked. While it is impossible to find "being" or a "universal," "being" is a necessary presupposition for developing a unified system. A good example of the use of ontological categories in theology can be found in Paul Tillich's work. Tillich seeks to discover the essence of being itself. This is possible, according to Tillich, because "there are concepts which are less universal than being but more universal than any ontic concept."[82] Tillich goes further to directly connect the ontological question with metaphysics.[83] This move to metaphysics is a result of the belief that beneath the language of faith resides a systematic, unifying concept to which all theological concepts refer. Theological words take on their meanings through their reference to the foundation of being.

In his attempts to secure a solid foundation for theology (and one that is philosophically defensible), Tillich, according to Holmer, sacrifices the language of faith. "It is surely very strange to have to say that you are referring to something when you talk about God, Jesus, and the Holy Spirit."[84] Language does not need "an accompanying ontological commentary which tells us how to take it."[85] The ontological move carries with it metaphysical presuppositions, since the question of being must then be asked of God (and in fact, for Tillich, God is the ground of being). All of these highly sophisticated, philosophical moves fail to take seriously the language of faith itself. The result is a theology about faith that replaces a theology of faith.

A second attempt to establish a foundation for the language of faith has been proposed by those who seek to uncover the fundamental facts. Since the onset of the historical–critical study, there has been an attempt to use scientific methods in order to discover a historical foundation. Holmer notes that, "Despite valiant attempts to find the foundations of theology in the facts about Jesus, nothing very conclusive ever appears to have been achieved."[86] Holmer believes that there are similar difficulties with the attempts to uncover a factual foundation as there are with the ontological approach. Facts do not exist independently of language. Neither is there a "master concept of 'fact'" which refers to a "master state of affairs."[87]

> The overwhelming point to remember, which lays to rest the ghost of those peculiar philosophical longings that grip us ever and anon, is that there is no indisputable, no indubitable starting point– no fact– for any and all inquirers.[88]

The search for a universal via an ontological or factual foundation is mistaken because it fails to take seriously the primacy of the language of faith or note its peculiarities. In its rush to discover a hidden meaning, it rushes over the meaningful acts and words of believers. The distinctiveness of the language of faith cannot be so easily overlooked or assimilated into a meta–system.

> One must never entertain, therefore, a picture of a Christian theology as a net of causes and reasons, an intellectual proposal, which by constant assimilation of novelties, by continual adaptation to new circumstances, will reclaim the masses by its sweet reasonableness.[89]

Holmer's emphasis on the language of faith is based on his commitment to the experiential nature of theology. Theology does not seek to be an end in itself, but "moves towards a present–tense, first person mood."[90] Only when personal appropriation takes place does this transfer occur and there is a move "to becoming solicitous, personal, and persuasive."[91] The existential nature of theology does not result in mere subjectivity. According to Holmer, there are basic concepts which function within theology. A concept is a meaning–complex which relate together "personal powers, like potencies, like skills and abilities."[92] These concepts are not dependent on definitions, but on ways of acting (or a form of life).

Concepts are the "ruled functions" which give guidance to our lives. Consequently, Christian concepts such as *agape* act as an interpretive key while at the same time calling for a form of life. "God" is another concept which calls for a response. A concept is learned when it is used properly in the context of one's life. Thus, prayer and worship show the proper use of the concept God (this underscores Holmer's insistence on theology as the language of faith as opposed to the language about faith). These concepts are learned through the language of faith and its accompanying form of life. The theological task becomes the "description and study of the religious concepts."[93] Holmer goes further to state that "theology is an accounting of how the concepts, including the concept of 'God,' hang together."[94] The result is an "informal consensus" that develops out of the study of the language of faith. Within the contexts of the Scripture, liturgy confession, etc., concepts and ideas are developed which bring the individual to the act of worshipping God.[95]

> Knowing God, then, is a matter of coming to know him in prayer, worship, praise, and much else that makes up the religious life. Theology, now thinking of it in the grammatical sense, is not a substitute for worship; and it is certainly not a lofty and sophisticated way to acknowledge God in contrast to vulgar modes of belief and submissive respect. it does not substitute new concepts for those in the story, for that again is no improvement but is invariably a radically different replacement. One might say that a new concept usually changes the entire grammar. Theology is a name, then, for the ruled way, the correct way of speaking about and worshipping God. ...The true God is known only when his identity is established in a tradition and by a ruled practice of language and worship. This is what the grammar, the theology, provides.[96]

Responses to Holmer

There is much to commend in Holmer's work. By taking his cue from Wittgenstein's definition of meaning as function and the adequacy of everyday language, Holmer makes a distinctive and significant rejoinder to much of academic theology. At this point, Holmer's work is an affirmation and extension of D'hert's critique of theologians who seek to tell believers what they "really believe." The presumptuousness of much of theology fails to consider that the language of faith *does* work for many believers. Parallel to Freudian theories of neuroses, theologians have based their theories on what they determined were "problematic areas" while ignoring the healthy function of worship and the vitality of faith in scores of Christian churches. Furthermore, Holmer's critique (based on his reading of Wittgenstein) of the metaphysical and ontological traditions is an important reminder of the presuppositions of many theologians. The task of theology is not to discover a hidden reservoir of meaning by supplying a unifying system. Instead, theology should show the relationships between the words and actions of believers. Holmer provides an important reminder that metaphysical and ontological options are actually changing the grammar which results in a distortion of the language of faith.

There are difficulties, however, with Holmer's understanding of "concepts" and their centrality to the language of faith. Holmer's own writings add to the confusion when he writes that, "Philosophy seems to arise because some people are intent upon conceptualizing...."[97] In an earlier essay, Holmer argues that concepts are a technical and sophisticated way of viewing the "vernacular language of everyday."[98] Given this understanding, philosophy (or theology) seeks to make explicit the concepts which are present in the language of faith.

Religion is learned through stories, liturgy, prayer, etc., but in these various activities reside a certain grid, which Holmer refers to as concepts.

> Once one has acquired a taste for concepts and conceptual meanings, the whole shape of popular religion seems quite different and inadequate. For then, the concepts seem to have been involved all along; they seem to have been there in some sense, maybe implicitly, prior to their discovery. It is as if they were meant all along, as if the concepts (i.e., the meaning complexes) were present in some immaterial and mysterious way long before the philosophically minded reader came along.[99]

The recognition of the implicit concepts allows one to expand upon them and conclude ("confidently") that "the God concept is of an 'immaterial substance,' 'omnipotent being' 'necessarily existing.'"[100] These are amazing conclusions from a theologian who has expressed skepticism about both academic theology and metaphysics. The reader is left wondering how Holmer jumps to such statements after his continued insistence on the adequacy of the language of faith.

While Holmer cites Wittgenstein for his use of concepts, one must note that concepts play a significantly smaller role in Wittgenstein than they do in Holmer's writings. Furthermore, the entire issue is clouded by controversy over a debate about Wittgenstein's use of concepts. Colin McGuin questions an understanding of concepts that is manifest from our actions (similar to Holmer's position) because of the impossibility of a supra-perspective vantage point. "For any behaviour that we take to manifest a given concept *could* be interpreted so as to constitute the manifestation of a different concept."[101] Holmer's understanding of concepts implies both a metalinguistic as well as a transcendent perspective that dramatically differs from his claim that in theology we cannot go beyond the game (which involves being attentive to the materials, i.e., Scripture, creeds, etc.).[102]

One must question whether or not Holmer forces himself into this predicament in order to avoid being left with mere subjectivity. Holmer's existentialist approach is highly individualistic. While denying that theology can be "yours" or "mine," Holmer insists that the move from language about to language of faith must be a personal achievement. The task of theology is to bring the listener to a new situation: "his self-evaluation; his subjectivity, his aims, wishes, hopes, desires, must be altered so that the grammar of faith becomes relevant."[103] While Holmer's desire is certainly noteworthy, there is a conspicuous absence of the role of the community throughout his writings. Indi-

viduals seem to be the focal point and at best the community is only the pre-
server of a kind of static tradition (made up of Holmer's concepts).

The emphasis on the individual leaves Holmer precariously open to the
charge of subjectivity. There is a lack of criteria for evaluating personal decisions. At this point, Holmer's concepts are employed to try to bridge the gap
between existential actualization and the core of Christianity. It is interesting
that Holmer is willing to place trust in language, but not in the community
which transmits it. The lack of place for the contextual power of the community leaves Holmer without a locus for theological action (action both as a result of the language about and of faith). The conceptual hypothesis provides
this basis, but only at the price of his previous gains. It seems almost tragic that
Holmer who has fought so valiantly for the validity of believers' experiences
and the adequacy of the language of faith, resorts to the necessity of concepts
in order to defend himself from accusations of subjectivity. The result is a
work that is highly commendable as a critique of much of modern theology,
but that in the end falls prey to many of his own criticisms. Holmer's writings
provide an interesting commentary on Wittgenstein. They are highly selective
and at times seem to be filtered through Kierkegaardian lenses (in particular,
the argument regarding concepts). There is a kind of implicit mysticism at
work which grows out of Holmer's existential, experiential commitment.
Holmer refers rather broadly to a "Christian form of life" and the language of
faith. This implicit reliance on a mystical foundation seems to be apparent
here. While a certain indebtedness to the community is noted, the major interest seems to be on individual experiences. Holmer avoids the temptations of
reading mysticism into Wittgenstein (or, as in Nieli's case, Wittgenstein into
mysticism), but he does seem to be more comfortable with reading Wittgenstein as a supporter of the adequacy of the individual's use of language rather
than in terms of the power of the community. Lacking in this approach is a
consistent recognition that language is based on a consensus that requires a
community.

Wittgenstein and the Philosophy of Religion

Another significant attempt to appropriate Wittgenstein for theological
purposes has been offered by Hugh Jones. In *Die Logik theologischer Perspektiven*,
Jones presents a compendium and commentary on both Wittgenstein and a
wide range of philosophers of religion. Jones includes John Wisdom, R. M.
Hare, John Hick and Ian Barbour as conversation partners in presentation

and is further stimulated by the theological interest in story developed by
Dietrich Ritschl and Paul van Buren. Amidst these array of resources, Jones
centers his discussion around the significance of perspective which he claims is
the central contribution of Wittgenstein's writings.[104] A major concern of
Jones' work is to facilitate a dialogue between analytical philosophy and the
hermeneutical tradition (based largely on Heidegger). Jones finds similarities
between the two schools of thought, "*denn sie sind alle Varianten des nachkan-
tischen Idealismus.*"[105] The discussion of Wittgenstein in terms of the philosophy of religion places Jones squarely in the post–Kantian tradition. Within
this framework, Jones seeks to interpret Wittgenstein (and interpreters of
Wittgenstein) in order to address questions regarding the perspective or
"*Weltbild*" of religious language.

Jones recognizes a continuity in Wittgenstein which begins with the centrality of the *sehen/zeigen* passages in the *Tractatus*. The *sehen/zeigen* motif includes two important elements for Jones. First, the emphasis on *sehen* (that
later moves to *sehen–als*) supplies the fundamental insight that perspective is
the key to recognizing how language (and religious language in particular)
functions. Secondly, the *zeigen* passages provide Jones with his claim that "*die
fundamentalen Gewissheiten sind im stillschweigenden Wissen.*"[106] This "*stillschweigendes Wissen*" is an implicit part of all language games.

> Hinter unseren Betrachtungsweisen ist ein System, ein Denkgebäude von Wissen,
> Überzeugung und Urteilen, von Begriffen und empirischen Sätzen, aus denen ein
> Weltbild entstanden ist.[107]

This *Weltbild* encompasses a kind of mythology that is learned through the
language, but is ultimately ungrounded. This underlying system provides the
believer with an interpretive schema that while not stagnant provides an implicit foundation. The significance of *zeigen* is due to its participation in the
grammatical structure of language (Jones interprets Wittgenstein's remarks on
theology as grammar in this light). In religious language, *zeigen* occurs because
God is "*letztlich verborgen.*"[108]

Jones finds it advisable to investigate perspective because theology cannot
attempt to articulate precisely what is ultimately impossible to state. Instead,
theology attempts to provide clarity in the "'*Tiefengrammatik*'" *in der
Alltagssprache christlicher Menschen.*"[109] Jones seeks to provide an overview of
language by taking note of the connections in a language game.

Wenn man die Sprache als eine alte Stadt ansieht, d.h., als "ein Gewinkel von Gäschen und Plätzen, alten und neuen Häusern, und Häusern mit Zubauten aus verschiedenen Zeiten..." (PU 18), liegt es auf der Hand, daß man nach dem Wesen der Sprache bzw. des Glaubens nicht fragen kann. Dies würde die "Altstadt" mit den neueren "Vororten" und ihren "geraden und regelmässigen Strassen und mit einförmigen Häusern" verwechseln (ebd.). Dies wäre, als ob wir darauf bestünden, unter jeder alten Stadt wie Frankfurt oder London oder Paris ein Gitter "gerader und regelmässiger Strassen" finden zu müssen.[110]

Attempts in the philosophy of religion to interpret Wittgenstein through the use of patterns, bliks, experience [*Erleben–als*], or interpretation have all fallen prey to the tendency to look beneath the language game for a structure of meaning. Jones correctly notes that Wittgenstein insists that meaning cannot be separated from (either "behind" or "beneath") the language game. In Wittgenstein's later writings there is an emphasis on the descriptive task of philosophy. For Wittgenstein, the philosophical task was not to produce hypotheses, but to analyze and describe the logical form of statements, questions, exclamations, etc. Wittgenstein went further to reject metaphysical arguments because they tried to state what cannot be said. Instead, Wittgenstein sought to provide an overview [*Übersicht*] which recognized the primacy of the language game.

Aufgabe des Philosophen ist es allerdings nicht, "feine Unterschiede" zu machen als ob er die Verschwommenheit der alltäglichen Sprache beseitigen könnte, sondern er versucht, sich Übersicht zu verschaffen durch Beschreibung von Begriffsunterschieden, Grenzfällen und dem Sich-Kreuzen unserer Begriffe.[111]

Consequently, the philosopher is less interested in the history of an idea than in the use of language and the connections that are made within the language game.

At this point, Jones makes an important distinction between *Sehen* and *Sehen–als*.

Beim Sehen hat man die Mitteilung einer Wahrnehmung, wird dadurch über die Außenwelt informiert wie bei den anderen Sinneserlebnissen (vgl. Z 474–477). Demgegenüber haben Mitteilungen eines Sehen–als zwar die oberflächliche Grammatik einer solchen Mitteilung, sind aber die Beschreibung eines Aspektwechsels wie einer Wahrnehmung "ganz als hätte sich der Gegenstand vor meinen Augen geändert."[112]

Sehen–als is similar to *Sehen* in so far as neither attempts to interpret the perceptual input that is received. It differs however in that it goes beyond sensory input and provides the individual with a framework which seeks to show the internal relationships between objects in the grammatical structure. In a certain sense, *Sehen–als* is a pre-condition of the language game. While it is implicitly learned by participation in a language game and the accompanying form of life, it establishes a framework for taking part in the language game. This allows Jones to conclude that, "der Bezugsrahmen des Redens und des Handelns ist zwar das Sehen–als."[113] *Sehen–als* draws its significance from its connection to the "*stillschweigende Formen*" which provide interpretive clues to the participant in a language game.

Since *Sehen–als* is not simply a sensory experience of the individual, the criterion for it cannot be found "inside" a person. Because this experience is integrally tied to the language game itself, the question of private experience is misplaced. Instead of an internal mechanism, we are returned to the language game and its form of life.

> Denn sie stellen keine *umständliche* Redeweise dar, die ersetzt werden könnte durch eine direktere Ausdrucksweise wie etwa eine metaphysische Beschreibung von inneren Erlebnissen.[114]

Jones connects this experience of *Sehen–als* with Wittgenstein's use of the term "*Weltbild*." The *Weltbild* develops out of the use of models, metaphors, parables, etc. and informs the believer about the form of life and the interpretive schema which is in the language game.[115]

In his concluding chapter, Jones develops the concept of story as an appropriate model for understanding the relationship between the believer's language and his/her experience. Story as a genre is able to include a wide variety of literature (myth, parables, sagas, etc.) that includes an historical point of view. While story can include historical narrative it is also able to carry its own interpretative process. This allows story to include certain aspects of history (or what is generally understood as history) while at the same time providing some flexibility, both in terms of literary structure and point of reference. An important aspect of a story is that it normally occurs as a part of everyday language.[116]

> Zusammengefasst: das story-Konzept hat gegenüber Begriffen wie "Geschichte", "Mythos", "Symbol" usw. den Vorteil, daß es die Teilnahme an verschiedenen überlappenden semantischen Feldern ermöglicht, daß es auf einen Interpretationsprozeß und die Unterscheidung zwischen fiktiven und realen Welten hindeutet und daß es die tatsächlich gebrauchte Sprache als natürliches Phänomen, d.h. als Ausdruck einer Lebensform hervorhebt.[117]

Since a story brings with it an accompanying perspective, the task of theology is to recognize and respond (and to seek connections with other stories) rather than to hypothesize over possible meanings of the story. The rejection of hypotheses or possible interpretations allows an escape from the charge of subjectivity. Jones views interpretation as occurring within the framework of a perspective rather than independently (in contrast to both John Hick and Paul Holmer).[118] This framework is part of the indirect basis of the story that we learn through participating in a language game. Jones brings us, here once again, back to the *"stillschweigendes Fundamente solchen Wissens."*[119]

Jones' argument allows him to reject traditional metaphysical arguments while leaving him room to embrace the place of the *"christlich–theistichen Perspektive, die ingesamt den logischen Raum christlichen Denkens und Tun darstellt."*[120] Reference to God should not be construed as the end of an inductive or deductive chain. Consequently, attempts at either a natural theology or apologetic metaphysics are misguided. Instead, Jones understands the word God to be part of the inner system of logic that is present in the language game as well as implicitly functioning in the fiduciary framework. Jones returns once more to the *sagen/zeigen* distinction for the language game's use of God as a kind of pointer to the place in language in which the grammar of God is present.

> Vielmehr hat dieses Wort [God] die Funktion, die gesamte Reichweite menschlicher Möglichkeiten offen zu halten und...uns in Zentrum des Vertrauensrahmens zu führen.[121]

Within this framework, Jones attempts to recover the use of metaphysical statements by claiming that it is possible to construct a "descriptive metaphysic." Such metaphysics cannot be true or false in an empirical sense, but nonetheless it attempts to serve as a directive in the believer's language.[122] To this end, the *Gottesbegriff* does not refer to an object, but to a point of orientation for the believer.[123]

The use of metaphysics within the theistic perspective is made with the recognition that verification is not possible.[124]

> Hier handelt es sich weder um objektiv feststellbare *Gründe* noch um ganz private Überzeugungen, sondern um die Überlappung verschiedener Lebensformen und deren sprachlichen Ausdrucksformen bzw. Sprachspiele.[125]

In this sense, metaphysics is the more modest attempt to focus the believers' direction on the language of the Sprachspiel and its accompanying form of life.

The movement within the language game allows for a certain freedom, so that the participants are not held captive by the game. It is this freedom that allows the hearer to understand his/her own story in terms of the story which is being told. The psychological and sociological elements play an important part in both shaping and responding to the story.

> Es kommt alles darauf an, *wie* die story gebraucht wird, *wie* sie unsere Lebensorientierung und unser Handeln, anders gesagt, unsere Identität erhellt.[126]

Response to Jones

Jones presents a helpful collection and critique of an assortment of responses to Wittgenstein that have developed in the philosophy of religion. By working his way through this collection of thinkers, Jones is able to glean strengths from their readings of Wittgenstein while at the same time noting weaknesses in the various perspectives. Jones' own reading of Wittgenstein is insightful and particularly helps overcome the tendency to find a dichotomy in Wittgenstein between the earlier and later writings. The thematic interest in perspective in Wittgenstein provides Jones with a strong basis for his argument for continuity (albeit with developments and alterations) in Wittgenstein. One could, however, raise the question of whether Jones' own interest in perspective has forced the issue. The claim that this is the over-riding theme in Wittgenstein is open to question.[127] At this point, one must note that Jones relies heavily on his interpretation of the distinction between *sagen* and *zeigen* in the *Tractatus* which provides him with a foundation for his approach. The later Wittgenstein writings are then interpreted through this schema and depend largely on Jones' parallel interpretation of *On Certainty*.

Jones is particularly helpful in pointing out the centrality of the language game and its accompanying form of life. He is able to highlight Wittgenstein's insistence on the autonomy of language and in particular on the ways in which religious language games function. Jones is able to eliminate the need for historical verification and thereby return the language game to a question of faith while avoiding individualistic subjectivity. Wittgenstein's metaphor of language as a city is extended by noting the task of theology of describing the appropriate uses of language and pointing to the rules which are implicit in the language game itself. In his closing remarks, Jones cites Bonhoeffer's use of the "*Gottesbegriff*." The attempts to develop metaphysical arguments pushed God to the boundaries of language and experience. Jones notes that,

> Bei der obigen Darstellung des konstituierenden Begriffs geht es nicht darum, von Gott zu sprechen, wenn menschliche Erkenntnis und Kräfte zu Ende sind. Hier wird kein Raum für Gott ausgespart, sondern gerade der Gottesbegriff schafft Raum für menschliches Denken und Tun.[128]

The attempt by Jones to argue within the context of the philosophy of religion brings with it a particular difficulty. Jones notes at the outset the attempts to read Wittgenstein in the terms of a "*neukantischen Idealismus*."[129] Wittgenstein's radical critique of the task of philosophy forces one to ask whether or not one can so readily place him in such a context. One consequence of Jones' reading is his own difficulty with metaphysical statements. Jones is ready to cite Wittgenstein's rejection of the claims of metaphysics: "*metaphysische Wahrheiten sind nicht nur unsagbar, sondern auch illusorische Wieder-spiegelungen grammatischer Konventionen*."[130] Given such a position, it is peculiar that Jones then attempts to salvage a place for metaphysics, albeit one that is severely reduced. This leads to a certain confusion in Jones' usage of the word "metaphysics." By attempting to redefine the term, Jones only creates uncertainty regarding his reading of Wittgenstein. Jones' ready acceptance of the "christlich-theistische Perspektive" of Christianity carries with it similar (but perhaps not quite as troubling) difficulties due to the abuse of theism and the often-accompanying questions of the existence of God.

Finally, one must question if Jones' preference for *zeigen* and the *still-schweigendes Element* of the language game allows him to still firmly embrace an incarnational understanding of Christianity. According to Jones, the believer's faith is in the *Deus absconditus* who can only be pointed to by the language of faith.[131] The doctrine of the incarnation, however, is a strong statement that God is *with* us in an immanent way. Christians confess with language and in doing so receive new life through the presence of God.

A Sociological Reading of Wittgenstein

In *Theology after Wittgenstein*, Fergus Kerr presents an exegetical and interpretive reading of Wittgenstein based largely on the *Philosophical Investigations* and the later writings. According to Kerr, there are two major themes of theological importance in Wittgenstein: (1) a rejection of metaphysics; and (2) a dismissal of the Cartesian mentalist-individualist approach. Kerr weaves these two themes together through a presentation of selected passages from the "late Wittgenstein."

Kerr begins with Descartes who remains the primary opponent throughout the work. Descartes' discovery of the rational "I" has become the basis for theological work of the past 350 years. Humanity defined in terms of consciousness and viewed from an egocentric perspective has been adopted and expounded upon in theological literature. Augmented by Kant, the Cartesian self remains an entrenched part of theological presuppositions.

> The picture of the self-conscious and self-reliant, self-transparent and all-responsible individual which Descartes and Kant between them imposed upon modern philosophy may easily be identified, in various guises, in the work of many modern theologians.[132]

It is this picture of the self that Wittgenstein (among others) sought to challenge. Through a reading of a variety of contemporary theologians (among them Rahner, Kaufmann, and Ogden), Kerr shows the central role that the Cartesian model of the self plays in a wide range of theological perspectives. The starting point for much of theology has become the individual who almost inevitably attains some kind of divine attributes.[133]

Kerr contends that Wittgenstein's main task was to expose the "myth of the worldless (and often essentially wordless) ego."[134] Descartes' connection of the certainty of the individual's own existence with an understanding that the existence of reality beyond one's own consciousness is guaranteed solely by God has resulted in a coupling of the mentalist–individualist perspective with a metaphysical perspective.[135]

> As Paul Feyerabend has pointed out, the very idea of a personal experience that would be infallible, self-authenticated, unprejudiced etc., because it was the result of sloughing off all received opinion, tradition, authority etc., in fact the very idea with which Descartes opens the *Meditations*, is remarkably reminiscent of certain tendencies in the history of Christianity that would put the individual believer directly and inwardly into a relationship with God which excluded in advance all mediation by a historical community with authoritative tradition, rituals, and the like.[136]

Once he has established the Cartesian view of the self as the point of attack, Kerr introduces the reader to Wittgenstein, starting with an overview of Wittgenstein's reception in theological circles. According to Kerr, Wittgenstein is best known for Kai Nielson's discussion of "Wittgensteinian fideism." This brand of fideism, attributed to Wittgensteinian theologians, argues that religious language is distinct and understandable only to those who participate in this "form of life." Consequently those outside the Christian faith are not able to comprehend or dismiss the claims of Christianity. The connection with Wittgenstein is usually made by understanding religion as a "form of life" which must be accepted, or by viewing religious language as a "language game" with its distinct set of rules (comprehensible only to those who participate in this game). Kerr dismisses this interpretation of Wittgenstein:

> The very idea that religion, or anything else on that grand scale, would count as a "form of life" in Wittgenstein's sense, although it keeps cropping up, has to be excluded on textual grounds.[137]

While Wittgenstein identified language with a "form of life" (see *PI*, §19), the examples he offers as constituting a form of life are much more specific (e.g., giving and obeying orders, telling a story, thanking, praying, etc., *PI*, §23). Consequently, to apply the term to such a broad and diverse phenomenon as religion or even Christianity is to extend it beyond credibility. Christianity is composed of a vast number of linguistic activities that cannot be so easily lumped together under one heading. In addition, Wittgenstein did not view language games as isolated from each other, but as integrally related to each other.[138] Unfortunately, this misunderstanding of Wittgenstein's terms has resulted in labeling him as a "fideist."

Wittgenstein greatly admired Augustine, and the *Investigations* begins with a quotation from Augustine's Confessions.[139] By beginning with Augustine, Kerr believes that Wittgenstein sought to portray the "interweaving of metaphysical anthropology with Christian faith that remains the background of modern Western thought."[140] The place of the soul and the egocentric perspective undergird the idea that meaning is something private that occurs "inside a head." The understanding of the ego as mental and as hidden away in the mind takes us away from the real world. Wittgenstein wants to remind Augustine, and us, of the place of the community. Meaning is not found within the individual's consciousness, but in the context of the "public world" that we share. "The 'essence' of human language is the round of collaborative activity that generates the human way of life."[141] By reminding us of how words function, Wittgenstein seeks to shift the place of meaning from the "ego's mental enclosure to the social world."[142] Wittgenstein's search for simple elements (manifest in the *Tractatus*) shifted to a focus on the forms of life. His emphasis on the forms of life underscores his passionate concern about

our existence together. Instead of resorting to a pre-linguistic place of consciousness, we find meaning and ourselves in the customs and practices of everyday life. It is our actions that constitute the place of meaning. The place of
meaning is not found in isolated individuals, but in "the whole hurly-burly of
human actions."[143]

> From the outset we are reminded that we are agents in practical intercourse with one
> another-not solitary observers gazing upwards to the celestial realm of the eternal
> forms, or inwards at the show in the mental theatre. ... is in our dealings with each
> other-in how we *act*-that human life is founded. ...Community is built into human
> action from the beginning.[144]

There is a tendency to isolate the misunderstandings or deception that we
may experience. This is not the norm. In most cases, we do understand each
other. Philosophy should seek to bring out the understanding which we share
because of our shared forms of life. Our commitment to each other brings
with it a way of life. It is in this context that we discover meaning.

> All meaning... must have conceptual links with the whole system of the human way of
> doing things together. There is nothing inside one's head that does not owe its exis-
> tence to one's collaboration in a historical community. It is established practices, cus-
> tomary reactions and interactions, and so on, that constitute the element in which
> one's consciousness is created and sustained: my sense of myself, not to mention the
> contents of my mind and memory, depend essentially on my being with others, my be-
> ing in touch with other, of my physical and psychological kind. ...Nothing is more
> foundational to the whole human enterprise than the community that we create in
> our natural reactions to one another as they have been cultivated and elaborated in a
> very contingent historical tradition.[145]

The interrelatedness of language and life makes all privatistic attempts illegitimate. Language is a shared activity and Wittgenstein spends a great deal of
time in the *Investigations* displaying the impossibility of a private language. Our
experiences are not private, isolated ones. The Cartesian understanding of the
self has led us to a dichotomy between soul and body. Consequently, we begin
to believe that our thoughts are the result of a hidden process to which we
alone have access. Such an understanding reaffirms the place of the Cartesian
"I," but it does so only at the cost of isolation and estrangement. In contrast,
Wittgenstein notes the fact that the self and consciousness are found in the
world (not outside of it or in one's head). "There is no world for me or anyone
else other than the world that the language gives us."[146]

Kerr dismisses both idealist and realist readings of Wittgenstein. In contrast to idealists, Wittgenstein presents a "radical anti–idealism" in which action takes precedence over ideas.

> The meanings that establish the house of reason are not inside our individual minds. They are out in the open, constituting the space, wherever two or three gather to exchange gifts or threats, or stories and songs.[147]

Realists share with idealists a common belief that language is dependent on ostensive definition. This basic premise is one that Wittgenstein rejects. Like the idealist, the realist also accepts a metaphysical premise that the individual can gain a supra–individual perspective.[148] The most common critique of Wittgenstein is to label him a behaviorist for rejecting the "mentalist–individualist mystifications."[149] But in contrast to behaviorists, Wittgenstein starts with the forms of life rather than the sense data.

> We have been tempted into the habit of thinking that either *die Dinge* or *unsere Vorstellungen* must be the primary thing, but the choice between realism and idealism overlooks *das Leben*: that is Wittgenstein's suggestion.[150]

Although Wittgenstein's only reference to theology in the *Investigations* occurs parenthetically, Kerr believes that it is a significant aside. Wittgenstein's notion of "theology as grammar"[151] makes a methodological claim.

> Theology as grammar is, then, the patient and painstaking description of how, when we have to, we speak of God. But why is it that we doubt it can be in mere words or signs or bodily activities that we discover anything interesting about out inner selves or about the divine?...Again and again Wittgenstein reminds us that we have no alternative to attending to the signs, the repertoire of gestures and so on that interweave our existence. We have no access to the divine, independently of our life and language. ... We have nothing else to turn to but the whole complex system of signs which is our human world.[152]

Wittgenstein believed in the sufficiency of signs and language. Although we can gain no divine access or assume a view–point outside our selves, Wittgenstein reminds us of our humanity. "Once and for all...we need to give up comparing ourselves with ethereal beings that enjoy unmediated communion with one another."[153]

The importance of language is tied to its incorporation in life. "Practice [*Praxis*] gives the words their sense."[154] In such a situation, the task of theology is to point out the place of language and to reclaim it from its mistaken metaphysical presuppositions. Kerr notes that questions about the existence of God are exemplary at this point. The believer seeks no causal explanation for God's existence. It is only non-believers or those who are seeking an additional proof who later turn to the question of God's existence. Belief in God is not based on a metaphysical analogy, but it develops out of a form of life. Wittgenstein wrote once that "Life can educate to a belief in God."[155] The existence of God is largely the result of how we have learned to talk about God. Through praying, blessing, cursing, etc., we are shown certain connections with "God." These connections are not fundamentally concerned with the question of God's existence. Wittgenstein concluded that, "Perhaps one could "convince someone that God exists" by means of a certain kind of upbringing, by shaping his life in such and such a way."[156]

Implicit in this discussion is Wittgenstein's belief that religion is a natural part of life. Wittgenstein views ceremony and ritual as an accepted part of human activity and as a foundation for religious involvement. This leads Kerr to conclude that for Wittgenstein, "Religions are an expression of human nature long before they give rise to reflections about the divine."[157] Understanding religious activities is seeing ourselves as ceremonial creatures. Wittgenstein sees a deep continuity between all religious practices. In such a context, Kerr refers to the need to develop a "naturalized theology" which begins with "the deep and sinister" in our own nature rather than starting from a "hypothesis about a deity."[158]

Kerr concludes by attempting to sketch out how a few theological problems might look in light of Wittgenstein. One example that he offers is a "scapegoat Christology" which seeks to place the doctrine of atonement in the context of a sociological understanding of human nature. Because humans share something sinister, Kerr believes that there has often been the need for a scapegoat (an arbitrary victim who is expelled by the community). The key for Kerr is connecting the atonement with "the natural history of human beings."[159] While Kerr offers this as only one of several suggestions which he briefly presents, the underlying desire is to discover ways that theology can work "within the bounds of the human condition."[160] Central to this task is a recognition (which he ascribed to Wittgenstein) of our own shared humanity and the impossibility of making metaphysical claims.

Response to Kerr

Kerr's book is a helpful introduction to Wittgenstein (particularly the later writings) that is centered on refuting the metaphysical presuppositions of most of theology. Kerr offers an impressive selection from Wittgenstein to make his point. Secondly, Kerr concerns himself with the Cartesian basis of philosophy and theology which is based on an individualist mentality. Kerr's arguments on this point often contrast with the readings of Wittgenstein in philosophical circles. There is a concerted attempt to point out the mistakes that have been made in both translating and interpreting Wittgenstein (particularly significant is Kerr's discussion of solipsism in Wittgenstein). In the light of the hyper-individualism of western society today, Kerr's reading of Wittgenstein is an important antidote to the predominant trend.[161]

There are certain difficulties, however, in Kerr's presentation. In his acceptance of the sociological givenness of religion, Kerr fails to provide a basis for making distinctions between religious communities. Are all religious groups fundamentally the same because they all are built on that which is sinister in us? Kerr's reading of Wittgenstein reminds one of the tendency of the *Religionsgeschichteschule* to view phenomenon together rather than to isolate what is distinctive. A possible argument could be based upon differences in language and rituals. Kerr fails to communicate what makes Christianity distinctive or to provide reasons why an individual would change religious traditions and communities.

Another difficulty is Kerr's emphasis on humans as reactors. Kerr repeatedly speaks of our being placed in a certain situation (with language and rules) in which we are called upon to respond. At what point can humans *act* creatively? Kerr notes that "it is occasionally possible for a man and woman to reflect and deliberate,"[162] but he fails to delineate when and how this occurs.[163] If Kerr cannot provide a stronger basis for human creativity, then the distinctions which he makes between Wittgenstein and behaviorism tend to blur.

Finally, Kerr's own theological sketches made in light of Wittgenstein are not very convincing. In particular, his attempt to reconstruct the doctrine of atonement in terms of a sociological reading of scapegoats is highly questionable. It is hard to imagine most Christians accepting such an arbitrary act as the basis for their faith. Kerr fails to show why this act (Jesus' death) breaks the cycle of human sacrifice. It is clear that the cycle is not broken due to a change in the sinister nature of human beings. What is the basis for change in the community that occurs (particularly the early Jewish/Christian community) and from whence does change come?

While his theological sketches may be questionable, Kerr has produced a convincing introduction to Wittgenstein. The most significant contribution is

Kerr's demonstration of the importance and availability of Wittgenstein to theologians. Kerr shows theologians that they have much to learn by reading Wittgenstein and that Wittgenstein was interested in challenging the presuppositions which we have often overlooked. By sorting through the Wittgenstein literature (both primary and secondary), Kerr is able to provide the reader with an insightful look as well as a challenging introduction to Wittgenstein's work and its significance for theology.

Conclusion

The preceding survey of theological readings of Wittgenstein showed the diversity of interpretations that exist. Due to the bipolarity of the mystical/sociological motif in Wittgenstein, there is a resultant diversity in the theological interpretations. It is important to note, however, that the majority of theologians have preferred to interpret Wittgenstein on the basis of mystical rather than sociological criteria. While Nieli's presentation (and even D'hert's) is a more extreme example, mystical themes underlie many of the uses of Wittgenstein in theology. Even in the philosophy of religion there is a preference for an implicit mystical approach, perhaps because of the interest in metaphysical and ontological claims and/or the predominance of existentialism. Kerr represents the major alternative with his radical emphasis on the sociological dimensions of Wittgensteinian thought. Whether or not this preference for mysticism is justified is something that can only be ascertained by a careful study of Wittgenstein. It does appear that to some extent philosophers and theologians have selected different themes in Wittgenstein to highlight. The result has been a wide divergence as well as a lack of dialogue. The best example of this phenomenon was the tendency of logical positivists to treat the *Tractatus* as a primer for their philosophical school. Theological readings of Wittgenstein have provided a helpful reminder that the *Tractatus* cannot be so readily classified. Perhaps theologians need to be reminded that their tendencies to emphasize the mystical portions of Wittgenstein also have resulted in a skewed interpretation. Wittgenstein's adamant rejection of a school of thought or of the possibility of *one* point of view are explicit claims which seek to show the danger of categorization.

There are certain areas of agreement shared by all of the theological interpretations. There is a consistent rejection of traditional metaphysics due to the rejection of a transcendental point of view.[164] The rejection of metaphysics is tied closely to the impossibility of ontological arguments. Wittgenstein clearly showed that such claims go beyond the possibilities of the religious language game and enter into another game. Metaphysical questions address religious language games from a supernatural perspective and raise questions which are not only beyond verification, but illegitimate within the context of the language game. The interpreters of Wittgenstein are also united in rejecting the need for scientific verification for a religious language game. The believers' participation is not bound to the confines of the arguments of the theologian or even the results of the archeologist and historian. The use of facts or other items as an external reference point is denied.

Closely tied to this point is the recognition by theological readers of Wittgenstein that the theological task is a horizontal one. Wittgenstein's own tertiary comments on theology as grammar point out the need for theology to accept the modest (but challenging) task of seeking out the connections within language games and the plausibility of extensions of the grammatical rules. Only at this point can the theological task be considered corrective. Theology can point out only when the grammar has been abused, but cannot try to alter the language itself or to determine what believers are really saying or meaning.[165]

The theologically oriented readers of Wittgenstein are united in their recognition of the primacy of the believer's language. There is a concerted effort to return to the language game(s) and the accompanying form(s) of life. Accompanying this move is a rejection of an academic pursuit of theology in which often the expert has gained priority over the believer. In its place is an awareness that believers' language is adequate and that the life of faith continues to survive. A closely related recognition is that praxis is the place of learning. Believers learn by their inclusion in the community and their participation in the language games and the accompanying acts.

The role of the community is underscored because of its importance as a bearer of the tradition. This return to tradition receives significance due to the communities' use of language and its form(s) of life. Consequently, even the extreme mystical interpretations of Wittgenstein remain indebted to the community for its appropriation of the language game and its inclusion of individuals. The place of the individual in the community remains open for debate among the theologians that were presented. There is, however, a general agreement that privatism must be rejected. The dependency of the individual on the community demands that participation cannot occur in an isolated context.

The divergent interpretations of Wittgenstein as well as the diversity within Wittgenstein himself should not result in despondency. Instead, the variety of interpretations offers a selection which must be carefully culled and refined. In spite of the divergence there are areas of agreement. With this in mind, the following chapter returns to an analysis of the place of the Apostles' Creed in the liturgy.

NOTES

1   Jens Glebe-Møller, "Two Views of Religion in Wittgenstein," in *The Grammar of the Heart*, ed. by Richard Bell (San Francisco: Harper & Row, 1988), p. 98. This subjective element may be responsible for the theological interpretations of Wittgenstein that are based on mysticism as an interpretive key.

2   Wittgenstein, *Zettel*, p. 124.

3   Glebe-Møller, p. 109.

4   Stanley Hauerwas and William H. Willimon, *Resident Aliens* (Nashville: Abingdon Press, 1989), p. 45.

5   Russell Nieli, *Wittgenstein: From Mysticism to Ordinary Language* (Albany: State University of New York Press, 1987), p. xii.

6   Carnap in Nieli, p. 64

7   Ibid., p. 66. See also Friedrich Waismann, *Wittgenstein und der Wiener Kreis* (Frankfurt am Main: Suhrkamp, 1984).

8   Carnap in Nieli, p. 68.

9   Wittgenstein in Nieli, p. 170.

10 Nieli credits the work of Bin Kimura for a presentation of the derealization-depersonalization experience. Kimura draws heavily from "the phenomenology of Husserl and the traditions of the Zen Buddhists." See Nieli, p. 17, Footnote 9.

11 Nieli notes the parallels to Kierkegaard's use of dread and seems tempted to include Kierkegaard in his list of supporters. Nieli does however draw attention to the differences in Kierkegaard's sense of dread (i.e., Kierkegaard emphasis is on the social world whereas Heidegger is concerned with the personal world). In spite of the noted differences, Nieli does conclude that Heidegger has adopted Kierkegaard's concept of dread and applied it in his own way. In particular, see Nieli, pp. 24–26 and Footnotes 37, 38, and 39.

12 Ibid., p. 28.

13 Ibid., p. 69.

14 Nieli, p. 71. Nieli cites Abraham Maslow's study of peak experiences as evidence for the existence of mystic flight. It must be noted that Maslow certainly would not accept Nieli's theocentric interpretation of the description. Maslow's humanism does include references to transcendence, however Maslow embraced atheism and did not understand a peak experience to be referring to a "theophanic Encounter." For a further description of Maslow's position, see my dissertation on "The Christology of the Gospels and Abraham Maslow's Characteristics of Self-Actualization," Baylor University, 1984.

15 Nieli, p. 82.

16 Ibid., p. 85.

17 Russell in Nieli, p. vi.

18   Nieli concludes that the experience that Wittgenstein described in the lecture on Ethics is
      the same experience that he told Malcolm that he had in association with seeing a play in
      Vienna when he was twenty-one. Malcolm records the incident with the following words:
          "In Vienna he saw a play that was a mediocre drama, but in it one of the characters ex-
      pressed the thought that no matter what happened in the world nothing bad could happen
      to him–he was independent of fate and circumstances. Wittgenstein was struck by this stoic
      thought; for the first time he saw the possibility of religion." (Norman Malcolm, *Ludwig
      Wittgenstein* (Oxford: Oxford University Press, 1984), p. 58.)
          It must be noted that in transmitting this incident Nieli removes the phrase "Wittgen-
      stein was struck by this stoic thought." One must question whether Nieli's selective reading
      of this anecdote does not dramatically alter its intention. In addition, Wittgenstein does
      not give any specific reference to this feeling of "absolute safety." The experience is listed as
      one of three examples and is not given a central place in the lecture.

19   Nieli, p. 91.

20   Ibid., p. 91. Nieli goes further to hypothesize that this experience could have resulted in
      Wittgenstein's shift from mathematics to philosophy! See p. 96, Footnote 14.

21   Ibid., p. 98.

22   Ibid., p. 109.

23   Even Engelmann, however, is criticized for his "inability to transcend psychologistic catego-
      ries." See p. 112. This is a remarkably presumptuous criticism since Nieli's interpretation is
      based largely on psychological categories and a psychoanalytical reading of both Wittgen-
      stein and the literature.

24   Ibid., p. 116.

25   Ibid, pp. 121–23, footnote 8.

26   Ibid., p. 133. Nieli goes further to cite Englemann for a defense of "wordless faith": "Any
      doctrine uttered in words is the source of its own misconstruction by worshippers, disciples
      and supporters."

27   Ibid., p. 135.

28   Ibid., p. 148.

29   See Nieli, pp. xiv–xv.

30   Ibid., p. 176.

31   Ibid., p. 185.

32   Ibid., p. 202.

33   Ibid., pp.219–20.

34   Ibid., p. 220.

35   Ibid., p. 240.

36   Ibid., p. 245.

37   Ibid., p. 240.

38   Ibid., p. 245.

39   Ibid., p. 91. Another line of argument is offered by Don Cupitt who refers to the "para-
      noiac fantasies of omnipresent threat [Nieli's reading of the late Wittgenstein?] and abso-
      lute security" as counter-productive. In this line of thinking, one would have to reject both
      the early and late Wittgenstein because of psychological instability. These categories are
      Nieli's psychoanalytical creation and need not (and should not) be accepted as the interpre-
      tive key to Wittgenstein. Don Cupitt, *The Long Legged Fly* (London: SCM Press, 1987), p.
      76. See also footnote 18 in this chapter.

[40] Nieli is actually more convincing and provides better evidence for Heidegger's relationship to mysticism than he does for Wittgenstein.

[41] Nieli, p. 123.

[42] Nieli's mysticism is one option which drives apart the "two Wittgensteins." The inclusion of Wittgenstein in the logical positivistic school is another such approach.

[43] Ibid. See the discussion on pp. 197ff. and p. 246 in particular.

[44] Ignace D'hert, *Wittgenstein's Relevance for Theology* (Bern: Peter Lang, 1974), p. 34.

[45] Wittgenstein, *Tractatus*, p. 187.

[46] Ibid., p. 189.

[47] D'hert, p. 33.

[48] Ibid.

[49] Ibid., pp. 32–33.

[50] Ibid., p. 38.

[51] Ibid., p. 39.

[52] Ibid., p. 59.

[53] Ibid., p. 72.

[54] Ibid.

[55] Ibid.

[56] Ibid., p. 78.

[57] Ibid., pp. 80–81.

[58] Ibid., p. 83.

[59] Ibid.

[60] Ibid., p. 115. This entire argument is then given additional support by a reading of Thomas Aquinas in an attempt to show a parallel between natural theology in St. Thomas and meaning in Wittgenstein. The result is an attempt to "indicate the possibility of elaborating something like a proof of the existence of God on the basis of his notion of meaning." See also p. 119.

[61] See p. 109. D'hert claims that according to Wittgenstein, "Theology is a proper language game with its own rules."

[62] See the discussion on page 164. D'hert then goes further to recover "being" and "essence" under the function of meaning made plausible to him by the equation of God as Meaning and Being. pp. 158–60.

[63] Ibid., p. 185.

[64] Ibid., p. 98.

[65] Wittgenstein's *Remarks on Frazer's Golden Bough* demonstrates his rejection of reductionistic attempts. It should be noted that D.Z. Phillips latest work attempts to overcome the reductionistic criticism that D'hert offers of his earlier work. See Phillips, *Faith after Foundationalism*.

[66] A recent attempt to address these questions is offered by Phillip Stein in *Logic and Sin in Wittgenstein* (Chicago: University of Chicago Press, 1993).

[67] Paul Homer, *The Grammar of Faith* (San Francisco: Harper & Row, Publishers, 1978), p. 22. Holmer goes on to declare that a major task of the theologian is to show the flexibility of "God's grammar" to the present situation.

[68] Holmer, p. 25.

[69] Ibid., p. 11.

[70] Ibid., p. 11.

[71] Ibid., p. 18,

72   Ibid., p. 21.
73   Ibid., p. 119.
74   Ibid.
75   Ibid., p. 130.
76   Ibid.
77   Ibid., p. 131.
78   There is a shift at this point from Wittgenstein's emphasis on meaning *as* use to Holmer's concern with meaning *in* its use.
79   Ibid., p. 133. Holmer does note that there are criterion for making distinctions in religious language. These distinctions can be made by being attentive to the grammar and by noting the significance of criterion such as the authority of Scripture. Theological criticism is appropriate in these instances.
80   Holmer claims that the analogy to buildings and their foundations breaks down at this point. "We do clearly have buildings without the builders; but there is an odd sense in which we do not have beliefs without believers. Without the latter, the beliefs are really nothing at all." Holmer, p. 84.
81   Ibid., p. 88.
82   Tillich, *Systematic Theology*, Vol. 1, p. 164.
83   Tillich notes that they are actually related to the same question (i.e., Why is there something), but he prefers to use ontology because of the connotations associated with the word metaphysics. See Tillich, Vol. 1, pp. 163-64.
84   Holmer, p. 91.
85   Ibid., p. 92.
86   Ibid., p. 100.
87   Ibid., p. 102.
88   Ibid., p. 106.
89   Ibid., p. 11.
90   Ibid., p. 24.
91   Ibid., p. 27. Holmer contends that "theology is directed to the essential spiritual core, our center of vitality and energy" (p. 34). Since he has dismissed the category of being in part because of its unavailability (i.e., being cannot be found, but only posited), it seems remarkable that Homer can speak so easily of an "essential spiritual core" and fail to tell the reader what it is.
92   Ibid., p. 140.
93   Ibid., p. 144.
94   Ibid., p. 194.
95   Holmer fails to delineate any distinction which he makes between "concepts" and "ideas." In an earlier essay he uses the words as synonyms. See Paul Holmer, "Religion from an Existential Standpoint," in *Religion in Philosophical and Cultural Perspective*, ed. by J. Clayton Feaver and William Horosz (Princeton: D. Van Nostrand Company, 1967), p. 154.
96   Ibid., pp. 203-4.
97   Holmer, "Religion from an Existential Standpoint," p. 151.
98   Ibid., p. 152.
99   Ibid., p. 155.
100   Ibid.
101   McGuin, *Wittgenstein on Meaning*, p. 148.
102   Holmer, *Grammar of Faith*, pp. 21-22.

103 Ibid., pp. 29–30.

104 Hugh O. Jones, *Die Logik theologischer Perspektiven: eine spachanalytische Untersuchung* (Göttingen: Vandenhoeck & Ruprecht, 1985), pp. 83ff.

105 Ibid., p. 16. Jones refers to several philosophers of religion who draw from the "Wittgensteinian metaphysics." This remarkable claim made in passing in the introduction will be discussed later in this work.

106 Hugh Jones, "Zum Verhältnis von Sprache und religiöser Erfahrung," Unpublished paper, p. 9.

107 Jones, *Logik theologischer Perspektive*, p. 128.

108 Hugh Jones, "Das Story-Konzept und die Theologie," in *"Story" als Rohmaterial der Theologie*, Dietrich Ritschl and Hugh Jones (München: Chr. Kaiser Verlag, 1976), p. 52, footnote 10.

109 Jones, *Logik theologischer Perspektive*, pp. 134–35.

110 Ibid., p. 212.

111 Ibid., p. 108.

112 Ibid., p. 111.

113 Ibid., p. 117.

114 Ibid., pp. 121–22.

115 Ibid., p. 136.

116 Ibid., pp. 213–215. See also "Zum Verhältnis zwischen Sprache und religiöser Erfahrung," p. 4. This seems to be an adaptation of his position in "Das Story-Konzept in der Theologie" where Jones rejects story as the appropriate theological construction in which to present theology. The difference appears to be resolved through Jones' employment of that which can only be shown. Thus Jones recovers the use of story as the appropriate activity of the believer while denying its validity as part of the task of theological analysis itself.

117 *Logik*, p. 215.

118 Ibid., p. 221.

119 Ibid., p. 221. Jones makes particular use here of Wittgenstein's statement that, "At the foundation of well-founded belief lies belief that is not founded." See Wittgenstein, *On Certainty* , p. 33e Note 253).

120 Ibid., p. 229.

121 Ibid.

122 I take this to mean that attempts to make explicit the "theistic" framework serve the function of helping the believer articulate and extend his/her language and actions. The results for Jones are metaphysical statements that seek to work as a road map rather than as an argument for the construction of this "city."

123 "Zum Verhältnis von Sprache und Religiöser Erfahrung," p. 16.

124 Jones also dismisses Hick's attempts to construct an eschatological verification.

125 Ibid., p. 227.

126 "Zum Verhältnis von Sprache und Religiöser Erfahrung," p. 6.

127 Cf. the critique of interpretations of religious language that are based on an understanding of the pictures provided by religious language in Hilary Putnam, "Wittgenstein on Religious Belief." In *On Community*, pp. 66ff.

128 Ibid., p. 225.

129 Ibid., p. 16, footnote 24.

130 Ibid., p. 104.

131 Ibid., p. 230.

132 Kerr, *Theology after Wittgenstein*, p. 5.

133 Kerr's reading of modern theologians illustrates that despite divergent opinions, much of theology is based upon an individualistic approach that through transcendence, decisive action, mystery, or a variety of other approaches is able to move beyond him/herself.

134 Kerr, p. 23

135 This perspective also serves as a central pillar for scientific theory. The desire to obtain an objective view-point results in a belief in the "ideal of the detached self." Consequently, while pursuing vastly different agendas, both scientific theory and theological investigation have agreed on the premise that reality begins with the isolated self. In both cases, however, the subject is required to transcend human emotions, cultural and historical particularity, and the like, in order to encounter, bare, that which is truly important (Kerr, p. 26).

136 Kerr, p. 24.

137 Ibid., p. 29. See discussion of this point in chapter two, note 2.

138 Kerr cites Wittgenstein's comparison of language and a medieval city to demonstrate the interrelatedness of language games (See p. 31).

139 It is recorded that he once called the *Confessions* the most serious book ever written. M. O'C. Drury in *Recollections of Wittgenstein*, ed. by Rush Rhees (Oxford: Oxford University Press, 1984), p. 90.

140 Kerr, p. 39.

141 Ibid., p. 58.

142 Ibid.

143 Wittgenstein, *Zettel* p. 99.

144 Kerr, p. 65.

145 Ibid., p. 76.

146 Ibid., p. 97.

147 Ibid., p. 118

148 Ibid., p. 128. This conclusion leads Kerr to state that realism is possible only from a theistic basis. Kerr claims that the realist decision of the truth or falsity of a statement when the evidence is unavailable necessitates the existence of a supratemporal perspective.

149 Kerr's term for the metaphysical Cartesian influence.

150 Kerr, p. 133.

151 *Philosophical Investigations*, p. 373. Wittgenstein further expounds on this note in his lectures recorded by Alice Ambrose between 1932–35 (see Kerr, p. 146). Here Wittgenstein infers that the task of theology is to point out what can be appropriately said about God (i.e., what is the proper use of the word "God"). Such an understanding shows the connection between the early and late Wittgenstein. In includes the investigation as to what can be properly said that predominates in the *Tractatus* and points to the contextual significance that is a leading theme in the late Wittgenstein.

152 Kerr, p. 147.

153 Ibid., p. 45.

154 Wittgenstein in Kerr, p. 152.

155 Wittgenstein in Kerr, p. 155.

156 Ibid.

157 Kerr, p. 162.

158 Ibid., p. 163.

159 Ibid., pp. 180–82.

160 Ibid., p. 189.

161   For a better understanding of the dominance of the individual in American society today, see the excellent sociological study by Robert Bellah, et. al., *Habits of the Heart: Individualism and Commitment in American Life* (Berkeley: University of California Press, 1985).

162   Kerr, p. 118

163   The only clue is Kerr's cryptic remark that speaks of the community which we create in "our natural reactions." In such a perspective, creativity is defined as a necessary reaction! Kerr, p. 77.

164   It is interesting to note how metaphysics seems to seep back into the discussion, particularly in D'hert and Jones.

165   Jones' extension of the Wittgensteinian analogy of the city is particularly insightful at this point.

Chapter Four
Creedal Interpretation in Light of Wittgenstein

The following chapter looks at the Apostles' Creed on the basis of Wittgenstein's work and in light of the theological discussion surrounding his work. Before attempting to apply the gleanings of our survey of Wittgenstein and his reception into the theological arena, there is a need to look at alternative interpretations of creedal statements. As was noted in chapter one, during the nineteenth century a series of conflicts erupted regarding the proper place and usage of the creed. The continuing skirmishes and widening confusion surrounding religious language has continued throughout this century and questions about the interpretation of creedal statements have continued to be discussed. In the midst of these deliberations, alternative approaches have been outlined. Before returning to an analysis of the creed in light of Wittgenstein, a brief survey of other approaches will be offered.

Dantine's Models of Creedal Interpretation

While several theologians in recent years have examined the meaning of creedal statements (and reflected on the Apostles' Creed in particular), the following chapter relies on Wilhelm Dantine as a conversation partner. Dantine's discussion in regards to the interpretation of creedal statements prompted a variety of responses that share significant similarities to and differences from an approach based on Wittgenstein's works.

Dantine begins by noting the common concerns shared by the differing approaches to creedal statements. Christian faith occurs in a linguistic context, i.e., language is an integral part of its arena.[1] Secondly, Christian faith is centered on the historical person of Jesus of Nazareth.[2] Finally, Dantine reminds us that Christian faith is not private or individualistic.[3] Christianity has a sociological context and is based upon consensus. This ecclesiological basis is a reminder that faith occurs not in isolation, but in shared reciprocal relationships. "Kirche Jesu Christi ist grundsätzlich eine soziologische Größe, denn der einzelne existiert nur in sozialer Bezogenheit zu anderen Christen."[4]

Given these presuppositions, Dantine contrasts three approaches to interpreting a confession. Dantine refers to the first approach of a confessional
statement as a dogmatic model. Dogma here is *fides quae creditur* or objective
statements that refer to specific facts or historical events. A confession in this
sense refers to statements that capture the truths of Christianity. In this sense,
God's acts in human history are defined as objective, descriptive truths which
not only summarize these events, but identify them as recognizable historical
truths which provide the foundation for faith.[5] By providing an objective basis,
dogma seeks to point to the results of specific events as the grounds for faith.
In making this move, the events (of salvation) are bound together in a closed
system.[6]

The development of statements that encapsulate dogmas leads to a logical
progression of dogmatic propositions. The move to encapsulate dogmas as
objective statements of truth produces a tendency to objectify God and logically classify God as the highest object. The logical movement in this process
grows out of the desire to determine specific statements which capture objective truths in a strict logical sense.[7]

Dantine identifies a second approach to creedal statements as the confessional model which developed during the time of the reformation. While this
approach has roots that go back to New Testament times, it was only in the
sixteenth century that it emerged as a contrasting approach to the dogmatic
model that had been traditional. In this new confessional understanding, the
emphasis was placed on the New Testament concept of *didache* as opposed to
kerygma. By building on a New Testament understanding of the *didache*, the
confessional model emphasized the place of doctrine as fundamental in its
understanding of creedal statements. The result of this approach led to a rapid
acceptance of the creeds as confessional statements [*Lehrbekenntnisse*] by reformation leaders and a later development in which the creeds were understood
as the norms and requirements [*Lehrgesetz*] for the faithful.[8]

The process of this new approach to creedal statements grew out of a consensus by those in the church. Instead of being developed by a select elite or
the hierarchical leaders, the reformation statements of faith developed out of a
democratic agreement by leaders and members of the church. The result of
this process was an understanding that the acceptance of the confessional
statements represented the fundamental criterion for recognition as a church
(a noted reversal from the dogmatic model in which the church established
the creed; in the confessional model the consensus on the creed legitimized

the church).[9] The increasing tendency towards intellectualizing the creedal statements received a sharpened focus in this process since the confessional model underscored the need for both leaders and laity to accept the creedal statements as a basis for inclusion into the life of the community. The historical by-product of this development was the movement by Protestants toward a required acceptance of the "pure doctrine" contained in the confessions which became the operative determinant for inclusion at the eucharistic table.[10]

Dantine's criticism of both the dogmatic and confessional models is based on three broad claims. First, both approaches to the creed fail to do justice to the human activity in the creation of these statements. The result of overlooking this crucial element leads to the negligence of the ethical dimension in favor of dogmatics. Secondly, the tendency to objectify the elements of the creed leads to a static view that tends to neglect the on–going historical dimension. Rather than noting the historical circumstances in which the statements develop, both the doctrinal and confessional models present them as eternally unchanged. Finally, both models grow out of a linguistic approach which understands the truth of the creedal statements only in terms of past events. This is further convoluted by a separation between knowledge and action that grows out of the lack of connection between past events and present decision.[11] In one form or another, each of these criticisms points to the failure to show the relationship between statements and their connection to ethical activities. When creedal statements are viewed as a summation of past events, one is left with a compendium of historical data. The place of the creed as a statement of faith points out the need to see the creed in light of its capacity as a *present* declaration of one's commitment which carries with it significant ethical implications.

Dantine notes that the problematic aspects of the dogmatic and confessional models can be seen by looking at the conflicts over creedal understanding in the nineteenth century (see chapter one). In particular, Dantine points to the *Apostolikumstreit* as exemplary of the impasse that existed in creedal interpretation. Only the development of an alternative model could allow the creed(s) to be approached with a new understanding. According to Dantine, the development of the new model occurred first with the Barmen Declaration.[12] This new approach to creedal statements grew out of the desire to emphasize the connections between confession and action.

The ethical implications of the Barmen confession are clear against their historical backdrop of the Third Reich. They emerge out of a context in which confession is made in explicit obedience to Christ (and in opposition to loyalty to the government). The radicality brought about by this historical necessity provided the impetus for a new approach to creedal statements. Dantine sees in this connection both a renewal and a re-interpretation of the traditional confessional statements.

> Erstmals in einem kirchlichen Text werden in umfassender und zugleich prinzipieller Weise Glaubensgehorsam und Handlungsgehorsam eng miteinander verbunden. Dogmatik und Ethik liegen hier ganz ineinander, nicht mehr beziehungslos neben- oder hintereinander.[13]

The new emphasis set out in the Barmen confession is further under-scored by the Leuenberger Concordance. The continued development of this approach to the creeds is seen in the renewed recognition of the historical development of the earlier creedal statements. This movement is accompanied by a new desire for confessions to be understood in terms of their present ar-ticulation of the faith of the believer(s). The transition from creedal interpreta-tions which view the creed as a statement of past factual components to the contemporary existential articulation of the faith makes it possible for believ-ers to recognize the ethical relevance of confessional statements.[14]

In this new approach to creedal statements, Dantine sees a return to the New Testament confessional approach which is pneumatic and doxological. The desire to recover these dimensions of the New Testament confessions leads Dantine to an investigation of the underlying intention [Grundinten-tion] of the confessional statement and act. Dantine describes the confessional intention as arising out of an internal compulsion to express one's faith.[15] The New Testament characteristics of confession are marked by the desire to con-fess faith in the midst of alternatives and opposition. This distinctive element of the early church (that one confesses this faith) is another reminder of the contextual dependency of any confessional statement. The statement that "Je-sus is Lord" was made by the early church in distinct contrast to other beliefs and consequently carried with it a present, existential dimension. Dantine contrasts this understanding with the development of later confessional state-ments (in particular those associated with the dogmatic model) which ex-changed the early existential/eschatological dimension for the security of a metaphysical dogmatic system.[16]

In addition to its expression of inner faith (in light of the work of the Holy Spirit), a confession provides a verbal structure for both the believer and those outside of the faith. Since the confession emerges in contrast to other beliefs, it provides a basic framework for the believer and acts as a form of proclamation. This aspect leads Dantine to claim that the creed provides a "logic of the faith."[17] In times of crisis, the creed serves as a continual reminder of the on-going presence of faith in light of "the Word made flesh."

In the place of this early creedal approach, which provided a form of guidance and support for believers, the dogmatic and confessional approaches to the creeds demand an acceptance of doctrinal compliance. This shift from the early pneumatic, existential confession of faith to a dogmatic insistence on conformity to creedal statements underscores for Dantine the problematic nature of both the dogmatic and confessional models. The movement from "dogma to dogmatic" culminated in the use of the creeds as standards of orthodoxy for ordination (a development which led to the series of skirmishes in the nineteenth century). This is in distinct opposition to the early usage in which confessions (e.g., "Jesus is Lord") were understood as an act of decision. In the early understanding, confession is integrally tied to the event of confessing faith rather than the reliance on creedal formulations. The later shift is marked by a grammatical distinction in which the verbal activity associated with "confession" diminishes in favor of the nominal presentation of salvific events. The early understanding of confession as an activity was marked by the act of confessing as a decisive moment of decision on the part of the believer ["das >Bekennen< als ein >Sichentscheiden<"] which highlights the ethical connections between the statement of faith and the event of stating one's faith.[18]

Dantine points out that the ethical connections which are necessarily associated with the confessional statements should not be confused with the status quo morality that is often associated with religious belief. In this regard, Dantine embraces the task of "Entmoralisierung" as a legitimate aim of theology. Furthermore, Dantine is concerned about the need to re-establish Christian ethics in the social dimension. The tendency to view ethics in individualistic terms and categories is a long-standing problem in Christianity. Dantine believes that the new approach to creedal statements marked by the Barmen Declaration signifies a shift from individualistic to social ethical concerns.[19]

The interpretation of creedal statements is marked by the meaning, sense, and boundaries [Grenzen] of the language of the statements.[20] These statements include the social-ethical dimension because dogmatics and ethics are inextricably wed. This inner connection is established by the language rules [Sprachregelung] themselves in which truth and action are inseparable. Dantine undergirds this approach to creedal statements by noting that confession is an act in which the believer takes a stand. In this sense, confessions represent not only truths but true action. This is human action in which the believer joins those who also confess the faith. The integration between truth and action in the creedal statements is so intensive that confessions become the model by which all other statements and activities can be judged.[21]

This new approach to creedal statements (which Dantine views as a return to the early confessional model) provokes Dantine to call for an "Entdogmatisierung" of theological thought. This step is necessary because dogma has become so closely associated with the dogmatic model and its inherent weaknesses. Similarly, Dantine believes that the confessional model has led to a fixed doctrinal understanding. The result of the connections made in the various approaches to creedal statements leads Dantine to claim that all theological statements will be interpreted in a manner that closely parallels the creedal approach.[22] At stake, then, in this discussion are not only important consequences in terms of creedal understanding, but significant repercussions for the entire theological method. The crux of the issue is that the dogmatic and confessional approaches to creeds bring with them philosophical presuppositions that are grounded in platonic and Aristotelian metaphysics.[23] As a result, both approaches to the creed fall victim to the dangers of objectivizing theological truth and presenting God as another thing. Similarly, both the dogmatic and confessional models fail to make ethics a primary part of the act of confession. In doing so, both approaches build up a system which attempts to provide the believer with concrete theological truths and a predetermined ethical system that removes the need for existential decision and action.

> Der Versuch, im Dogma oder im Lehrbekenntnis eine Manifestation einer objektivierbaren theologischen Wahrheit zu besitzen, verzerrt die Wahrheit des Evangeliums. Es verführt dazu, aus dem Glauben ein Für-Wahrhalten zu machen und aus dem Gehorsam ein bloßes Befolgen.[24]

Confessing one's faith must move beyond these misunderstandings and return to its earlier (New Testament) practice in which it was understood as an act that reflects both an historical situation and a contextual connection. Confessions find particular forms of expression which provide theological knowledge that reflects both the person and work of Jesus Christ. These forms are based on the need to express one's faith in a particular setting rather than to try to develop eternal truths and doctrinal standards for Christendom as a whole. Earlier confessions retain their significance as markers and milestones that deserve and respect attention. The task of confessing is not, however, one which requires recitation of particular formulas, but one in which believers find the appropriate manner to confess faith in their historical situation. To the extent that past statements reflect similar present circumstances, a certain continuity exists. Equally important is the ability of creedal statements to provoke believers to formulate contemporary expressions of their faith.[25]

These factors coalesce at the point in which the church is recognized as a "creatura verbi." In light of Luther's understanding, the church is not another object of faith, but the place in which confession occurs and in which it finds its meaning. For Dantine, this meaning is balanced between the dynamics of a subjective, existential expression of faith and the sociological, ethical dimensions of a group of believers. As a result of this dynamic tension, the church must be a place in which Christians are moved to confess their faith in both word and deed. In providing both the context and cause for the act of confessing, the Church is challenged to fulfill its calling as a confessing community.[26]

The possibility of the church living out its calling occurs when the church is able to function as both institution and event. Confessing one's faith is the act which moves the church beyond its institutional domain. Confession provides the example and the basis that makes church as a present event possible. Consequently, the act of confessing one's faith carries with it the possibility of a new reformation of the church. This reformation does not seek to deny or diminish the creedal formulations that have been developed out of its past history and context, but seeks to claim them as appropriate for the present encounter. The possibility for this to occur rests on a willingness to move from dogmatic and confessional models to an understanding of the creeds that seeks to re-appropriate the patterns of New Testament formulations. In doing so, the emphasis shifts from eternal, metaphysical encapsulations of truth to present, existential expressions of faith that mark and provoke the believer to action. The return to confession as an event (rather than a passive reiteration of timeless truths) can occur when the church recognizes the connections in the liturgy between the creed and the eucharist. The doxological foundation which holds these together serves as a reminder that this connection is not intended as a proof test (in terms of dogma and doctrine that must be accepted before further participation is allowed), but as an expression of gratitude and grace by the people of God for the continued sustenance which they receive.[27]

Responses to Dantine

Dantine's essay prompted a collection of responses from a variety of theological perspectives. The following section critically summarizes significant aspects of some of these responses which clarify, critique or contribute to the discussion of creedal interpretation in light of Wittgenstein.

In response to Dantine's essay Karl Rahner discusses the distinction between "*Fides qua–fides quae*" and the need of the church to select the essential elements of the content of faith. Rahner recognizes that a shift has taken place and that dogma is not accepted merely because it is presented by the church. Instead, the need is for the church to draw attention to those parts of the *fides quae* which make existential commitment possible.[28] In spite of shifting the emphasis to the need for selectivity by the church and the importance of avoiding blanket acceptance (*cart blanche*) of all church declarations, Rahner fails to move beyond the early dogmatic model of creedal understanding. The *fides quae* remains as the foundation, albeit a smaller, more selective one (how this selection occurs remains unexplained; is it based on usefulness for experience?). From such a perspective, the church is the keeper of tradition which it passively passes on. The church's involvement with the content of faith, however, remains minimal. This content consists of past events which are recorded and preserved in order that faith may be actualized by those who accept them as a factual foundation for faith. There is no attempt to rethink the function of *fides quae*, only an attempt to adjust it to a more modest scope.

Schmidt–Lauber's reaction to Dantine's suggestion is based on his desire to reflect upon the place of confession in ecumenical encounters. In the discussion of the place of tradition and the search for areas of unity between denominations, Schmidt–Lauber proposes that the solution is to attempt to recapture the intention of the older statements in a new way.[29] Such a solution postulates the ability to separate intention from language as well as the possibility of being able to identify the original intention of an historical statement. While the proposal avoids the difficulties encountered with the dogmatic position, which claims a static propositional approach to creedal statements, Schmidt–Lauber's solution encounters similar hermeneutical difficulties. How can we travel back in time to discover historical facts that are the basis for faith (Rahner) or discover the intent in the minds of the writers of the creed? It is ironic, that these two distinctly different proposals share the same weakness. Much more helpful is Schmidt–Lauber's conclusion underscoring the central place of the eucharist as the setting in which language and deed come together.[30] Here is an intersection where past and present meet (and the future is open) wherein confessional statements are at home.

Claus Westermann investigates the historical development leading to creedal statements in the Hebrew Scriptures. While recognizing that there is not a confession in the strictest sense of the word (until much later), he portrays the backdrop that led to the later development of creedal formulations. His study leads him to draw conclusions regarding the genre and use of confessions. For Westermann, a confession grows out of a doxological context which binds the community together in the act of praise. In this context, a confession recalls the acts of God from which the community draws its existence.[31]

Curiously, Westermann concludes that:

> Sowohl das nominale wie das verbale Bekenntnis bleibt in seinem Kern gleich durch alle Zeiten. In seiner Sprache aber muss es sich wandeln, weil Gott sein Volk durch die Geschichte führt.[32]

Westermann's point appears to be that the use of confessions has remained the same although the language has changed. Unfortunately, such an interpretation leads to a bi-furcation between meaning and language. The result is an understanding of language in which the words become insignificant so long as the meaning is the same.

Westermann's search for meaning (apart from language) may have been fueled by assumed presuppositions. Christofer Frey notes that the search for meaning [*Sinn*] occurs in conjunction with a classical metaphysical perspective.[33] Similarly Christian Link observes that theology as a western academic discipline has been based upon the categories of Greek philosophy.[34] Both Frey and Link raise the question of whether or not the Gospel is bound to such a framework.

In contrast to the elusive search for meaning, Frey raises the question of the truth criterion that are a part of Dantine's categories. The dogmatic approach recognizes truth as objectively describable. Dogma (and in this context a creed) is a correct presentation of these eternal truths. Dantine's second model (doctrine) seeks to modify this perspective by including the notion of consensus as the criteria for truth.[35] Dantine's desire is for ethics to become part of the basis for truth. Consequently, the third approach underscores the centrality of *Handeln* and *Verhalten* in truth criterion.[36] Such an understanding does not allow meaning and language to be separated, but recognizes the inner connections between them.

Christian Link is specific in noting that the church does not confess abstractly, but always "*in concretissimo*." Confessions are contingent upon specific times and places.[37] They are imbedded and imbued in a context. The contextual nature of a confession is two-fold. It expresses a particular understanding of the life of faith at a particular historical time. To this extent Schmidt-Lauber (among many others) is correct in noting the historical nature of the statement. An important contribution in dealing with this factor has been made by George Lindbeck who underscores the connection between time and language in *The Nature of Doctrine*. Equally important, though is the recognition of the relationship and context of the present use of a confession. Here, too, Link is helpful by pointing out that confessional statements are not simply repetitions of past events. "Denn Bekennen is etwas anderes als die Bestätigung folgenloser Richtigkeiten, etwas anders auch als die Ratifizierung gemeinsam anerkannter Lehre."[38] Link provides an example in noting the Lutheran decision in 1977 in regards to South Africa. In making its decision, the Lutheran church recognized the connection in confession between language and act. Consequently, Link distances himself not only from the dogmatic model outlined by Dantine, but also from the classical doctrinal approach. In noting the hermeneutical problems of other approaches to creedal statements, Link draws attention to the "*ungleichzeitig*" dimension of worship.[39] Knowledge of the historical bound statement as well as a recognition of our own context are starting points for discovering an alternative approach to creedal statements.

Link applauds the correlative between dogmatics and ethics and faith and act made by Dantine. In so doing, Link finds similarities between Martin Luther and Dantine.

> Luther hat das ökumenische Kriterium nicht historisch oder juristisch, auch nicht eigentlich dogmatisch, er hat es-mit dem energischen Hinweis auf den "Häuptartikel von Jesu Christo"-axiologish bestimmt: Das Bekenntnis zur einen Kirche wird dort gesprochen, wo die Wahrheit des Evangeliums in Geltung steht und zu sichtbarer Darstellung findet.[40]

This connection is possible because Link recognizes that confessional activity is a part of and grows out of confessional language.

Critique of Dantine's Approach to Creedal Statements

Several aspects of Dantine's essay have been highlighted in the responses. It is important to note both the contributions and weaknesses of Dantine's approach in preparation for a discussion of creedal interpretation in light of the discussion of Wittgenstein and the reception of his work in theological circles. The analysis of creedal interpretations by Dantine is particularly helpful in highlighting the circumstances that have led to skirmishes and confrontations about the use and understanding of the creeds. Dantine's assessment of the historical approaches to the creed that led to both dogmatism and doctrinal rigidity present valuable "corroborating evidence" for the need to develop a new approach.

Equally significant is Dantine's questioning of the metaphysical presuppositions that have been interpreted as a part of the creedal statements. The alignment of the dogmatic and doctrinal models with Greek metaphysical presuppositions led to the questioning of the meaning of the creeds once the historical–critical method emerged. Of primary importance is Dantine's reminder of the historical–cultural development of any statement of faith. By drawing attention to the contextual dependency of a statement of faith, Dantine highlights the time–bound language of a creed as opposed to the attempts to turn the creeds into statements of timeless truth. In particular, the Apostles' Creed tells us about the life and significance of one historical person. The return to historical models grows out of a recognition of both the historical period in which the creed was written and the events in history which are being presented. A word of caution seems warranted at this point. Any discussion of the historical dimensions of creedal statements runs the danger of being understood as a desire to go back to particular events (be they first century or fourth century). Dantine's use of New Testament confessions avoids a simplistic "back to the Bible" approach, while at the same time insists on a biblical pattern for interpreting creedal statements. While the creeds refer to particular historical events, Dantine ably points out that there is no desire to understand the creeds as an accumulation of past "factual" statements. Surely the hermeneutical discussions of the past century point out the impossibility of isolating past historical events that provide a "safe basis for faith." While the theological community has been virtually unanimous in its recognition that historical events cannot provide a foundation for faith, there remains a danger that hermeneutics will seek answers to questions of meaning in the minds of the authors. In such a scenario, creedal statements could be interpreted only by conjecturing what the authors had intended when writing these words. The call for recognizing the historical-contextual milieu of the creedal statements should in no way be confused with an attempt to posit meaning in the minds of the authors. Instead, Dantine reminds us of the historical backdrop of faith and its expression. This relationship seeks to underscore the on-going present tense of faith ("I believe") rather than to resort to inaccessible pasts. Dantine's emphasis on the historicity of the creedal statements is based on his conviction that the creeds are not timeless truths, but are actions and responses of past believers that express their beliefs.

The importance of the present expression of faith in the creedal formulation is underscored by Dantine's emphasis on the need to restore the ethical dimension. Dantine relentlessly attacks the dogmatic and doctrinal approaches to creeds for their failure to highlight confession as an act that carries with it ethical ramifications. Since he has made his claim against faith as an acceptance of propositional truth and rejects any attempt to remove faith from an historical dimension, Dantine has prepared a strong foundation for confessions as ethical proclamations. The creeds represent the act of stating one's faith; an act that is already ethical in orientation. By returning to a biblical approach to confessions, Dantine demonstrates that a confessional statement is already an act which sets the believer apart from others and establishes him/her as a part of a new community. In the first century, such an act often carried with it dramatic consequences.

Similarly, the historical circumstances which surrounded the Barmen Declaration caused great difficulty for those who joined together to confess their faith via these words. In such an event, ethics is not an afterthought, but a first-order phenomenon which is a part of the event and extends beyond it to the ethical consequences that grow out of the act of confessing one's faith. Dantine returns us to a place where the creed is a dynamic event rather than a passive reiteration of past events. This event begins an ethical process of uniting with a community of faith which seeks to live out its faith in a particular historical situation. Such a situation demands ethical actions that are made in light of one's confession of faith. Ethics become a primary, foundational and on-going part of the confessional act in Dantine's presentation.

While Dantine's dramatic reclamation of the integral nature of ethics and dogmatics is laudable and noteworthy, there remains a certain inconsistency in this regard throughout his presentation. The desire to emphasize ethics as a primary activity is undermined by Dantine's division between an "inner faith" and one that later expresses itself in words. Drawing distinctions between faith and language returns ethics to a secondary position which Dantine is trying to avoid! Furthermore, Dantine's presentation of an inner faith runs the risk of making faith first and foremost a private concern which only later is expressed in word and deed. If ethics is integrally related to dogmatics and if action is inseparable from language, then faith cannot be mystified and privatized away from the arena of action. Dantine holds up two separate portraits; in one portrait, he shows the need to rediscover and re-connect ethics with statements of faith; in the other, the connection is cut short in favor of an "internal" experience.

A related difficulty emerges in Dantine's presentation of the place of faith. In the private, internal portrait of faith the individual becomes the decisive unit. While pointing out the need for ethics to return to the social dimension, Dantine presents us with an individualistic model of faith which only later expresses itself in the language of faith. But from where does this language come? Are these words of the confession a mystical coincidence? Does the Holy Spirit who brings us to speech (according to Dantine) give us these words? Where is the turning point for Dantine that takes us beyond ourselves and into a community of faith which seeks to live out the faith in ways that challenge the status quo of societal practices? Instead of strengthening the tie between language and act and returning ethics to its primary role, Dantine has given us another model which separates faith from language and action and relegates both speech and deed to secondary events (possible only after an internal change). When faith is presented as an attitude, mental state or internal decision, then ethics and language are separated regardless of the attempts to re-claim them as primary. While Dantine's motivation to emphasize ethics, particularly in the social dimension, is necessary, it is possible only by building upon an understanding of language that rejects privatism and individualism as a basis.

Creedal Interpretation in Light of Wittgenstein

The critique of Dantine's presentation has prepared and already foreshadowed the presentation of creedal interpretation in light of Wittgenstein. The study began with an over-view of the impasse reached during the nineteenth century regarding the meaning and interpretation of the creeds (an impasse that was underscored in Dantine's essay). The presentation of major elements in the later writings of Wittgenstein and the analysis of the reception and interpretation of Wittgenstein by the theological community have sought to lay the groundwork and sort out options for the application of Wittgenstein's approach to language for creedal statements.

Language

The appropriation of Wittgensteinian themes in regards to creedal statements begins with a recognition of the diverse ways in which language functions. Wittgenstein used Augustine's picture of language to critique a limited understanding of language that was based on ostensive reference.

In a similar way, the historical controversies surrounding the interpretation of the Apostles' Creed pointed out the difficulty in reaching an agreement over the proper use of creedal statements. The irony of the discussions is that despite bitter disagreements about the meaning and appropriateness of the creed, both sides remained enmeshed in interpretations of the creed that were based primarily on historical/ostensive reference. The creed was approached as an historical window through which one could look back to earlier times in order to gain an awareness of certain historical events that were believed to be central to the Christian faith. Conservatives remained insistent on interpreting the creed as a summary of past historical events which must be protected since it represented the core of Christianity. Rationalists argued over which of the events truly belonged to the core of Christian faith. Neither side seemed to question whether it was actually possible to move so quickly "behind" the creeds. Wittgenstein's discussion of language games and their diversity points to the importance of recognizing that language cannot be understood primarily in terms of historical reference.[41]

The return to human life as the center of activity is a return to participation in language games. These shared activities point to a level of trust that is fundamental to the language game(s). In such an approach, belief is not a private matter, but is a participatory action on the part of a group. Such an understanding of faith draws on the community as providing both the context and content of faith. The community as the bearer of tradition as well as the place of continued participation stands in dramatic contrast to private, individualistic portrayals of faith. The emphasis on the shared sociological dimensions of the community also raises significant questions about the value of existential categories which primarily concentrate on isolated individuals.[42] Such an approach highlights the significance of identity as central to matters of faith. Creedal statements are of particular importance in this regard since they provide a common language for believers as they confess their identity as Christians.

It is also central to the investigation of doxological language to insist that the liturgical domain is not one of sophisticated philosophical nuance which needs clarification by professionals in order for the faithful to adequately understand what they are saying. In contrast, Wittgenstein's pointing to the whole "hurly-burly" is a reminder that language does work. Doxological language games have this in common with other language games. What is needed is not a new interpretation of doxological language, but a rediscovery of the connections that are a part of the language game(s).

The connections that are a part of any language game are highlighted in Wittgenstein's discussion of the "forms of life" that accompany any language game. These forms are not external or secondary to language, but are bound to the language game(s). They begin in the act of participating in the language game and extend beyond that act.

Rules

The extension of a form of life is possible due to the rules that are established as a part of the language game. These rules are significant in establishing boundaries and point to the on-going connections between language and action. Once again it should be noted that in speaking of boundaries Wittgenstein was not claiming that stringent divisions could be maintained between language games. Instead, rules act as a kind of guidance system which lead participants in a language game in certain directions.[43]

The significance of Dantine's emphasis on the inseparability of dogmatics and ethics as well as the need to understand confessions in ethical ways was underscored above. Such relationships are possible when no separation between thinking and action is posited. Rather than viewing the creed as a later event which expresses in an external fashion what has already occurred "inside" the person, a Wittgensteinian approach to creeds recognizes the language game(s) which makes up the confession of faith as an act in itself which both points to and participates in a host of shared and related activities (in the first stage they are related to other liturgical activities, but beyond that seek to relate to all areas of life).[44]

The rationalists were helpful in their concerted efforts to underscore the beliefs/acts which they held in common with other Christians. In contrast, the conservative response was misleading when they proclaimed that the boundaries of acceptable interpretations of the creeds were clearly demarcated. In addition, conservatives were adamant that the rules which they had identified allowed for only one response, namely an adherence to a literal, historical appropriation of a creed (in a particular dogmatic light). In so doing, there was little concern for understanding rules as that which allows one to participate in the community. The conservatives' concern was not about action or shared praxis, but about a proper recitation of the creed.

Karsten's commentary on the similarities in praxis between the *Lichtfreunde* and their conservative opponents is a reminder of the way in which shared praxis can provide an application of rule usage. An emphasis on common activity can provide a basis for discovering shared language games.[45] Unfortunately, Karsten's decision to emphasize "inner experience" over "external forms" made language secondary rather than primary. A more consistent application of rule usage allows one to emphasize the integral relationship between speech and praxis. It also underscores once again the centrality of the community as that which teaches and models language games.

Meaning as Use

The Wittgensteinian insistence on "meaning as use" stands in sharp contrast to the attempts to uncover the meaning in some historical layer or tradition. The use of the creed points again to the doxological context. The confession of faith via a creed is an act by the believers to respond to the grace of God in their lives and to align themselves in solidarity with the community of faith. In its liturgical placement, the creed can be understood as an act which sets the community apart, gives it an identity (as those who believe in this particular God), and prepares them for the eucharistic meal.

In the midst of the *Apostolikumstreit*, Ferdinand Kattenbusch offered a remarkably similar commentary on the need to redirect the discussion away from the elusive search for meaning. As an alternative Kattenbusch proposed that the creed could be approached differently by the laity than by the clergy. While the laity would be expected to exhibit a naive understanding of the creed (that was based primarily on historical reference), the educated clergy would be allowed a more sophisticated, scientific approach to interpreting the creed. While such an approach avoids the danger of reducing meaning to a mental state or an inner feeling, it runs the risk of bi-furcating the language games of clergy and laity. If the solidarity of the community is central to the establishment and transmission of language games, then surely an attempt to separate members of the community could only lead to further confusion.

"Meaning as use" not only re-orients the hermeneutical task away from the elusive search for meaning, it also makes metaphysical inquiry secondary. If the interpretation of the creed is based primarily on its context and function in the liturgy, then metaphysical speculation is no longer a matter of vital concern.[46] The survey of possible interpretations of Wittgenstein by the theological community pointed to distinct differences in regard to the legitimacy of metaphysics in light of Wittgenstein's work. To some extent, the discussion is colored by a preference for the early or late Wittgenstein writings. Those who rely heavily on the *Tractatus* are more open to the possibility of continued use of metaphysical categories, while those who draw primarily from the *Philosophical Investigations* seem more reluctant to place continued reliance on metaphysical presuppositions.

Contextuality

The place of context in determining the meaning is a helpful starting point in this process. Wittgenstein's approach to the meaning of statements is centered upon the context of the statement. Words and sentences belong to systems which provide them a setting in which they operate. In such an interpretation, any understanding of creeds would look to liturgy as a primary focal point. This would cause a significant shift from the points of inquiry that were noted in the nineteenth century debates (and remain prevalent, if not predominant today). There has been a growing recognition of the place of doxological language in recent years.[47] Dantine hinted at the significance of both doxological language and the eucharist in the conclusion of his essay. It is important to note that creeds are doxological acts that are connected to other parts of the liturgy. Since liturgical differences between various denominations exist, the connection between the creed and other parts of the service will vary.[48] In spite of the variations in liturgical order, the inter-relationship between creed, sermon and eucharist are of particular importance in establishing a context or "system" to which they belong.[49] Consequently, any interpretation of a creed must look at the other components of the context. Such an approach is markedly different from the attempts to dredge up an earlier historical meaning (often perceived to have been in the mind of the author).[50]

While Harnack shared an interest in examining the historical circumstances that led to the formulation of the creed, he also noted the importance of approaching creedal interpretation in terms of the appropriateness of its usage. During the *Apostolikumstreit*, Harnack remarked that while an educated theologian would take exception to certain statements in the Apostles' Creed, he/she would also recognize the historical significance and truths of the creed. Harnack's further attempts to emphasize that the creed could not be used as a litmus test for orthodoxy in the ordination of ministers or as a test of the maturity of Christians in the congregation serve as a preliminary portrait of what Wittgenstein would discuss in terms of the significance of contextuality in the interpretation of language. While there was a new appreciation for certain contextual factors in Harnack, there remained a certain naiveté which curiously divided the creed into appropriate and questionable statements (e.g., Harnack's rejection of the statement that Jesus was "born of the Virgin Mary").

Religious Belief

A related shift occurs in the understanding of faith. Faith is not mental acquiescence to a list of historical, doctrinal, or factual statements. The creeds must not be considered as lists that require intellectual assent. Wittgenstein harshly criticized the notion of meaning as a mental state. Similarly, faith cannot be conceived as simply a matter of feeling that precedes or accompanies a statement of faith. By following the Wittgensteinian approach to language and its denial of language as a private, subjective matter, there is a return to a praxis oriented faith. Wittgenstein's cursory comments on Christianity serve as a guide at this point. "Christianity is not a doctrine, not I mean a theory about what has happened and will happen to the human soul, but a description of something that actually takes place in human life."[51]

In the debate surrounding the *Protestantenverein*, Rothe sharply criticized an understanding of faith which was based upon intellectual assent to historical statements of the church. Rothe argued that Christians who are aware of the changes occurring in the world must move beyond dogmatic proclamations that reflect the understanding of earlier and different historical periods.

Ich habe dem heutigen Christen das Recht und nicht minder auch die Pflicht vindiciert, ein Dogma beiseite zu legen, das ihm also thatsächlich seinem heiligsten Glauben widersprechend, seiner freilich gerade entgegengesetzten Intention ungeachtet, bewußt geworden ist.[52]

In this regard, Rothe served as a precursor to Dantine's call for an *Entdogmatisierung* of Christianity. Both share a common interest in an understanding of faith which has striking similarities to that which has been developed in light of Wittgenstein. The way in which the process occurs for Rothe, however, is dramatically different than that which could be followed after an application of Wittgenstein.

For Rothe, dogma is given up because it no longer reflects the understanding of a present *Weltanschauung*. In its place, a new expression of faith is formulated in keeping with modern-day views and in light of the historical basis of Christianity and the continued presence of Christ.

> Heutigen Tages kann der Christi seinen Herrn und seinen Glauben an ihn wahrlich auf eine bessere Weise bekennen, als durch die Zustimmung zu theologischen Sätzen und Formeln. Der Herr hat durch die Geschichte größere und bleibendere Dinge hervorgebracht, als Dogmen und Liturgieen und kirchliche Institutionen aller art.[53]

The dismissal of dogma and liturgy leaves one without a basis for recognizing the centrality of language for the faith community.

Throughout this study a wide variety of interpretive options have been explored in an attempt to discover what provides for both continuity and change within the faith of the Christian community. Following his reading of Wittgenstein, Paul Holmer criticized any attempt by theologians to provide a foundation. While a secure basis for faith cannot be developed, it is possible to describe the ways in which theologians have attempted to apply Wittgenstein to a discussion of the development of faith. As alternatives we have noted the attempts to shift to an "inner" mystical experience (Nieli and D'hert), existential application (Holmer), a grammatical framework which points to the presence of God (Jones), and ceremonial expressions of human nature (Kerr). While each of these proposals has attempted to develop its argument on the basis of certain aspects of Wittgenstein's work, the weaknesses of each approach has been pointed out.

Dantine's discussion of creedal interpretation is particularly significant because it returns us to praxis as the place of orientation for the Christian community. Dantine demonstrates that this approach to confession is one that has much in common with that of the early church. But the critique of Dantine noted that praxis can only be properly reclaimed at the center of Christian faith when language and action are held in inseparable conjunction.

An application of Wittgenstein's work to an understanding of creedal language grows out of an awareness of language, rules, meaning as use, and con-

textuality. This approach to creedal language recognizes the distinctive attributes of doxological language. It avoids the temptation of reducing or clarifying
statements of faith on the basis of historical or scientific presuppositions. It
has the distinct advantage of recognizing that words and actions are intertwined. It affirms the place of the community as the bearer of faith while
avoiding an understanding that is static or passive. It underscores the participation of individuals, while rejecting attempts to base truth on internal, existential experiences.

Faith is recognized as a dynamic exchange in which learning to be Christian includes knowledge of how to express faith in word and deed. Discovering
the connections and forms of life within the language games is an on-going
process in which Christians seek to develop a more mature faith. Doxological
language is rudimentary because it provides a grammatical starting point from
which faith develops.

Theology as Grammar

The interpretation of creedal statements must refocus its investigation on
the actions of the community and the connections that are being made between the statements of faith and other actions of the believers. The investigation of the grammatical structure seeks to point to these connections (which
could be called "language events") and to note the areas of agreement within
the community. The theological task from this perspective is to point out connections that have been made and could be made, as well as to point out discrepancies in the connections that are present.[54] Such a study of the grammatical structure is freed from the attempts to dig "beneath" language, to
hypothesize about previous layers of tradition, or to conjecture about the intent of the authors. Instead, the theologian is returned to the midst of the
Christian community and is challenged to use his/her skills to explore ways of
living faithfully as a part of a group whose identity is founded on its confession
of faith that God has acted decisively in Jesus the Christ!

To the extent that the participants in the controversies over the interpretation of the Apostles' Creed sought to clarify an understanding of the creed
and its connections, then we can look at their discussions as noble attempts to
discover the implications of confessing faith. One can be thankful to those
who courageously spoke out for truth. However, the danger that theologians
will seek to prescribe a certain interpretation of creedal statements is not only

evident through a reading of the nineteenth century literature, but remains present in theological work today.

The need to clarify and re-orient the role of the theologian is underscored by Dietrich Ritschl in *The Logic of Theology*. Ritschl refers to the need for the theologian to "stand in" story and doxology.[55] The identification of the believer is established in the confession of faith in solidarity with the community. As a starting point, the act of confessing one's faith via the creed places the believer(s) as part of an on-going story of God's redemptive work. The continued usage of the creed not only re-affirms this identity but plays a significant grammatical role in the articulation of the faith. In this sense, the grammatical rules act as a guidance system for the community. Wittgenstein refers to rules as a kind of brake which restricts one's movement rather than as a wall which sets distinct limits.[56] Similarly, the grammatical structure of the creed both limits and directs the believers.[57]

Doxological language invites the participant to enter a narrative world in which the stories of the believers (both individual and corporate) become a part of a wider story. "Doxological language not only establishes a link with tradition but at the same time represents a sketch of our own future and God's."[58] Participation in the story of God's saving work usurps individual stories and claims precedence, not only in the doxological moment, but in all of life's moments. The theologian as a participant in this story is similarly called to regulate his/her work and action in light of this story. The recognition of the over-arching guidance provided by story(ies) has led to the recent emergence of "narrative theology."[59]

If "narrative theology" or "doxological theology" is defined as a simplistic repetition of narrative or liturgical formulations, then Ritschl is quite right in rejecting them as "misleading."[60] However, a narrative theology which seeks to provide a way of re-establishing the priority of the Christian story on the lives of the believers and insists on a method in which theological work grows out of this understanding and commitment shares many similarities with Ritschl's own approach. An area of disagreement remains, however, in regard to the relationship between doxology and theology. Ritschl argues that doxological statements are the end result of "standing in" the story and that theology shares that movement towards doxological language.[61] In contrast, the investigation of the function of the creed as a doxological event pointed out its role as an initiatory act which sets the believer(s) apart and is an on-going act of renewal and regulation. In such a situation, doxology functions as a starting point which establishes and confirms the identity of the believers as well as acting as a guidance system. The theologian works out of this doxological commitment and seeks to test and confirm the connections that have been made or suggested by the community. Such an order reaffirms that the work of the theologian grows out of the life of the community.

More recently, Ritschl has expressed an openness to the movement **from** doxological language. Ritschl offers the following summary of the differences in the discussion: "*Ereignis–Reflexion–Doxlogie*" (Ritschl's own position) versus "*Ereignis (bzw. Erfahrung)–Doxologie–Reflexion*" (Wainwright/Teresa Berger). He concludes, though, that, "Vielleicht liegen beide Sequenzen vor."[62] Even with this qualification, my conclusions have followed a different sequence. The rudimentary nature of doxological language that has been developed in this study does not allow for a separation between event and doxology. Instead, doxological language **is** the place of event and experience.[63]

"Dogmatik ist eine theologische Disziplin. Theologie ist aber eine Funktion der Kirche."[64] When doxological language is recognized as a starting point then theology is returned to its proper setting of working for clarification within the "circle of faith."[65] The investigation of the creed has pointed to its function within the liturgical context and its significance as an act which places the believers in the story of God's ongoing work of redemption. This approach to the creed differs from those which seek meaning solely through historical research, metaphysical speculation, or in terms of an "inner" existential commitment. In place of these options, the community stands as an ever-present witness to the dynamic transformation of a "chosen people" who confess their faith in word and deed.

NOTES

[1]   While making the claim for the primacy of language, Dantine appears to flirt with a Kantian perspective by including "religious forms." Dantine gives priority to the language by insisting that the forms occurs within linguistic contexts. Even with this qualification, it is curious that Dantine chooses such language, particularly in light of his resistance to idealism (see the following footnote). Wilhelm Dantine, "Bekennendes Bekenntnis" in *Bekennendes Bekenntnis: Form und Formulierung christlichen Glaubens*, eds. Eric Hultsch and Kurt Lüthi (Gütersloh: Verlaghaus Gerd Mohn, 1982), p. 15.

[2]   Dantine's position is actually even stronger than this statement. The initial aim of Dantine is to contrast historical and idealistic perspectives. Dantine is insistent that Christian faith and language is not language about something (or some idea), but is language that is grounded in the historical ("*geschichtlichen, historischen*") person, Jesus of Nazareth. But be-

yond Dantine's initial goal of avoiding abstract idealism lies a more problematic claim: Does Christian language have the historical Jesus as its sole content and context? If such a claim is true, then how does Christian faith embrace the present and future (and avoid being trapped in the past)?

3   For a critique of the dangers of individualism, see Bellah, et. al., *Habits of the Heart*. For an analysis of theological changes brought about by individualism, see Paul Galbreath, "Protestant Principles in Need of Reformation," *Perspectives: Journal of Reformed Thought* (October 1992), pp. 14–17.

4   Dantine, p. 16.

5   Ibid., p. 21.

6   Ibid., p. 22. "Das Heil erscheint als verschnürtes, fertiggemachtes Heilspaket, das übrigens dann wieder einer eigenen Transmission bzw. eines eigenen Transportes bedürftig ist, als die man dann die sog. >zueignende< bzw. >aneignende< Gnade auswählte (*die gratia applicatrix*)."

7   Ibid., p. 23.

8   Ibid., p. 25.

9   Ibid., pp. 26–27. "Wenn eine Kirche sich ein bestimmtes Bekenntnis zu eigen macht, dann erst tritt sie damit automatisch durch ihren Consensus in die Heilsgemeinschaft ein."

10   Ibid., p. 27.

11   Ibid., p. 28. Dantine notes that this develops a particular metaphysical approach to language which makes it impossible to show the interdependence between truth and conduct.

12   Ibid., p. 29.

13   Ibid., p. 30.

14   Ibid., p. 31. Dantine observes that this is a transition from the objective factual aspect of the dogmatic model or the doctrinal objectivity of the confessional model to a confessional act in which believers express their faith. The recognition of the historical dependency of all creedal statements allows one to accept the past expressions of the faith as appropriate for their context while also relativizing their present usage. A similar argument for recognizing the cultural–linguistic dependency of doctrinal statements is presented in Lindbeck *The Nature of Doctrine*.

15   Ibid., p. 33. Dantine speaks of an "*innerliches Überwältigwerden, auf eine innere zwingende Nötigung*" which moves the individual to speech. Such a claim will be later analyzed in terms of its understanding of language as a secondary event as well as its emphasis on the primacy of the individual.

16   Ibid., p. 34. It must be noted here, however, that Dantine's use of metaphysics is unclear. At one point he speaks of the capacity of the early (New Testament) confessions to reach the metaphysical depths [*metaphysische Tiefendimension*], while later he criticizes the Athanasian Creed for relying on metaphysical categories. The ambiguity of Dantine's use of metaphysics is apparent in his description of the internal metaphysical dimension of the early confessional statements as opposed to a later external metaphysics that employs mythical space dimensions ["*...in der Vorstellungswelt des Dogmas das ewige Heil zur metaphysischen Raum–Dimension geworden ist*"].

17   Ibid., p. 37.

18   Ibid., p. 40.

[19] Ibid., p. 43.

[20] Ibid., p. 44.

[21] Ibid., p. 46-47. "In ihm [Bekennen] erscheint das Ur-und Grundmodell allen Ethos."

[22] Ibid., p. 48. "Theologische Wahrheit will im Grunde genommen nichts anderes besagen als einen von der Problematik des Modells A und B oder C freien Ausdruck."

[23] Ibid., pp. 48-49.

[24] Ibid., p. 53.

[25] Ibid., pp. 55-56.

[26] Ibid., p. 59. "Man könnte geradezu davon sprechen, daß Bekennen eine heilsnotwendige Lebensfunktion kirchlicher Existenz sei."

[27] Ibid., pp. 59-60. "Echtes, lebendiges Bekennen ist die lebendige >eucharistia<, die öffentliche Danksagung des Volkes Gottes für das Widerfahrnis der Gnade."

[28] Karl Rahner, "Fides qua fides quae," in *Bekennendes Bekenntnis*, pp. 70-71.

[29] Hans-Christoph Schmidt-Lauber, "Ökumenisches Bekennen in Kontext der Gemeinde," in *Bekennendes Bekenntnis*, p. 75.

[30] Ibid., pp. 78-80.

[31] Westermann, p. 108. Great care must be taken at this point in order to avoid the dangers of resorting to a dogmatic understanding of the statement. If these acts are understood as just past events, then creedal statements are subject to the hermeneutical problems that have already been discussed.

A related concern is that an emphasis on the acts [*Taten*] of God could be interpreted in light of the early Wittgenstein (*Tractatus*) so that the acts become the simples which are the basis for all else. Westermann qualifies his position by noting the existential context of confessional statements in which the community confesses its present faith. In spite of this modification, there remains an implicit presence of the dogmatic approach hidden in the presentation.

A qualification that could possibly be useful at this point is offered by Koloman Micksey who claims that

> Bekenntnisse sind nicht primär zur theoretischen Information da, sondern sie sind Zeugnisse menschlicher Ganzheitsakte, existenzieller Taten, nämlich des Bekennens von damals und rufen in der Entscheidungssituation nicht zur Wiederholung, sondern zum neuen Bekennen. Koloman Micksey, "Analyse der generativen Kompetenz der systematischen Theologie in Wilhelm Dantines Vorlesung 'Bekennendes Bekenntnis,'" in *Bekennendes Bekenntnis*, p. 210.

The attempt to understand these acts as equally present releases one from the hermeneutical dilemma and recognizes that the confession is imbedded (past and present) in the act of confession.

[32] Westermann, p. 108.

[33] Christofer Frey, "Die Bedeutung des Bekentnisses für die Gestalt der Kirche," in *Bekenndes Bekenntnis*, p. 130.

[34] Link, p. 86.

[35] If Frey is correct here, then Rahner's approach could fall somewhere in between the dogmatic and doctrinal models, since one could assume that the church could operate on a basis of consensus in selecting that which is foundational.

36   Frey, p. 137.

37   Christian Link, "Das Bekenntnis zur Okumene als Bekenntnis der Okumene," in *Bekennendes Bekenntnis*, p. 82.

38   Link, p. 82.

39   Ibid., pp. 85–86. "Die Zustimmung zu einem Bekenntnis is mehr als die formale Anerkennung einer Lehre. Kirchen, die die Bekenntnisse der Kirche unterschrieben haben, verpflichten sich damit, durch ihr tägliches Zeugnis und ihren täglichen Dienst zu bekunden, daß das Evangelium sie ermächtigt hat, als Gottes Volk zu leben."

40   Ibid., p. 91.

41   Putnam notes that even words like "reference" have different meanings in different contexts. The uses of "reference" share similarities, but are not uniform.

> The use of religious language is both like and unlike ordinary uses of language to refer; but to ask whether it is "really" reference or "not really" reference is to be in a muddle. There is no essence of reference. Hilary Putnam, Wittgenstein on Religious Belief, in On Community, p. 73.

42   Thomas Peterson makes a helpful distinction between individuality and individualism. Individuality tells us "what kind of thing" we are, whereas individualism isolates us from the community. See *Wittgenstein for Preaching* (Lanham, MD: University Press of America, 1980), pp. 160–164.

43   Cf. the conclusions of Christian Link, in *Bekennendes Bekenntnis*, p.64.

44   The statement of faith establishes the community as believers in a particular God (the God of Abraham, Isaac, and Jacob). The agreement helps define and delineate the community and prepares the way for further participation in the liturgical order (e.g., the sharing of the sacraments). But beyond this the confession claims to extend to all areas of life by providing the believers with an identity that they belong to God and to one another.

45   This approach has become increasingly significant in the ecumenical movement.

46   Cf. Putnam, p. 73. "The way to understand religious language is not to try to apply some metaphysical classification of possible forms of discourse."

47   Geoffrey Wainwright's *Doxology: The Praise of God in Worship, Doctrine and Life* (New York: Oxford University Press, 1980) marks a particularly significant attempt to rediscover the significance of doxological language in systematic theology.

48   The creed is listed before the sermon in the order of worship in the *Evangelisches Kirchen-Gesangbuch* (Karlsruhe: Verlag Evangelischer Presseverband für Baden e. V., 1983), p. 2. It traditionally occurs after the sermon in the order of worship in *The Book of Common Prayer* (New York: Seabury Press, 1979), p. 54 and *The Book of Catholic Worship* (Washington: The Liturgical Conference, 1966), p. 386 and *The Book of Common Worship* (Louisville: Westminster/John Knox Press, 1993), p. 38. The variation in placement could point to significant differences in the interpretation of the creed because of the importance of contextual dependency.

49   *Zettel*, p. 41. "...it all depends on the system to which the sign belongs."

50 "The affirmation underlying most of the practice of historical criticism has been some form of historicism..." Jon D. Levenson, "Theological Liberalism Aborting Itself, *The Christian Century* (Feb. 5-12, 1992, Vol. 109, No. 5), p. 139.

51 Wittgenstein, *Culture and Value*, p. 28.

52 Rothe, "Zur Debatte," p. 118.

53 Ibid., p. 124.

54 How is it possible to maintain a belief that God is the "creator of heaven and earth" without a concern for the maintenance and care for this creation? Theologians cannot solve discontinuities like this one, but it is their task to point to discrepancies in the connections that are being made by the community of faith.

55 Dietrich Ritschl, *The Logic of Theology* (London: SCM Press, 1986), p. 286.

56 Wittgenstein, *Culture and Value*, p. 28.

57 Ritschl also notes the dependence on the creed which provides a specific content for the believers and direction for ethical action. See *The Logic of Theology*, p. 237.

58 Ibid., p. 279.

59 For a summary of the early discussions and contributions of narrative theology, see George Stroup, *The Promise of Narrative Theology* (Atlanta: John Knox Press, 1981). An analysis of the hermeneutical division within the narrative approach can be found in my thesis "Hermeneutical Options: A Comparison of the Narrative Approaches of Paul Ricoeur and Hans Frei," Austin Presbyterian Theological Seminary, 1985.

    A similar discussion about the relationship between doxology and story can be found in Berger, *Theologie in Hymnen?*, p. 193. Berger notes the doxological context of biblical stories.

60 *The Logic of Theology*, p. 285.

61 Ibid., p. 285. "If ideas appear in chains of statements with a clearly marked difference between beginning and end, in the thought of believers doxology comes at the open end, not at the beginning."

62 Dietrich Ritschl, "Lehre," in *Theologische Realenzyklopädie*, Vol. 20, ed. Gerhard Müller (Berlin: Walter de Gruyter, 1991).

63 At times Berger speaks similarly about the way in which doxology includes ethical action (see esp. p. 196). In other places, the relationship is less clear. In particular, the reliance on the importance of "*Intention*" carries certain difficulties. "Sicher wird man an unterschiedlichen Zielsetzungen von Doxologie und Theologie auf der Ebene der direkten Intention festhalten müssen." (p. 207) (See also p. 198 where Berger raises the question of whether doxology is the "authentischer Ausdruck der zugrundliegenden Intention.")

    Berger concludes that both doxology and theology are based on the experience/event of God's activity. The difference between the two is that doxology praises God whereas theology reflects upon the relationship between God and humanity (p. 194). In assuming experience as a starting point, Berger is able to claim an underlying relationship between doxology and theology. Unfortunately, both become secondary to the foundational experience to which they point. It seems ironic that in an otherwise highly commendable work on the significance of doxology, that in the end doxology is implicitly relegated to a status that is secondary to experience and further qualified by a reliance on the intention of the participants.

64 Barth, Vol. 1/1, p. 3.

65   Tillich, *Systematic Theology*, Vol. 2, p. 23.

Afterword

In the fifteen years since the body of this work was completed, relatively little has been published in the area of liturgical theology that advances the work of linguistic analysis on liturgical language. Wittgenstein's work on language remains largely ignored by many liturgical theologians. In 2004, Larry Hoffmann provided a helpful, succinct introduction to Wittgenstein in a plenary address to the North American Academy of Liturgy, the major academic gathering for liturgical scholars.[1] That such a primer on one of the major philosophical figures of the twentieth century was needed is in itself indicative of the limited impact that Wittgenstein's work has made on liturgical studies.

One major exception to this norm can be found in the field of ritual studies where scholars are increasingly taking note of Wittgenstein's writings and integrating portions of his philosophical gleanings into their own work. Fergus Kerr's own insightful reading of Wittgenstein served as a precursor in this direction. While Kerr's own interests in ritual studies led him to adapt Wittgenstein's philosophy in the direction of the work of René Girard, it nevertheless points to the significant intersection between Wittgenstein's insistence on the contextual role of religion and language in one's life, and the broad interests of those in ritual studies to observe and examine ritual actions.[2] Significant voices in the field of ritual studies continue to build on the insights of Wittgenstein. Tom Driver cites and explicates Wittgenstein frequently in his helpful work Liberating Rites: Understanding the Transformative Power of Ritual.[3] Other scholars in the field of ritual theory, like Stanley Tambiah's work on performance ritual, build more implicitly on Wittgenstein's approach.[4]

Closely related to these concerns are the recent works of scholars who examine the social history of the liturgy in order to determine its meaning, function, and purpose. Recent work in this area has recognized the importance of moving beyond liturgical texts and the debates about historical and theological meanings that may lie "behind" the texts (and which seem to need scholarly explanations). A new focus is emerging about the role of texts and acts in the lives of the participants. Karen Spierling's brilliant work on baptism in reformation Geneva is a wonderful example of the importance of such an approach.[5] Careful attention to the social history and the way that liturgical texts were embodied in worship services and understood in the life of the participants shares a deep concern for the importance of liturgical context and an integral connection to the daily lives of participants in the assembly. In this sense, the careful work of social historians can help avoid the drastic alternatives that some interpreters of Wittgenstein have advocated. In the attempt to reject the absolute claims of academic metaphysical systems or a dependence on the ability of theologians to explain doctrinal systems that lie underneath liturgical texts, some interpreters of Wittgenstein have emphasized mystical readings (especially of the Tractatus). Surely, though, there are other alternatives between these positions. A social historical approach to the liturgy offers a promising possibility that avoids the dangers of a highly individualistic, mystical interpretation.

Scholars in ritual theory and social history both help point us back to the centrality of the community in teaching us language games and showing us connections to this in our daily lives. Work in ritual studies and social history also encourages us to pay closer attention to the role of embodiment and gesture that accompanies the assembly's act of reciting a confession.

Many of the theological interpreters of Wittgenstein's work share a common consensus in locating the liturgical context as the hermeneutical focus for interpretation. Ignace D'hert called for an investigation of the grammar of the forms of life that are located in liturgy, prayer, and preaching.[6] Similarly, Paul Holmer's attention to the grammar of faith pointed back to the use of language in prayer worship as the central concepts that serve as interpretive keys for analyzing forms of life.[7] Fergus Kerr echoed this emphasis with his concern for analyzing the customs and practices of everyday life. On this point, major theological interpreters of Wittgenstein find common ground with Dantine's emphasis on the doxological character of creedal statements. Here, the existential act of confession is related to the assembly as it gathers for Eucharist. The experience of receiving grace at the communion table frames the language of creedal affirmation in the act of thanksgiving.[8]

I share all of the concerns about understanding liturgical language in the act of gathering at the table. Here gesture and response, language and action, come together to provide a context in which the act of confession is grounded in the lives of the participants. The sheer density of these communal acts, which vary not only among ecclesial bodies but also among individual congregations, makes precise interpretation frustratingly difficult.[9] But, it is this ongoing act of regular thanksgiving that sustains (and informs) the lives of faithful people around the world.

Missing from the discussion, though, is any recognition of baptism as the central act of confession and of particular significance for the Apostles' Creed. This is especially clear in the Easter Vigil liturgy. The assembly's procession into the sanctuary behind the newly lit paschal candle establishes the connection that the celebration of Christ's resurrection is ritually connected to the actions around the baptismal font. The extended readings of Scripture from creation through the prophets to the Gospel place the community's identity squarely in the biblical narrative of God's covenant with creation. The baptismal liturgy underscores this movement as it invites the participants to confess their faith through a series of steps: a presentation of the candidates, a prayer of thanksgiving over the water, and a profession of faith that includes renunciations of evil and sin. These acts lead to the congregation joining the baptismal candidates by professing "their faith in the words of the Apostles' Creed."[10] The creed itself can take on a dialogical character as it is framed by the insertion of questions that underscore the trinitarian elements of the creed (e.g., "Do you believe in God, the Father almighty?"). The act of baptism immediately follows the recitation of the creed. The pouring of water on the candidates is followed by the laying on of hands and the anointing of oil. The use of baptismal garments and baptismal candles can further heighten the celebration of newness of life that is celebrated.[11] Recent work in the Presbyterian Church underscores the integral relationship of the baptismal rite with life-long discipleship.[12] All of this broadens the liturgical context so that associations with a creedal statement draw on (and interplay with) a variety of ritual acts and linguistic expressions.

This broader understanding of context will also need to move beyond the walls of the church to examine significant cultural and political influences that shape and color the ways that we write, hear, and respond to texts. Dantine (among many voices) pointed to the Barmen declaration as a primary example of linking a confessional statement to present ethical demands. The Belhar Confession in South Africa is another example of recognizing the broad relationship between confessional statements and social and political contexts.

All of this comes together to underscore the importance of interpreting confessional statements as liturgical acts of faith that are colored and shaped by their connections and associations with language and events inside and outside the walls of the church. Following Wittgenstein, we are returned to the "hurly-burly" of life in all of its richness and diversity. Shared statements of faith do not result in uniformity of belief and action. Instead, careful examination of the language and actions of faith communities shows patterns that coalesce around liturgical language and actions in which the lives of participants are grounded and guided in their daily actions.

My recent work in sacramental ethics seeks to uncover central connections between word, water, bread and wine and our daily lives.[13] In this regard, the language of our confession (the Apostles' Creed) as a part of our baptismal pilgrimage seeks to orient us in our decision making process (e.g., to believe in God the Father, the creator of heaven and earth is to learn to care for this creation). Such an approach requires a kind of modesty in scope as it leaves dogmatic pronouncements behind in favor of theological portraits that illumine the shape and places that liturgical language connects (or fails to connect) with our daily lives.

An essay by Ron Grimes serves as a helpful guide along the way. Grimes offers a harsh critique of the abuses of liturgical authority that dictates an invariable approach. "Liturgy's felicitousness does not arise from ecclesiastical, biblical, conciliar, or traditional alone but also on the basis of a rite's ability to meet fundamental human need."[14] In place of this approach (which he refers to as liturgical erectitude), Grimes proposes the need for liturgical supinity, of being rooted, adaptable, open and close to the ground. Such an understanding of ritual is "... rooted in, generated by, and answerable to its infrastructures–bodily, cultural, ecological, spiritual."[15]

The work and meaning of liturgical language and ritual gesture are ultimately grounded in the lives of participants and believers. These words and actions shape and suggest ways of comprehending, reflecting, and acting both within the walls of the church and beyond the church. Wittgenstein's careful examination of language provides a way for the church to reinvigorate its understanding and use of liturgical language. While liturgical scholars can certainly help point out connections within language that is used in church (and perhaps more importantly help avoid misappropriations or errant connections in language), it is not the task of scholars to extract and explain the meaning of liturgical language. Wittgenstein's examination of language games serves to underscore the broader context(s) and association of language within the complex systems in which it functions. The connection of language with behavior and forms of life offers profound insights into ways that the claims of liturgical language place on the participants of a congregation. Ritual gestures provide opportunities for directing and clarifying the claims of language on our lives.

The recognition of the way that implicit rules lie within the grammatical structure of language provides a way to help navigate the theological map of Christian faith. Inter-relationships between the elements of worship offer an approach and orientation with the structure of the worship assembly that also points beyond the assembly's walls. Gordon Lathrop's use of juxtaposition has made much of this possibility. In Holy Things: A Liturgical Theology, Lathrop writes of the way the stuff of worship, primarily book, bath, and table, "take on meaning in action as they are used, especially as they are intentionally juxtaposed."[16] Meaning, then, is grounded in grammatical rules that undergird the assembly's gathering and yet at the same time is transformed by the freedom of movement and new meanings that are exposed as liturgical responses and objects are placed side-by-side. To cite, but one example, note the theological difference in the placement of a statement of faith in the liturgy. When placed after the reading of Scripture and before the sermon, it functions as an historical bridge from the ancient world of the Bible to the post-modern world(s) of the listener. In this placement, it provides a hermeneutical framework for the proclamation of the text.[17] By contrast, when the statement of faith is placed following the sermon it provides an opportunity for the assembly to respond to the claims of Scripture on their lives.[18] The ordering of the liturgy serves as a grammatical guide to the implicit rules (or pictures as Wittgenstein suggested) of the language game in which the assembly participates. Thus, participants may be guided to hear Scripture interpreted through confessional statements or invited to respond to the word read and proclaimed by reaffirming their faith and Christian identity by reciting a confessional statement.[19] In these ways, the liturgical placement of confessional statements functions in different ways to provide boundaries of the language game(s).

The return to the whole hurly-burly of life does not leave us with out resources. Instead it pushes us back into the nexus where meaning rises out of the context and connections that surround us. Recovering the significance of meaning as use is fundamental to the shift that Wittgenstein advocated. Liturgical language is grounded in sets of practices that are surrounded by ritual gestures. As we have seen, the attempts to provide historical or metaphysical explanations of liturgical language have only brought further confusion and at times division to the church. Wittgenstein helps point us back to the way that beliefs are shown in our language and in our lives. Our shared participation in language games and ritual practices provides a framework out of which faith develops. Participation in interconnected systems provides a context for discovering ways of acting that embody the language of faith.

Scripture, creedal statements, prayer, hymnody, liturgical responses, and other uses of language (and silence) in worship provide a contextual setting out of which religious belief takes root. Participation in the assembly's gathering provides a way of seeing and living. Participants learn to navigate within the inherent logic of these systems. Theology as grammar works to clarify the language that is used in order for the connections to become clearer.

In the end, our journey goes full circle. We are taken back to the church where Karl Barth reminds us is the place that theology is done. But it is not just the church. It is always a particular place, a peculiar people, and a specific service in which the community gathers to speak, listen, read, preach, sing, pray, and act in order that the faith we confess and the words that we say may come to life in us and among us. In these moments, the words of the Apostles' Creed and other liturgical texts seek to serve as guides by providing us linguistic maps that are grounded in our actions as a community of faith and point to ways to live out our faith together.

NOTES

[1]   Lawrence Hoffman, "A Rendezvous of Ancestors: Wrestling with Ritual Truth." Proceedings of the North American Academy of Liturgy (2004), *pp. 19–40*.

[2]   See René Girard, "Violence and Sacred: Sacrifice," in *Readings in Ritual Studies*, ed. by Ronald Grimes (Upper Saddle River, N.J.: Prentice-Hall, 1996), pp. 239–256.

[3]   Tom Driver, *Liberating Rites: Understanding the Transformative Power of Ritual* (BookSurge: 2006).

[4]   Note the similarities in Tambiah's analysis of ritual events as performative acts that follow certain logical rules and are integrally connected to social actions. See Tambiah, "A Performative Approach to Ritual," in *Readings in Ritual Studies*, ed. by Ronald Grimes (Upper Saddle River, N.J.: Prentice-Hall, 1996), pp. 495–511.

[5]   Karen Spierling, *Infant Baptism in Reformation Geneva: The Shaping of a Community, 1536–1564* (Hants, England: Ashgate, 2005). Or for a sweeping overview of the possibilities of this approach, see Frank Senn, *The People's Work: A Social History of the Liturgy* (Minneapolis: Fortress Press, 2006).

[6]   D'hert, p. 98.

[7]   Holmer, *The Grammar of Faith*, p. 144. "... the very meaning of a word like *holiness* is grasped and exerted not by discourse alone but by a new quality and form of life."

[8]   Dantine, pp. 59–60.

[9]   For example, note how little work has been done on the social history of the altar's relocation and transformation into a table around which people frequently gathered for communion during the reformation. While significant analysis of Calvin's writings has underscored the central place of Eucharist in his theology, there remains a pressing need for reflection about how the dramatic changes in worship practice fundamentally shaped the

lives of the faithful. For the theological analysis, see especially, Brian Gerrish, *Grace &* *Gratitude: The Eucharistic Theology of John Calvin* (Minneapolis: Fortress Press, 1993). For an analysis of the shape of Eucharistic prayer as it forms the lives of the assembly, see my recent work *Leading from the Table* (Herndon, VA: The Alban Press, 2008).

10   *Book of Common Worship*, p. 426. This order is based on the baptismal liturgy prepared by the Consultation on Common Texts. It is worth noting that the Apostles' Creed is placed before the prayer of thanksgiving over the water in the primary baptismal liturgy in the book.

11   For Presbyterians, it is worth noting that Calvin's objection to the use of salt, candles, oil and other objects in association with baptism is a concern that these ritual actions would overshadow the act of baptism itself. The Directory for Worship states that "water should be applied visibly and generously." *The Constitution of the Presbyterian Church (U.S.A.), Part II, Book of Order* (Louisville: The Office of the General Assembly, 2005-2007), W-3.3605. Spierling also notes that Calvin's objections to the use of other elements were related to their association with pagan customs. Spierling, p. 41. Thus, the relationship between ritual action and forms of life provides a determinative critique in the process of liturgical reformation in Calvin's practice.

12   *Invitation to Christ*, Report of the Sacramental Study Task Force (Louisville: Congregational Ministries Publishing, 2006).

13   See "Doing Justice with a Sacramental Heart," *Hungry Hearts*, Fall 2005, Volume XIV, Number 3 and "Making Public Worship Public Again," *Call to Worship: Liturgy, Music, Preaching & the Arts*, Vol. 40.2, November 2006.

14   Ronald Grimes, "Liturgical Supinity, Liturgical Erectitude: the Embodiment of Ritual Authority" in *Reading, Writing, and Ritualizing: Ritual in Fictive, Liturgical, and Public Places* (Washington, DC: The Pastoral Press, 1993), p. 52.

15   Grimes, p. 56.

16   Gordon Lathrop, *Holy Things: A Liturgical Theology* (Minneapolis: Augsburg Fortress Press, 1993), p. 10.

17   *Evangelisches Kirchen-Gesangbuch* (Karlsrühe: Verlag Evangelischer Presseverband für Baden, e.V., 1983), p. 2.

18   Recent liturgical books have generally used this as the suggested placement for the statement of faith. See the *Book of Common Worship* or *Evangelical Lutheran Worship* (Minneapolis: Augsburg Fortress, 2006).

19   The question of identity is particularly highlighted in creedal statements that begin with the words: We/I believe.

Bibliography

Allerhöchste Antwort Sr. Majestät des Königs Friedrich Wilhelm IV. auf die von dem Berliner Magistrat in der Audienz vom 2. Oktober 1845 in Betreff der kirchlichen Angelegenheiten überreichten Immediat-Eingabe. Magdeburg: Albert Falckenburg, 1845.

Altmann, Alexander. "The God of Religion, the God of Metaphysics and Wittgenstein's 'Language Games'." *Zeitschrift fur Religions und Geistesgeschichte* (No. 4, 1987): 289-306.

Anscombe, G.E.M. "Wittgenstein: Whose Philosopher?" In *Wittgenstein Centenary Essays.* ed. A. Phillips Griffiths. Cambridge: Cambridge University Press, 1991.

Apel, Karl-Otto. *Transformation der Philosophie.* Vol. 1. Frankfurt: Suhrkamp Verlag, 1973.

Baker G. P. and P. M. S. Hacker. *Wittgenstein: Meaning and Understanding.* Oxford: Basill Blackwell, 1980.

———. *Wittgenstein: Rules, Grammar and Necessity.* Oxford: Basil Blackwell, 1985.

Baltzer, Eduard. *Erinnerungen: Bilder aus meinem Leben.* Frankfurt am Main: Deutschen Vegetarier, 1907.

Bambrough, Renford. "Fools and Heretics." In *Wittgenstein Centenary Essays.* ed. A. Phillips Griffiths. Cambridge: Cambridge University Press, 1991.

Barth, Hans-Martin. "Apostolisches Glaubensbekenntnis II: Reformations-und Neuzeit." *Theologische Realenzyklopädie.* Vol. 3. ed. Gerhard Krause and Gerhard Müller. Berlin: Walter de Gruyter, 1978, pp. 554-66.

Barth, Karl. *Die Kirchliche Dogmatik: Die Lehre vom Wort Gottes. Prolegomena zur kirchlichen Dogmatik.* Vol. 1/1. Zürich: Theologischer Verlag, 1970.

Bearsley, Patrick. "Augustine and Wittgenstein on Language." *Philosophy* 58 (1983): 229-36

Bell, Richard. "Theology as Grammar: Is God an Object of Understanding?" *Religious Studies* 11 (1975): 307-317.

———. "Wittgenstein and Descriptive Theology." *Religious Studies* (October 1969): 1-18.

Bellah, Robert, et. al. *Habits of the Heart: Individualism and Commitment in American Life.* Berkeley: University of California Press, 1985.

Besier, Gerhard. *Preussische Kirchenpolitik in der Bismarckära: Die Diskussion in Staat und Evangelischer Kirche um eine Neuordnung der kirchlichen Verhältnisse Preußens zwischen 1866 und 1872.* Berlin: Walter de Gruyter, 1980.

———. *Religion-Nation-Kultur: Die Geschichte der christlichen Kirchen in den gesellschaftlichen Umbrüchen des 19. Jahrhunderts.* Neukirchen-Vluyn: Neukirchener, 1992.

Bezzel, Chris. *Wittgenstein zur Einführung.* Hamburg: Junius Verlag, 1988.

Binkley, Timothy. *Wittgenstein's Language.* The Hague: Martinus Nighoff, 1973.

Birkner, Hans-Joachim. *Spekulation und Heilsgeschichte: Die Geschichtsauffassung Richard Rothes.* München: Chr. Kaiser, 1959.

The Book of Catholic Worship. Washington: The Liturgical Conference, 1966.

The Book of Common Prayer. New York: Seabury Press, 1979.

Book of Common Worship. Louisville: Westminster/John Knox Press, 1993.

Brederlow, Jörn. *"Lichtfreunde" und "Freie Gemeinden": Religiöser Protest und Freiheitsbewegung im Vormärz und in der Revolution von 1848/49.* München: R. Oldenbourg Verlag, 1976.

Browarzik, Ulrich. "Der Grundlose Glaube." *Neue Zeitschrift für systematische Theologie und Religionsphilosophie* 30 (1988): 72–100.

Burke, T. E. "Wittgenstein's *Lectures on Religious Belief:* A Re-consideration." In *Wittgenstein and His Impact on Contemporary Thought.* Proceedings of the Second International Wittgenstein Symposium. Vienna: Hölder, Pitcher, Tempsky, 1978.

Celebrate God's Presence: A Book of Services for The United Church of Canada. Etobicoke, Ontario: The United Church Publishing House, 2000.

Chappell, V. C., ed. *Ordinary Language.* Englewood Cliffs, N.J.: Prentice-Hall, 1964.

Charakterbild Jesu von Dr. Daniel Schenkel oder Bibel? Karlsruhe: Gutsch, 1864.

Churchill, John. "Beliefs, Principles, and Reasonable Doubts." *Religious Studies* 23 (June 1987): 221–232.

The Constitution of the Presbyterian Church (U.S.A.), Part II, Book of Order 2005–2007. Louisville: The Office of the General Assembly, 2005.

Cook, John. "Wittgenstein on Privacy." In *Wittgenstein: The Philosophical Investigations.* ed. George Pitcher. Notre Dame: University of Notre Dame Press, 1968.

Coope, Christopher, Peter Geach, Timothy Potts, and Roger White. *A Wittgenstein Workbook.* Oxford: Basil Blackwell, 1971.

Cremer, Hermann. *Warum können wir das apostolische Glaubensbekenntnis nicht aufgeben?* Berlin: Wiefandt and Grieben, 1893.

Cupitt, Don. *The Long Legged Fly.* London: SCM Press, 1987.

Dalferth, Ingolf. *Religiöse Rede von Gott.* München: Chr. Kaiser Verlag, 1981.

———. *Sprachlogik des Glaubens: Texte analytischer Religionsphilosophie und Theologie zur religiösen Sprache.* München: Chr. Kaiser Verlag, 1974.

Dantine, Wilhelm. "Bekennendes Bekenntnis." In *Bekennendes Bekenntnis: Form und Formulierung christlichen Glaubens.* eds. Eric Hultsch and Kurt Lüthi. Gütersloh: Verlaghaus Gerd Mohn, 1982.

David, Ian. *A Theology of Speech.* London: Sheed and Ward, 1973.

de Pater, Wim. "Der Sprechakt, seinen Glauben zu bekennen." In *Möglichkeiten des Redens über Gott.* Düsseldorf: Patmos Verlag, 1978.

Delius, Walter. *Die evangelische Kirche und die Revolution 1848.* Berlin: Evangelische Verlagsanstalt, 1948.

D'hert, Ignace. *Wittgenstein's Relevance for Theology.* Bern: Peter Lang, 1974.

Downey, John. *Beginning at the Beginning*. Lanham, MD: University Press of America, 1986.

Drews, D. "Lichtfreunde." *Die Religion in Geschichte und Gegenwart*. 1st ed. Vol. 3. ed. Friedrich Michael Schiele and Leopold Zscharnack. Tübingen: J. C. B. Mohr, 1912, pp. 2113-2117.

Driver, Tom. *Liberating Rites: Understanding the Transformative Power of Ritual*. BookSurge, 2006.

Engelmann, Paul. *Ludwig Wittgenstein: Briefe und Begegnungen*. Vienna: R. Oldenbourg, 1970.

Evangelical Lutheran Worship. Minneapolis: Augsburg Fortress Press, 2006.

Evangelisches Kirchen-Gesangbuch. Karlsruhe: Verlag Evangelischer Presseverband für Baden e. V., 1983.

Fann, K. T. *Wittgenstein's Conception of Philosophy*. Oxford: Basil Blackwell, 1969.

Findeis, A. R. *Ueber die Gesellschaft der protestantischen Freunde und ihre Grundsätze*. Magdeburg: Albert Falckenburg, 1844.

Flew, Anthony (ed.). "Wittgenstein." In *A Dictionary of Philosophy*. New York: St Martin's Press, 1979.

Fogelin, Robert. *Wittgenstein*. Boston: Routledge and Kegan Paul, 1976.

Frei, Hans. *The Eclipse of Biblical Narrative*. New Haven: Yale University Press, 1974.

Frey, Christofer. "Die Bedeutung des Bekentnisses für die Gestalt der Kirche." In *Bekenndes Bekenntnis*. eds. Eric Hultsch and Kurt Lüthi. Gütersloh: Verlaghaus Gerd Mohn, 1982.

Galbreath, Paul. "The Christology of the Gospels and Abraham Maslow's Characteristics of Self-Actualization." Ph.D. Dissertation. Baylor University, 1984.

——. "Doing Justice with a Sacramental Heart." *Hungryhearts*. Fall 2005, Vol. XIV, Number 3.

——. "Hermeneutical Options: A Comparison of the Narrative Approaches of Paul Ricoeur and Hans Frei." Th.M. Thesis. Austin Presbyterian Theological Seminary, 1985.

——. *Leading from the Table*. Herndon, VA: The Alban Press, 2008.

——. "Making Public Worship Public Again." *Call to Worship: Liturgy, Music, Preaching & the Arts*. Vol. 40.2, November 2006.

—— "Protestant Principles in Need of Reformation." *Perspectives: A Journal of Reformed Thought* (October 1992): 14-17.

——. "Sacramental Ethics: Doing as Remembering." In *Theology in Service to the Church*. Louisville: Westminster/John Knox Press, 2008.

Gerhard Goeters, J.F. and Rudolf Mau (eds.). *Die Geschichte der Evangelischen Kirche der Union: Die Anfänge der Union unter landesherrlichem Kirchenregiment (1817-1850)*. Vol. 1. Leipzig: Evangelische Verlagsanstalt, 1992.

Gerrish, Brian. *Grace & Gratitude: The Eucharistic Theology of John Calvin*. Minneapolis: Fortress Press, 1993.

Glebe -Møller, Jens. "Two Views of Religion in Wittgenstein." In *The Grammar of the Heart.* ed. by Richard Bell. San Francisco: Harper & Row, 1988.

Gollwitzer, Helmut. "Das Bekenntnis will mehr, als es sagt." In *Bekennendes Bekenntnis.* eds. Eric Hultsch and Kurt Lüthi. Gütersloh: Verlaghaus Gerd Mohn, 1982.

——. "Die Bedeutung des Bekenntnisses für die Kirche." In *Hören und Handeln.* eds. Helmut Gollwitzer and Hellmut Traub. München: Chr. Kaiser Verlag, 1962.

Grimes, Ronald, ed. *Readings in Ritual Studies.* Upper Saddle River, N.J.: Prentice-Hall, 1996.

Grimes, Ronald. *Reading, Writing, and Ritualizing: Ritual in Fictive, Liturgical, and Public Places.* Washington, DC: The Pastoral Press, 1993.

Guericke, E. F. *Allgemeine Christliche Symbolik.* 2nd ed. Leipzig: Winter, 1846.

Habermas, Jürgen. *Nachmetaphysisches Denken.* Frankfurt: Suhrkamp Verlag, 1988.

Hacker, P. M. S. *Insight and Illusion.* London: Oxford University Press, 1972.

Hallett, Garth. *A Companion to Wittgenstein's "Philosophical Investigations."* Ithaca: Cornell University Press, 1977.

——. *Essentialism: A Wittgensteinian Critique.* Albany: State University of New York Press, 1991.

——. *Wittgenstein's Definition of Meaning as Use.* New York: Fordham University Press, 1967.

Harms, Claus. *Ausgewählte Schriften und Prediten.* Vol. 1. ed. Peter Meinhold. Flensburg: Christian Wolff, 1955.

Harnack, Adolf von. *Das apostolische Glaubensbekenntniß.* Berlin: Haack, 1892.

——. *Reden und Aufsätze.* 2 Vols. Gießen: Ricker, 1904.

Harned, David. *Creed and Personal Identity.* Philadelphia: Fortress Press, 1981.

Hartnack, Justus. *Wittgenstein and Modern Philosophy.* trans. Maurice Cranston. Garden City, NY: Anchor Books, 1965.

Hase, Karl. *Kirchengeschichte: Lehrbuch zunächst für akademische Vorlesungen.* Leipzig: Breitkopf und Härtel, 1877.

Hauck, Ph. G. *Dr. Schenkel, seine Freunde und seine Gegner.* 2nd. ed. Karlsruhe: Gutsch, 1865.

Hauerwas, Stanley and William H. Willimon. *Resident Aliens.* Nashville: Abingdon Press, 1989.

Hausrath, Adolf. *Richard Rothe und seine Freunde.* 2 Vols. Berlin: G. Grote'sche Verlagsbuchhandlung, 1906.

Hermelink, Heinrich. *Das Christentum in der Menschengeschichte.* 3 Vols. Stuttgart: J. B. Metzler, 1953.

Heyer, Friedrich and Volker Pitzer, eds. *Religion ohne Kirche: Die Bewegung der Freireligiösen.* Stuttgart: Quell Verlag, 1977.

Hick, John. Review of *The Edges of Language* by Paul van Buren. *Journal of Theological Studies* 24 (October 1973): 634.

High, Dallas. *Language, Persons and Beliefs*. New York: Oxford University Press, 1967.

——. "Wittgenstein on Doubting and Groundless Believing." *Journal of American Academy of Religion* 49 (1981): 249–266.

Hill, Patrick. "Religion and the Quest for Community." In *On Community*. ed. Leroy Roumer. Notre Dame: University of Notre Dame Press, 1991.

Hilmy, S. Stephen. *The Later Wittgenstein*. Oxford: Basil Blackwell, 1987.

Hintikka, Merrill and Jaakka. *Investigating Wittgenstein*. Oxford: Basil Blackwell, 1986.

Hönig, W. *Die Arbeit des deutschen Protestantenverein während seines fünfundzwanzigjährigen Bestehens*. Berlin: A. Haack Verlag, 1888.

——. *Der deutsche Protestantenverein*. Berlin: 1904.

Hoffmann, G. "Apostolikum II: Im Protestantismus." *Die Religion in Geschichte und Gegenwart*. 3rd ed. Vol. 1. ed. Kurt Galling. Tübingen: J. C. B. Mohr, 1961, pp. 514–16.

Hoffman, Lawrence. "A Rendezvous of Ancestors: Wrestling with Ritual Truth." *Proceedings of the North American Academy of Liturgy* (2004), pp. 19–40.

Hofmeister, Heimo. *Wahrheit und Glaube: Interpretation und Kritik der sprachanalytischen Theorie der Religion*. Wien: R. Oldenbourg Verlag, 1978.

Hohlwein, H. "Protestantenverein, Deutscher." *Die Religion in Geschichte und Gegenwart*. 3rd ed. Vol. 5. ed. Kurt Galling. Tübingen: J. C. B. Mohr, 1961, pp. 645–47.

Holmer, Paul. "Religion from an Existential Standpoint." In *Religion in Philosophical and Cultural Perspective*. ed. by J. Clayton Feaver and William Horosz. Princeton: D. Van Nostrand Company, Inc., 1967.

Holmer, Paul. *The Grammar of Faith*. San Francisco: Harper & Row, Publishers, 1978.

Hudson, Donald. "The Light Wittgenstein Sheds on Religion." In *Ludwig Wittgenstein: Critical Assessments*. Vol. 4. ed. Stuart Shanker. London: Croom Helm, 1986.

——. *Ludwig Wittgenstein*. Richmond: John Knox Press, 1968.

Hunter, J. M. F. "'Forms of Life' in Wittgenstein's *Philosophical Investigations*." In *Essays on Wittgenstein*. ed. E. D. Klemke. Urbana: University of Illinois Press, 1971.

Jones, Hugh. "Das Story-Konzept und die Theologie." In *"Story" als Rohmaterial der Theologie*. Dietrich Ritschl and Hugh Jones. München: Chr. Kaiser Verlag, 1976.

——. "Zum Verhältnis von Sprache und Religiöser Erfahrung." Unpublished paper. Mainz.

——. *Die Logik theologischer Perspektiven: Eine spachanalytische Untersuchung*. Göttingen: Vandenhoeck & Ruprecht, 1985.

Kampe, Ferdinand. *Geschichte der religiösen Bewegung der neueren Zeit*. 2 Vols. Leipzig: Otto Wigand, 1852.

Karsten, H. *Die Kirche und das Symbol in ihrem innern Zusammenhange so wie in ihrem Verhältnisse zu Staat und Wissenschaft.* Hamburg: Johann August Meißner, 1842.

Kattenbusch, Ferdinand. *Zur Würdigung des Apostolikums.* Leipzig: Grunow, 1892.

Katzenbach, Friedrich. "Der erste Apostolikumstreit." *Zeitschrift für Kirchengeschichte* 86 (1975): 86–89.

Kerr, Fergus. *Theology after Wittgenstein.* Oxford: Basil Blackwell, 1986.

Kessler, Paul. *Glaube und Gesellschaftsgestaltung: Die Bedeutung Richard Rothes für das Verhältnis von Kirche und Welt im 20. Jahrhundert.* Essen: Reimar Hobbing, 1969.

Köhler, Karl. "Die Amtsentsetzung des Pfarrers Schrempf vom kirchenrechtlichen Standpunkt aus betrachtet." *Die Christliche Welt* (15 September 1892): 868–75.

——. *Der königliche Ausspruch: "daß die Kirche sich durch sich selbst zu gestalten habe" und die Bekenntnisfrage.* Berlin: C. Grobe, 1846.

Kramer, Wolfgang. *E. W. Hengstenberg, die Evangelische Kirchenzeitung und der theologischen Rationalismus.* Erlangen-Nürnberg: Diss. phil., 1972.

Kripke, Saul. *Wittgenstein on Rules and Private Language.* Oxford: Basil Blackwell, 1982.

Lacey, A. R. "Philosophy and Analysis." In *A Dictionary of Philosophy.* ed. Anthony Flew. New York: St Martin's Press, 1979.

Lange, Ernst Michael. "'Einer Regel folgen'–zu einigen neuen Interpretationen Wittgensteins." *Philosophische Rundschau* (1987): 102–24.

Lapointe, Francoise (ed.). *Ludwig Wittgenstein: A Comprehensive Bibliography.* Westport, CT: Greenwood Press, 1980.

Lathrop, Gordon. *Holy Things: A Liturgical Theology.* Minneapolis: Augsburg Fortress Press, 1993.

Leese, Kurt (ed.). *Der Protestantismus im Wandel der neuen Zeit.* Stuttgart: Alfred Kröner Verlag, 1941.

Levenson, Jon D. "Theological Liberalism Aborting Itself." *The Christian Century* 109 (Feb. 5–12, 1992): 139–149.

Lindbeck, George. *The Nature of Doctrine: Religion and Theology in a postliberal Age.* Philadelphia: Westminster Press, 1984.

Link, Christian. "Das Bekenntnis zur Okumene als Bekenntnis der Okumene." In *Bekennendes Bekenntnis.* eds. Eric Hultsch and Kurt Lüthi. Gütersloh: Verlaghaus Gerd Mohn, 1982.

Lisco, E. G. *Das apostolische Glaubensbekenntnis.* Berlin: Henschel, 1872.

Lochman, Jan. *Das Glaubensbekenntnis: Grundriß der Dogmatik im Anschluß an das Credo.* Gütersloh: Verlaghaus Gerd Mohn, 1982.

Loewenich, Walther von. "Kritischer Bericht über Entstehung und Sinn des Apostolicums." In *Das Glaubensbekenntnis: Aspekte für ein neues Verständnis.* ed. Gerhard Rein. Stuttgart: Kreuz Verlag, 1968.

Lüthi, Kurt. "Bekennen und Bekenntnis und das Problem einer Sprache unserer Zeit." In *Bekennendes Bekenntnis*. eds. Eric Hultsch and Kurt Lüthi. Gütersloh: Verlaghaus Gerd Mohn, 1982.

Malcolm, Norman. *Ludwig Wittgenstein: A Memoir*. Second Edition. Oxford: Oxford University Press, 1984.

——. *Thought and Knowledge*. Ithaca: Cornell University Press, 1977.

——. *Wittgenstein: A Religious Point of View?* ed. with a response by Peter Winch. Ithaca, NY: Cornell University Press, 1994.

Martin, Dean. "Learning to Become Christian." *Religious Education* 82 (Winter 1987): 94–114.

——. "On Certainty and Religious Belief." *Religious Studies* 20 (1984): 593–613.

McGuin, Colin. *Wittgenstein on Meaning*. Oxford: Basil Blackwell, 1984.

McGuiness, Brian. *Wittgenstein: A Life. Young Ludwig (1899–1921)*. London: Duckworth, 1988.

Mehlhorn, P. "Protestantenverein." *Realencyklopädie für protestantische Theologie und Kirche*. Vol. 16. 3rd ed. ed. Albert Hauck. Leipzig: Hinrichs'sche Buchhandlung, 1902, pp. 127–35.

Mehnert, Gottfried. *Programme Evangelischer Kirchenzeitung im 19. Jahrhundert*. Wittenberg: Luther Verlag, 1972.

Meinhold, Peter (ed.). *Studien zur Bekenntnisbildung*. Wiesbaden: Franz Steiner Verlag, 1980.

Micksay, Koloman. "Analyse der generativen Kompetenz der systematischen Theologie in Wilhelm Dantines Vorlesung 'Bekennendes Bekenntnis.'" In *Bekennendes Bekenntnis*. eds. Eric Hultsch and Kurt Lüthi. Gütersloh: Verlaghaus Gerd Mohn, 1982.

Migliore, Daniel. *Faith Seeking Understanding*. Grand Rapids: William B. Eerdmans Publishing Company, 1991.

Mirbt, Carl. "Lichtfreunde." *Realencyklopädie für protestantische Theologie und Kirche*. 3rd ed. Vol. 11. ed. Albert Hauck. Leipzig: Hinrichs'sche Buchhandlung, 1902, pp. 464–74.

Monk, Ray. *Ludwig Wittgenstein: The Duty of Genius*. New York: Penguin Books, 1990.

Müller, Gotthold. *Botschaft und Situation*. Stuttgart: Calwer Verlag, 1970.

Neuser, Wilhelm. "Agende, Agendenstreit und Provinzialagenden." In *Die Geschichte der Evangelischen Kirche der Union: Die Anfänge der Union unter landesherrlichem Kirchenregiment (1817–1850)*. Vol. 1. eds. J. F. Gerhard Goeters and Rudolf Mau. Leipzig: Evangelische Verlagsanstalt, 1992.

——. "Landeskirchliche Reform-Bekenntnis-und Verfassungsfragen: Die Provinzialsynoden und die Berliner Generalsynode von 1846." In *Die Geschichte der Evangelischen Kirche der Union: Die Anfänge der Union unter landesherrlichem Kirchenregiment (1817–1850)*. Vol. 1. eds. J. F. Gerhard Goeters and Rudolf Mau. Leipzig: Evangelische Verlagsanstalt, 1992.

Nieli, Russell. *Wittgenstein: From Mysticism to Ordinary Language*. Albany: State University of New York Press, 1987.

Nielsen, Kai. "Wittgensteinian Fideism." *Philosophy* 42 (1967): 191–209.

——. *Contemporary Critiques of Religion.* New York: Herder and Herder, 1971.

Nigg, Walter. *Die Geschichte des religiösen Liberalismus: Entstehung, Blütezeit, Ausklang.* Zürich: 1934.

Nippold, Fredrich (ed.). *Richard Rothes aus seinen letzten Lebensjahren.* Elberfeld: R. L. Friderichs, 1886.

Obst, Helmut. "Lichtfreunde, Deutschkatholiken und Katholisch -apostolische Gemeinden." In *Die Geschichte der Evangelischen Kirche der Union: Die Anfänge der Union unter lande sherrlichem Kirchenregiment (1817–1850).* Vol. 1. eds. J. F. Gerhard Goeters and Rudolf Mau. Leipzig: Evangelische Verlagsanstalt, 1992.

Olmsted, Richard. "Wittgenstein and Christian Truth Claims." *Scottish Journal of Theology* 33 (1980): 121–132.

Oppermann, Karl–Friedrich. *Christus und der Fortschritt: Richard Rothes Versuch einer Vermittlung von geschichtlichen Umgestaltungsprozess und christlichem Glauben.* Göttingen: Theol. Fak. Dissertation, 1983.

Pannenberg, Wolfhart. *Das Glaubensbekenntnis: ausgelegt und verantwortet vor den Fragen der Gegenwart.* Hamburg: Siebenstern Taschenbuch Verlag, 1972.

Peacocke, C. "Rule–Following: The Nature of Wittgenstein's Arguments." In *Wittgenstein: To Follow a Rule.* eds. S. H. Holtzman and C. M. Leich. London: Routledge and Kegan Paul, 1981.

Petersen, E. "Protestantenverein." *Die Religion in Geschichte und Gegenwart.* 1st ed. Vol. 4. ed. Friedrich Michael Schiele and Leopold Zscharnack. Tübingen: J. C. B. Mohr, 1913, pp. 1894-99.

Peterson, Thomas. *Wittgenstein for Preaching.* Lanham, MD: University Press of America, 1980.

Phillips, D. Z. *Faith after Foundationalism.* London: Routledge, 1988.

——. "Religion in Wittgenstein's Mirror." In *Wittgenstein Centenary Essays.* ed. A. Phillips Griffiths. Cambridge: Cambridge University Press, 1991.

——. "Religious Belief and Language Games." In *Ludwig Wittgenstein: Critical Assesments.* Vol. 4. ed. Stuart Shanker. London: Croom Helm, 1986.

Pitcher, George, ed. *Wittgenstein: The Philosophical Investigations.* Notre Dame: University of Notre Dame Press, 1968.

——. *The Philosophy of Wittgenstein.* Englewood Cliffs, N.J.: Prentice-Hall, 1964.

Putnam, Hilary. "Wittgenstein on Religion Belief." In *On Community.* ed. Leroy Roumer. Notre Dame: University of Notre Dame Press, 1991.

Rade, Martin. "Die Amtsentsetzung des Pfarrers Schrempf." *Die Christliche Welt* (18 August 1892): 761-66.

——. *Der rechte evangelische Glaube.* Leipzig: Grunow, 1892,

Rahner, Karl. *"Fides qua fides quae."* In *Bekennendes Bekenntnis.* eds. Eric Hultsch and Kurt Lüthi. Gütersloh: Verlaghaus Gerd Mohn, 1982.

Rhees, Rush, ed. *Recollections of Wittgenstein.* Oxford: Oxford University Press, 1981.

Ritschl, Dietrich. *Konzepte: Ökumene, Medizin, Ethik; gesammelte Aufsätze.* München: Chr. Kaiser Verlag, 1986.

——. *"Lehre." Theologische Realenzyklopädie.* Vol. 20. ed. Gerhard Müller. Berlin: Walter de Gruyter, 1990, pp. 608–21.

——. *The Logic of Theology.* London: SCM Press, 1986.

——. *Theologie in den neuen Welten: Analysen und Berichte aus Amerika und Australien.* München: Chr. Kaiser Verlag, 1981.

——. and Hugh Jones. *Story als Rohmaterial der Theologie.* München: Chr. Kaiser Verlag, 1976.

Rössler, Dietrich. "Richard Rothe." In *Theologen des Protestantismus im 19. und 20. Jahrhundert.* ed. Martin Greschat. Stuttgart: W. Kohlhammer, 1978.

Rothe, Richard. "Durch Welche Mittel können die der Kirche entfremdeten Glieder ihr wieder gewonnen werden? In *Gesammelte Vorträge und Abhandlungen Dr. Richard Rothes aus seinen letzten Lebensjahren.* ed. Friedrich Nippold. Elberfeld: R. L. Friderichs, 1886.

——. "Eröffnungsrede, gehalten bei der Gründung des Heidelberger Protestantenvereins am 5. November 1863." In *Gesammelte Vorträge und Abhandlungen Dr. Richard Rothes aus seinen letzten Lebensjahren.* ed. Friedrich Nippold. Elberfeld: R. L. Friderichs, 1886.

—— "Zur Debatte über den Protestantenverein." In *Gesammelte Vorträge und Abhandlungen Dr. Richard Rothes und seinen letzten Lebensjahren.* ed. Friedrich Nippold. Elberfeld: R. L. Friderichs Verlag, 1886.

Rupp, Julius. *Die Symbole oder Gottes Wort? Ein Sendschreiben an die Evangelische Kirche.* Leipzig: Wigand, 1846.

Russell, Bertrand. "The Philosophy of Logical Atomism." In *Logic and Knowledge: Essays 1901–1950.* ed. R. C. Marsh. London: George Allen and Unwin, 1956.

Sauter, Gerhart (ed.). *Theologie als Wissenschaft.* München: Chr. Kaiser Verlag, 1971.

Savigny, Eike von. *Wittgenstein's Philosophische Untersuchungen: Ein Kommentar für Leser.* 2 Vols. Frankfurt: Vittorio Klostermann, 1988.

Scharlemann, Robert and Gilbert Ogutu (eds.). *God In Language.* New York: Paragon House, 1987.

Schenkel, Daniel. *Der Deutsche Protestantenverein und seine Bedeutung in der Gegenwart.* Wiesbaden: C. W. Kreidal's Verlag, 1868.

——. *Die Protestantische Freiheit in ihrem gegenwärtigen Kampfe mit der kirchlichen Reaktion.* Wiesbaden: Kreidel, 1865.

——. *Gutachten der theologischen Fakultät der Universität Heidelberg über den durch Pastor R. Dulon angeregten Kirchensteit in Bremen.* Heidelberg: Karl Groos, 1852.

Schmidt, M. "Lichtfreunde." *Die Religion in Geschichte und Gegenwart*. 3rd ed. Vol. 4. ed. Kurt Galling. Tübingen: J. C. B. Mohr, 1961, pp. 359–361.

Schmidt –Lauber, Hans–Christoph. "Ökumenisches Bekennen in Kontext der Gemeinde." In *Bekennendes Bekenntnis*. eds. Eric Hultsch and Kurt Lüthi. Gütersloh: Verlaghaus Gerd Mohn, 1982.

Schneider, Theodor. *Was wir glauben: Eine Auslegung des Apostolischen Glaubensbekenntnisses*. Düsseldorf: Patmos Verlag, 1985.

Schrempf, Christoph. *Eine Frage an die evangelische Landeskirche Württembergs*. Göttingen: Vandenhoeck & Ruprecht, 1892.

——. *Religion ohne Religion*. 5 Vols. Stuttgart: Frommanns Verlag, 1947.

Schröer, Henning. *Unser Glaubensbekenntnis heute: Versuch einer theologischen Bilanz*. Hamburg: Furche Verlag, 1971.

Schulte, Joachim. *Wittgenstein: Eine Einführung*. Stuttgart: Philipp Reclam, 1989.

Senn, Frank. *The People's Work: A Social History of the Liturgy*. Minneapolis: Fortress Press, 2006.

Sherry, Patrick. "Learning How to be Religious." 77 *Theology* (January 1974): 81–90.

——. *Religion, Truth and Language–Games*. New York: Harper and Row, 1977.

Shibles, Warren. *Wittgenstein, Language and Philosophy*. Dubuque, IA: Kendall Hunt Pub. Co., 1969.

Shields, Philip. *Logic and Sin in the Writings of Ludwig Wittgenstein*. Chicago: University of Chicago Press, 1993.

Spierling, Karen. *Infant Baptism in Reformation Geneva: The Shaping of a Community, 1536–1564*. Hants, England: Ashgate, 2005.

Stegmüller, Wolfgang. *Hauptströmungen der Gegenwartsphilosophie*. 5th ed. Vol. 1. Stuttgart: Alfred Kröner, 1989.

Stoevesandt, Hinrich. *Die Bedeutung des Symbolums in Theologie und Kirche*. München: Chr. Kaiser Verlag, 1970.

Strauß, D. F. *Die Halben und die Ganzen: eine Streitschrift gegen die HH. Schenkel und Hengstenberg*. Berlin: Duncker, 1865.

Stroup, George. *The Promise of Narrative Theology*. Atlanta: John Knox Press, 1981.

Suter, Ronald. *Interpreting Wittgenstein*. Philadelphia: Temple University Press, 1989.

Sydow, Adolph. *Aktenstücke: betreffend das vom königlichen Consistorium der Provinz Brandenburg über mich verhängte Disciplinarverfahren wegen meines Vortrags "Ueber die wunderbare Geburt Jesu"*. Berlin: Henschel, 1873.

Tanesini, Alessandra. *Wittgenstein: A Femnist Interpretation*. Cambridge: Polity Press, 2004.

Thierbach, C. *Gustav Adolf Wislicenus: Ein Lebensbild aus der Geschichte der freien, religiösen Bewegung*. Leipzig: 1904.

———. *Die Throne im Himmel und auf Erden und die protestantischen Freunde.* Deßau: Fritsche, 1845.

———. *Thronrede bei der Eröffnung der sächsischen Ständesversammlung am 14. September 1845 und die den kirchlichen Bewegungen unsrer Tage gemachten Vorwürfe.* Leipzig: Gustav Brauns, 1845.

Tillich, Paul. *Systematic Theology.* Vol. 1. Chicago: University of Chicago Press, 1967.

Tischhauser, Christian. *Geschichte der evangelischen Kirche Deutschlands in der ersten Hälfte des 19. Jahrhunderts.* Basel: 1900.

Tominaga, Thomas. "A Wittgensteinian Analysis of the Depth Grammar of Religious Belief and Practice." In *Philosophy of Religion.* Vienna: Hölder–Pitcher–Tempsky, 1984.

Track, Joachim. "Schrift, Bekenntnis und Erfahrung." In *Lebendiger Umgang mit Schrift und Bekenntnis.* ed. Joachim Track. Stuttgart: Calwer Verlag, 1980.

———. *Sprachkritische Untersuchungen zum christlichen Reden von Gott.* Göttingen: Vandenhoeck und Ruprecht, 1977.

Traub, Gottfried. *Meine Verteidigung gegen den Evangelischen Oberkirchenrat.* Bonn: Carl Georgi, 1912.

Trigg, Roger. *Reason and Commitment.* Cambridge University Press: Cambridge, 1973.

Tschirn, Gustav. *Zur 60 jährigen Geschichte der freireligiösen Bewegung.* 1904.

Uhlich, Leberecht. *An ihren Früchten sollt ihr sie erkennen: Anmerkungen zu einer Erklärung des Hrn. Prof. Dr. Hengstenberg in Berlin gegen die protestantischen Freunde in dem Vorwort zu seiner evangelischen Kirchenzeitung 1845.* Leipzig: Kirchner, 1845.

———. *Bekenntnisse.* Leipzig: Böhme, 1845,

———. *Dissidentische Denkschrift.* Gotha: Stollbergsche, 1859.

———. *Predigten gehalten in der St. Catharinen Kirche zu Magdeburg im Jahre 1846.* Magdeburg: Creutz, 1846.

———. *Die protestantischen Freunde.* Deßau: Julius Fritsche, 1845.

———. *Sein Leben von ihm selbst beschrieben.* Gera: 1872.

———. *17 Sätze in Bezug auf die Verpflichtungsformel protestantischer Geistlicher, ausgegangen von der Synode zu Berlin 1846.* Wolfenbüttel: Holle'schen, 1846.

———. *Die Throne im Himmel und auf Erden und die protestantischen Freunde.* Deßau: Fritsche, 1845.

———. *Ueber den Amtseid der Geistlichen.* Leipzig: Otto Klemm, 1846.

Uhlig, Christian. "Lichtfreunde." *Theologische Realenzyklopädie.* Vol. 21. ed. Gerhard Müller. Berlin: Walter de Gruyter, 1991, pp. 119–121.

Völker, Alexander. *Gemeinsames Glaubensbekenntnis.* Gütersloh: Verlaghaus Gerd Mohn, 1974.

Wainwright, Geoffrey. *Doxology: The Praise of God in Worship, Doctrine and Life.* New York: Oxford University Press, 1980.

Waismann, Friedrich. *The Principles of Linguistic Philosophy*. ed. R. Harré. London: Macmillan, 1965.

——. *Wittgenstein und der Wiener Kreis*. Frankfurt am Main: Suhrkamp, 1984.

Wallmann, J. *Kirchengeschichte Deutschlands seit der Reformation*. Tübingen: J.C.B. Mohr, 1988.

Weitz, Morris. "Analysis, Philosophical." In *The Encyclopedia of Philosophy*. Vol. 1. New York: Macmillan Co., 1967, pp. 97–105.

Welch, Claude. *Protestant Thought in the Nineteenth Century*. 2 Vols. New Haven: Yale University Press, 1972.

Westermann, Claus. In *Bekennendes Bekenntnis*. eds. Eric Hultsch and Kurt Lüthi. Gütersloh: Verlaghaus Gerd Mohn, 1982.

Williams, Bernard. "Wittgenstein and Idealism." In *Understanding Wittgenstein*. ed. G. Vesey. London: Macmillan, 1974.

Wintzer, Friedrich. *Claus Harms: Predigt und Theologie*. Flensburg: Christian Wolff, 1965.

Wislicenus, Adolf Timotheus. *Beitrag zur Beantwortung der Frage Ob Schrift? Ob Geist?* Leipzig: Otto Wigand, 1845.

Wislicenus, Gustav. *Ob Schrift, Ob Geist?* Leipzig: Otto Wigand, 1845.

——. *Ob Schrift, Ob Geist? Verantwortung gegen meine Ankläger*. Leipzig: Otto Wigand, 1845.

Wislicenus und seine Gegner. Leipzig: 1845.

Wittgenstein, Ludwig. *The Blue and Brown Books*. Oxford: Basil Blackwell, 1975.

——. *Culture and Value*. ed. G.H. von Wright in collaboration with Heikki Nyman. Oxford: Basil Blackwell, 1980.

——. *Lectures and Conversations on Aesthetics, Psychology and Religious Belief*. ed. Cyril Barrett. Oxford: Basil Blackwell, 1966.

——. *Notebooks 1914–16*. ed. G.E.M. Anscombe and G.H. von Wright. Oxford: Basil Blackwell, 1961.

——. *On Certainty*. ed. G.E.M. Anscombe. Oxford: Basil Blackwell, 1969.

——. *Philosophical Grammar*. ed. Rush Rhees. Oxford: Basil Blackwell, 1974.

——. *Philosophical Investigations*. New York: Macmillan Company, 1953.

——. *Philosophical Remarks*. ed. Rush Rhees. Oxford: Basil Blackwell, 1975.

——. *Remarks on Frazer's Golden Bough*. ed. Rush Rhees. trans A.C. Miles. Cross Hill Cottage: Brynmill Press, 1979.

——. *Tractatus Logico–Philosophicus*. trans. D.F. Pears and B.F. McGuinness. London: Routledge, 1986.

——. *Zettel*. Berkeley: University of California Press, 1967.

Wuchertl, Kurt. "Religionsphilosophie nach Wittgenstein." In *Wittgenstein Symposium, Kirchberg.* Vienna, 1989.

Zabeeh, Fahrang. "Our Language Games and Forms of Life." In *Essays on Wittgenstein.* ed. E. Klemke. Urbana: University of Illinois Press, 1971.

Zahn-Harnack, Agnes von. *Adolf von Harnack.* Berlin: Hans Bott Verlag, 1936.

——. *Der Apostolikumstreit des Jahres 1892 und seine Bedeutung für die Gegenwart.* Marburg: N. G. Elwert, 1950.

Zeugnisse gegen das Buch des evang. Predigerseminardirektors zu Heidelberg, welches läugnet daß die Bibel Gottes Wort und daß Jesus Gottes Sohn sei. Karlsruhe: Gutsch, 1864.